POSTMODERN THEOLOGIES

The Challenge of Religious Diversity

Terrence W. Tilley

with
John Edwards
Tami England
H. Frederick Felice
Stuart Kendall
C. Brad Morris
Bruce Richey
Craig Westman

ORBIS BOOKS

Maryknoll, New Y

The Catholic Foreign Mission Society of America (Maryknoll) recruits and trains people for overseas missionary service. Through Orbis Books, Maryknoll aims to foster the international dialogue that is essential to mission. The books published, however, reflect the opinions of their authors and are not meant to represent the official position of the society.

Library of Congress Cataloging-in-Publication Data

Tilley, Terrence W.
    Postmodern theologies : the challenge of religious diversity /
Terrence W. Tilley with John Edwards . . . [et. al.].
       p.   cm.
    Includes bibliographical references and index.
    ISBN 1-57075-005-X (pbk.)
    1. Postmodernism—Religious aspects. 2. Postmodernism—Religious
aspects—Christianity. 3. Religions—Relations. I. Title.
BL65.P73T55   1995
200—dc20
                                           94-47927
                                            CIP

Contents

A Note on Authorship

Authorship is a problematic concept in postmodern writing. Although I make no pretense to "solve" the problems of authorship generally, perhaps a bit of light can be shed on the process that led to this book.

Postmodern Theologies: The Challenge of Religious Diversity is the product of a remarkable seminar held in the Religion Department of the Florida State University in the fall of 1993. The nine participants came from the departments of religion, humanities, and philosophy. There was one faculty member, four doctoral students, three M.A. students, and one undergraduate. I had intended to use the seminar as a springboard for developing a book I planned to write examining and evaluating postmodern and postliberal theologies as indicated in the introduction below (an early version of which served as part of the "syllabus" for the seminar). As the seminar began to develop, it became clear that it would make more sense to incorporate all the participants' research, insofar as their research and writing could conform to the shape anticipated for this book, rather than to have me repeat the research (or take credit for the others' work) in order to write it on my own. Seven of the other participants in the seminar developed research projects which lent themselves to inclusion in the book.

I designed the basic shape of the research projects and revised the papers submitted, sometimes rewriting them substantially, sometimes adding material, sometimes deleting digressions, sometimes simply smoothing the prose and attempting to bring some consistency to the style among the chapters. I then returned the revised versions to the other participants for their comments and criticisms. They made some further suggestions, most of which have been incorporated, and agreed to be acknowledged as co-authors of the chapters on which they worked. Of the eleven chapters of this book, then, seven are co-authored.

I would like to thank Orbis Books, and especially our editor William Burrows, for allowing me to make the offer to the members of the seminar to join me in this project. As primary author and designer, I am to be held responsible for the errors, oversights, omissions, and other blunders which remain in this work. The insights, of course, are to be attributed to all the participants, as they emerged from our discussions together. I hope you will find that this experiment in writing is useful.

We have all agreed that any royalties from this book will be given to the Graduate Fellowship Fund of the Department of Religion at Florida State University to help graduate students in the future.

Terrence W. Tilley

Introduction

The "Post-Age" Stamp

Much theoretical discourse stamps the contemporary era with a peculiar prefix: it is a *post*-age. Manifestos appear with disheartening regularity, announcing that our era is postmodern, postchristian, postreligious, postcolonial, postindustrial, postideological, postmoral, postanalytic, postliterate, postnarrative, postauthorial, postpersonal, poststructuralist, postliberal, etc. Moral theorists situate us *after* virtue or *after* Babel. Philosophers theorize *beyond* objectivism and relativism. Sociologists construe modern culture as beyond belief. Christian theologians move far beyond theism. Contemporary theologians write *after* Freud, *after* Wittgenstein, *after* Auschwitz, *after* Christendom, *after* the death of God. The signpost marking our age is the "post" sign.

A paradox stamps each post-age. Each distances our present from our past. The post-age marks us as situated beyond, living after, even being done with the past. Hence, the prefix, "post." Yet each "post"-age inevitably shows the present power of the transcended past. Whatever x we slip into "our post-x age" that x perversely drags that past x into the present. By declaring our era beyond x or post-x, we ironically display the present power of x to define our era. For every x in "the post-x age" signifies a power that has determined us and determines us still. X marks the spot from which we must start. This very nomenclature for the present recollects that past and highlights its present significance. A "post"-age is a paradoxical age, an unstable era, both denying and affirming the present power of the past.

Ambiguity and uncertainty stamp the post-age. For the post-age signifies where we've been. It does not signify where we are. Nor does it point to where we're going: "the post-x era" fails to signify what y might be dominant now or anticipated next. We do not live in a y age, but in a post-x age. We can't say what our era is, only what it is not. What it is and will be, remains unsaid.

In the past, before the "post"-age, paradigms of discourse shaped the "mind," the discourse practices, of an age. They signified where "we" were, the direction in which to cut our path, and the goal we sought. In the 1770s, for instance, Americans did not live in a "postcolonial" era, but in a revolutionary age[1] struggling for independence and for freedom. The 1790s were not a "postcolonial" period for the new country, but a "republican" era. The 1870s were not so much the "postwar era," as a time of "reconstruction." However ideological and deceptive such paradigms be, they shape the significance of a present because they show "the right ways" to remember the past and anticipate the future. In a post-age, the future is indeterminable and invisible, and the past paradoxically both dismissed and kept. Hence, ambiguity about where we've come from, uncertainty about where we are, and suspicion of where we're going are connected in every post-age.

What could stamp a theology for a post-age? Is theology after the death of God like biology after the end of life: a discipline without a subject? Have our sacred canopies been so rotted out by the acid rains of modernity that only a useless skeleton of bare rigging remains? Are theologians homeless wanderers blindly trekking in a barren wilderness? The point of this book is to show that the theologians' landscape is not so barren, their trek not so blind, their tents perhaps torn and tattered, but hardly irreparable.

For a post-age can be stamped with adventure as well as anxiety. And the adventure is the subject of this book: How are the theologians stamping the post-age?

The three chapters in Part 1 deal with the postmodernism of completion. This postmodernism finds the contemporary problematic not how to reject or repudiate the intellectual categories and social practices of the modern world, but how to *extend and complete* the modern project. The erosion of the religious world has not been a destruction but a purification. The task now is to build a critical theology.

Theologians often take off from the work of critical social theorists and philosophers, e.g., Jürgen Habermas. Many accept his argument that modernity is an incomplete project awaiting completion. They then go on to show that without religious *praxis* the modern project cannot be completed (not to mention that without accepting modernity, religious communities wither and institutions remain hollow shells). Helmut Peukert, David Ray Griffin and David Tracy are some leading theologians in this area.

Part 2 deals with postmodernisms of dissolution. These postmodernisms intensify the erosion of Christendom begun in the modern period. Some authors embrace deconstructive tactics, such as Jacques Derrida's, to show how all apparent necessities and absolutes given in our social and ideological structures can be taken apart to be seen as nothing but contingent and

---

[1] Sometimes, of course, such labels are retrospectively stuck on an era by historians. One might claim that such labels "objectivize" or "stabilize" the central elements of that era. They also reflect or create the marginal of that era. But when those labels stick fast, they do so, I suspect, because they capture the paradigm which shaped the era both in terms of what was valorized and what marginalized.

relative constituents of contingent and relative structures. Others use the genealogical moves of Michel Foucault to reveal the systems of domination and discipline which shape our loves, hates, fears and hopes—and every action which these emotions motivate. These theologians dissolve what is left of the humanly constructed cathedrals of thought which had once seemed eternal and immovable. In, through, and beyond the rubble which litters the ground, there remains an empty space for the Light, no longer blocked by human edifices; or perhaps it is just that the gaps, fissures, holes, and tears that are the present (as emptiness and absence at the heart of every thing) may show the absence of any Other. Or so I would interpret both such postmodern theologians of presence like Thomas J. J. Altizer and postmodern theologians (or a/theologians) of dissolution like Mark C. Taylor and Edith Wyschogrod. Their new and radical intellectual asceticism employs distilled and concentrated modern acids on religious and theological constructs.

The third part details the approach of theological postliberalism. Like the deconstructive postmoderns, postliberals find the humanism of religious liberalism to be religious pretense. Postliberal theologians are inspired by the work of Clifford Geertz in cultural anthropology and Ludwig Wittgenstein in linguistic philosophy. George Lindbeck has proffered an important approach which distinguishes the discourse practice of Christian theology from the discourses of the world. The point is neither to complete, reject, dissolve or resolve the modern world. The point is to see how to live in God's world and how all other "worlds" fit or fail to fit in the world God has made.

The three chapters of Part 4 discuss theologies of communal praxis (or practice). These theologians form a rather disparate group. What joins them is that they leave behind the endless debates of modernity about the foundations of religious belief in true or warranted doctrines. What is key for this postmodern approach are the practices which constituted shared religious life. True belief is, for them, not the foundation of religious life, but its result. Latin American theologians such as Gustavo Gutiérrez and North American theologians such as James McClendon and Sharon Welch take different approaches but share this postmodern "practical" turn.

Chapter 11 provides a test case for these theologies: how do they deal with the diversity of religions? The modern liberal paradigm has been soteriocentric. The liberal problem was whether salvation is available in other religions. Given the classic Christian position, *extra ecclesiam nulla salus*, what could one say about believers in other traditions? Three answers classically had been given. Exclusivism said salvation is not available through other religions because ours is final and sufficient. Inclusivism saw salvation as available through other religions, but only because they (unwittingly) share in the salvation that our religion finally and sufficiently provides. Pluralism found salvation available in various ways in each of the religions, that each offers a different "path to the Center," so that many may be sufficient, but none final. Each postmodern approach finds both this modern way of understanding what the problem is and its theoretical solutions terribly skewed. Exploring briefly the postmodern strategies for coping with religious diversity in this final chapter offers us a way for assessing the strengths and weaknesses of postmodern theologies.

And now for a couple of salutary warnings to the reader.

First and foremost, I am not neutral in these matters and will not attempt to assume the pretense of uninterested objectivity in what follows. I have learned from and appreciate the strengths and weaknesses of each of these theological approaches. They present themselves as viable options for Christian (or other) theology in our era. However, I do think that versions of the theologies of communal practice can incorporate most of the strengths and avoid the pitfalls of the other three options; indeed, some theologians whom we discuss in Part 1 would find themselves (mostly) at home in Part 4. However, for the constructive theologians, universal solidarity is a requirement, while for the theologians of communal praxis, it is a hope. The difference this makes will be shown below. On the other hand, the practical theories run the risks of being un-self-critical and of allowing practices (which can become deformed) a controlling role in theology. So no theological approach is *clearly* "the best" in our post-age. The choice of theological styles is a matter open for dispute, as are most matters in postmodern theology. Whether we have been fair enough in our accounts and balanced enough in our assessments must be judged by our critics.

Second, I omit a number of options others might include here. An area many find fascinating includes "ecological," "ecofeminist," and "cosmological" theologies. I exclude these here simply because these approaches are more at home where "religion and science" meet rather than where "foundational" issues about the possibility or modes of theology are central (although their criticisms of approaches considered here will not be ignored). I also make no pretense to survey every thinker and every position within the general types constructed here. That would make this relatively short book into a very long one.

Other patterns are not directly relevant to our task. These include postreligious, modern, and premodern religious approaches. The arguments of theologians represented in Chapter 1 succeed in showing that the most viable form of postreligious humanism necessarily is plagued with an inconsistency so fundamental that it must either collapse into incoherence or accept a religious completion. The argument of Chapter 7 claims that postmodern antihumanism finally reverts to a Nietzschean valorization of raw power; it is a viable position intellectually, but one incompatible with almost any religious view (despite the claims of writers surveyed in Chapters 4 through 6). The modern theological approaches carry on as if the acids of modernity have been neutralized when they have not; their arguments often strike me as fighting for territory already won or lost. It is not that their work does not continue to be of interest. It does. But the modern world in which modern theology was at home died somewhere in the quarter century that began with the allied acceptance of the strategy of obliteration bombing (including using nuclear weapons) in World War II, that continued with the slowly dawning realization of the magnitude of the destruction of European Jewry under Hitler and its manifold significances, that included the revolution of the Second Vatican Council and its remarkable effects on worldwide Catholicism, that saw the emergence of many independent nations in the colonized worlds and the tragic involvement of the super-powers in postcolonial warfare (especially in Indochina), that included a profound sexual revolution which provided easy control of human fertility without using aesthetically unappealing means, and that concluded with the variety of cultural revolutions and assassinations which afflicted the NATO world in 1968. Premodern retreats to authority, to commitment, to a world even longer dead than the modern one require religious communities to become exclusivist sects in cultural ghettoes, irrelevant to contemporary life and too weak to provide for a viable continuing religious tradition. Given the emergence of postmodernity, premodern theologies are simply not viable, save in a remnant community as isolated from contemporary life as the Amish want to be.

Third, much postmodern work is filled with convoluted jargon. Although some postmodernists may say I miss the point, where possible, we will unabashedly translate the jargon into more accessible terms. However, some theologians work at an unalleviated high level of abstraction, and this text will, at times, reflect that.

Fourth, it is not the approach of most postmodern theory to "make arguments," but to bring a reader to see what she has always seen in a new way. The jargon and wordplay can contribute to this new vision. We will attempt to avoid domesticating postmodernisms by attributing arguments where none are made; and we will also try to follow such a postmodern tactic: We will seek to share visions and not to make debaters' arguments herein. However, in those instances where arguments can highlight the weaknesses and show ways to develop a writer's strengths, we will utilize them as well as we can.

Finally, no book of this sort can be comprehensive. It must be selective in choosing positions to examine. Those which appear here are viable modes for theology in a "post"-age. I do not expect everyone to agree with all the specific choices, but do claim that the patterns of theological practices described herein are fair to the authors and to our age.

This book examines a set of new and exciting approaches to understanding, creatively transforming (when needed), and proclaiming (Christian) faith in a post-age. It is meant to encourage you to consider these theologies, to provide you with some critical questions to ask when you read works in this area, and to help you find which paths (among the many) might most interest you.

Welcome to the work.

PART 1

CONSTRUCTIVE
POSTMODERNISMS

Wesley Kort (1992) has argued that the meanings of theological discourses are best understood "oppositionally." What he means by this is that
the *referents* of theological discourses—God, the church, Jesus Christ, etc.—
do not determine the *meaning* of the theological discourse. Nor do the
authors of a theological text—scholars, ministers, bishops, etc.—give a
theology its meaning. Nor does the way an audience understands and
appropriates a theology give that theology its meaning. Rather, Kort claims
that the ways in which a theology or theological position distinguishes itself
from relevant alternative theological (and antitheological) positions determines its meaning.

Each theology defines itself by distinguishing itself from others. Of
course, schools and families of theologies are similar in that they share a
pattern or cultural context for defining themselves. The oppositions between theologies make sense only if there are also presumed similarities—
otherwise the different theologies might not connect with each other at all.
For instance, "process" theologies, however different, acquire their meanings especially through their opposition to what they call "classical theism"
or "substance theology." Process theologians oppose their views of the
ways the world affects God and God affects the world to the doctrines of
divine immutability and omnipotent sovereignty, central constituents in
their envisioned opponents. Protestant neo-orthodox theologies define
themselves by their opposition to Protestant liberal theologies. Neo-orthodoxy distances itself from liberalism by opposing liberalism's "capitulation
to" modern culture and the modern academy and by turning away from
human experience as a foundation for their thought and to the Word of God
as a firm rock upon which to build. Much nineteenth-century magisterial
Catholic theology defined itself over against European liberal political and

social thought and the cultural theologies that valorized liberalism. In contemporary North American theology, postliberal, intratextual theology (as discussed in Chapter 7) explicitly defines itself over against theological liberalism with its supposed "extratextual" interpretive strategies and over against genealogical and deconstructive forms of postmodern thought. Like neo-orthodoxy, postliberals see revisionist liberalism as capitulating to the modern world. Postliberals also use the criticisms of genealogical postmodernists, but think that there is a way to avoid the chaos and nihilism most postmodernists carry in their wake.

Self-definition by opposition also occurs within theological traditions. Within each theological "school," a theology defines itself by setting itself off from other similar theologies on various key issues. Thomistic philosophies and theologies in the twentieth century provide a prime example of a tradition having internal positions that define themselves by oppositions within Thomism (e.g., neo-Thomism vs. transcendental Thomism). Some process theologies see God as ambiguous or ambivalent, incorporating light and darkness, good and evil. Others see God as ultimately redeeming all that can be redeemed into the light of divine beauty. These, too, define themselves by opposition. In short, theologies acquire their central and distinctive meanings by their key oppositions to other articulated positions.

On first glance, Kort's approach seems demeaning and disconcerting. It seems to require that theologians must fight each other in order to establish their own "territorial hegemony." Irenic and inclusive theologians need not apply for work, as Kort would find that they cannot define themselves except that they become non-irenic and define themselves by *excluding and opposing other*, non-irenic forms of theology. So even irenic and inclusive theologies define themselves in opposition to agonistic and exclusivist theologies! An oppositional approach disturbs those who think that theologians are dedicated to telling the truth about God, the world and humanity, the referents of her or his theology.

Kort's oppositional analysis seems to degrade doing theology to violent jousting for territory in the theological countryside. But we must point out that just because oppositional analysis shows the way theologians define their positions with regard to others does not mean that at least one of those theologies may be telling what is true most adequately. The agonistic genesis of distinctive claims (by opposition) does not entail that those claims are true or false. That's another question.

Moreover, oppositional analysis is immensely useful for understanding how different theological understandings are related. It can bring out the latent patterns of influence and opposition in and among theological discourses. It understands these patterns of opposition as exercises of theological imagination, not merely as moves in social, psychological, or institutional power games. Theology develops, in this perspective, by the sort of dialogue that sharpens the theologians' wits. Oppositional analysis does not deny that one or more theologies might reflect God or the Church of eschatology adequately or construct its framework illuminatingly. Theologies may both contain and reveal what is true—but "the real" is not what gives them their meaning. The True or The Real or Being is not the ground of theological meaning, but may be shown or indicated by theological discourses when they do their work right. Revelation of and adequacy to God, the world, and humanity is not a *foundation* for theological discourse, but may be a *result* of theologians' doing their work well.

Oppositional analyses provide necessary working tools not only for understanding contemporary theologies in general, but also for showing the relationships of postmodern theologies to modernity and to other postmodern theologies. As indicated in the introduction, postmodern theologies explicitly define themselves in opposition to modernity and to other postmodern theologies.

The range of positions considered in the three chapters in this part of the book can be labeled constructive postmodernisms. These positions define themselves by their opposition to theologies which "abandon" the gains of the Enlightenment, whether those theologies are reversions to premodern authoritarianism and obscurantism or valorizations of postmodern antihumanism and deconstructive anarchy which can hide repressive and conservative polities.

What distinguishes constructive postmodernisms is the way in which they position themselves against central premodern, modern and deconstructive claims. The result is that they tend to retain central characteristics of modern liberal humanism and remain deeply indebted to specific philosophical systems. Of course, they also "oppose" each other and draw some of their distinctiveness from these oppositions as well.

Chapter 1

Toward a Theology of the Practice of Communicative Action

God's dominion means the abandonment of the domination of human beings over each other.

—Helmut Peukert

It might seem odd to begin a chapter in a book on postmodern theological discourses by analyzing the work of philosopher and social theorist Jürgen Habermas. This critical theorist generally rejects most of the arguments and positions of contemporary theologians (Habermas 1987). His prejudices against institutional religion are often exemplified (see, for example, Habermas 1994 on the Catholic Church in Poland). He has rejected the categorization of his work as "postmodern" because he finds that category preempted by the antimodern positions typified by Jacques Derrida, Michel Foucault, et al. That preemption is challenged by David Griffin and others, as we shall show below. Yet his analysis of modern society, based in the revisionist Marxism of critical theory, provides an intellectual framework unsurpassed as a critique of some of the same characteristics of modernity which the antimodernists also criticize. Moreover, many theologians working in this vein are explicitly or implicitly indebted to his work, so we turn to it to set the stage for the theological discourses which follow.

Habermas especially does not want to abandon the gains of the Enlightenment. He finds crucial gains to be the development of a universal morality and of critical reason. Rather, in the tradition of Hegel and Marx, he can be seen as a humanist dedicated to a "radical enlightenment" (Lakeland 1990:41) or to a "second enlightenment." The first Enlightenment achieved an intellectual emancipation for the knowledge elite in Western society. What is needed is not the rejection of this freedom, but the extension of emancipation to include all the spheres—personal, social, economic, political—in which humans live and move, and to include all the people—not just Western elites—in this emancipatory process. The problem with liberal democracy, one might say, parodying G. K. Chesterton on Christianity, is not that it has been tried and failed; the problem is that true liberal democracy has never really been tried.

The Enlightenment of the seventeenth century is the commencement of modern Western societies. It brought both boon and bane. The bane is described by earlier critical theorists, Theodor Adorno and Max Horkheimer as the multiple forms of human alienation. As Paul Lakeland shows (1990:33), the forms of alienation are basically twofold. First, we take ourselves as autonomous individuals over against our environments. It is not merely that we define ourselves "oppositionally," but that we are inclined to treat our environment and the items in it—including people—as instruments to be used. Second, we place ourselves as competitors who seek to dominate parts of nature—the larger the part we can dominate, the better. Modernity, then is a discourse which creates a "society" in which alienation of each from the other and competitive domination of nature dominate. Lakeland comments as follows:

> Both sets of assumptions are myths fostered by the system of capitalism, through which individuals have been led to believe what the system needs them to believe, namely, that they are first and foremost individuals, secondly in community, and that they are (economically) successful manipulators of technology. In reality, the system has deprived them of their essential humanity (Lakeland 1990:33).

The final upshot of alienation and domination is self-alienation. But once one has exposed the disasters of modernity, what does one do? Since one cannot return to a premodern life, after one diagnoses the sickness of modernity, one must prescribe an antidote.

The key to the sickness of modernity in Habermas's view is the *colonization of the lifeworld by the system.* The lifeworld is the everyday world in which we live together and communicate with each other. We are born into a lifeworld. It shapes us into the people we become. We share aspects of our lifeworld with family, friends, school chums, co-workers, gang members, etc. For living together in a lifeworld to be possible, we must share a set of social meanings and values. These are not always, perhaps not even often, articulated explicitly. Nonetheless, these shared meanings and values appear in and through our ordinary interactions.

Unlike some social theorists, Habermas does not construe a lifeworld as static. Rather, lifeworlds are reshaped and reformed by those who have been shaped and formed within them. For example, the civil rights movement in the United States was a truly American phenomenon, born in the American lifeworld, shaped by the shared values highlighted in the slogan "all people are created equal," and effective in reshaping that lifeworld to ameliorate some of the conditions of racial discrimination. By showing that the American way of life was distorted and discriminatory against a few when it prescribed liberty and justice for all, disenfranchised members of that lifeworld reformed it from within.

Sometimes implicitly, sometimes explicitly, we engage in a dialogue—not always a polite or peaceful one—in which we seek a consensus on ways to act, believe and live together. Again, the civil rights movement can be seen as an agonistic vehicle of dialogue in which an old set of presumptions, prejudices, and habits which had formed the American lifeworld after World War II was challenged and found wanting. The result was a new national consensus that discrimination on the basis of race in (at least) education, jobs, housing (i.e., in the lifeworld) was wrong. (That the nation has refused to act adequately to live up to this consensual value is at least sad, at worst a tragedy, and has led to much litigation, partly to continue working out what the consensus means and partly to force those who do not wish to live by non-discriminatory values to act civilly). The lifeworld in which we live provides standards for action (a morality), for recognizing when a person's claims are warranted (an epistemology), and for legitimating the society (a polity).

The "system" is (mostly) an invention of modernity. As societies become increasingly complex and as people have to interact with others who are not members of their own lifeworld, a pattern of systematization emerges. Francis Schüssler Fiorenza gave a clear summary of Habermas's concept of the "system":

> System refers to those administrative areas of modern society coordinated by money and power. Society is considered a self-regulating system. The media of this self-regulation are money and power. On the level of system, money and power—rather than consensus—coordinate and steer human action; they not only replace language as a medium of coordination, but they also coordinate human action in a way that differs considerably from that which takes place linguistically through communication. On this point Habermas . . . emphasizes that only money and power are steering-mechanisms on the level of systems, rather than influence and value commitment [which properly function in the lifeworld] (Schüssler Fiorenza 1992:68).

In the lifeworld, people use language in discussion and argument to achieve a consensus about what should be believed and done. However, in a complex society, systems of exchange (money) and control (power) are also needed to "steer" our behavior. The money system makes trade of otherwise incomparable things possible (e.g., a typical city dweller trades 25 percent to 40 percent of her or his labor for shelter by earning the money to pay for it). Power makes it possible to keep the lifeworld and the trade system relatively stable.

However, modernity has become pathological because money and power have become values in and of themselves in the lifeworld, rather than tools to be used for realizing values that we agree should be achieved. "Money, power, and the market become the facts of life, before which culture, consensus formation, and even personality must bend" (Lakeland 1990:59). People in late capitalist society develop personalities and personal value systems such that they desire money and power for their own sake, not as tools. They treat all interactions between people as if they were transactions in the market. Even marriage and the family come to be seen as basically contractual relationships. Success in the educational system is understood as having controlling power over people, and those who achieve power receive the lion's share of the financial reward (as exemplified in one major American university, where it is taken as perfectly defensible that the upper level administrative salaries rank in the top 5 percent of comparable universities, and faculty salaries rank in the bottom 25 percent). In modernity, money can buy you love; if it can't, power can.

In the lifeworld colonized by the system, money and power become the controlling values. "*Everyday consciousness* is robbed of its power to synthesize; it becomes *fragmented*" in such a system (Habermas 1987:355). Even the intellectual freedom achieved by the Enlightenment is undermined by such fragmentation. Knowledge becomes power, a tool to extend our own hegemony and domination over others rather than a tool to further the good of the commonweal. Knowledge becomes a commodity to be bought, sold, and controlled. And as our consciousness is fragmented, we become impotent in the face of the systems which control us. Some of us turn to drugs; others to protest; others to beating the system criminally. Lakeland summarizes this clearly:

> Above all, perhaps, Habermas is speaking to the pervasive feeling in developed capitalist societies that much is beyond the control of individuals or of community action, and that certain realities—money or the market, for example—are simply givens for which communicative praxis has no option but to make space. Genuinely human interrelationships, the sphere of communicative action, is then progressively diminished ... (Lakeland 1990:59-60).

Our creative attempts to solve our problems through discussion, argument, and resolution—the key to Habermas's communicative praxis—are infiltrated by questions of money and power. It is not that money and power issues have no place in deciding how to solve problems; it is rather that they become the only or primary questions asked in confronting problems.

As the human sphere is diminished, we develop not only "individual" problems, but social pathologies. We blithely use unemployment (a dislocation of people destructive to human relations) to cure inflation (a disequilibrium in the system). Keynesian and other economists find this perfectly acceptable, if painful for some (not themselves, of course) as a matter of national policy. We allow a poorer residential neighborhood to be invaded by heavy industry. Yet the city council which implements such zoning laws is constituted by members who live in more affluent neighborhoods, where industry is intolerable. Indeed, Habermas's diagnosis is that the proliferation of technical rationality to solve human problems, of the expertise of "systems management," has so refigured our lives that we have no human or humane way to defend our natural world and our human communities from degradation by those who control the system of power and money. The problem is not with Enlightenment humanism as the deconstructive "postmodernists" suggest, but with the failures to radicalize the emancipation of the Enlightenment and to extend it to all humans.

The prescription for an antidote to increasing degradation of the lifeworld, political impotence and frustration, social inertia, and economic stratification cannot be found in the realm of the system: neither power nor money can provide adequate solutions to the problems created by money and power. Americans should need no Habermas to educate them on this point: the failure of many of the Great Society programs of the 1960s shows the inability of money and power alone to solve problems in the lifeworld of marginalized people. We need practically "to promote a vigorous communication community dedicated to a public ethic that will win back control for the lifeworld of the system that is, inevitably, a good servant but a very bad ruler" (Lakeland 1990:69). But how is this possible? Our lifeworld has been colonized by the system. And everything, as the Nietzschean postmodernists point out, is a matter of power.

The theoretical answer Habermas offers as a basis for showing that winning back control of the lifeworld is necessary (and therefore possible) is his theory of communicative action, a complex theory of language-in-use-for-communication. The details of this complex theory occupy over 800 pages of dense prose (Habermas 1984,1987). For our purposes, three of its key claims are crucial. First, the simple fact is that we do communicate with each other. Sometimes it is halting, sometimes misunderstood, sometimes incomplete. But mostly we do communicate and understand each other well enough to be able to get through the day. Communication is the norm; miscommunication the deviation. Second, for us to communicate implies the priority of honesty and sincerity over dishonesty and deception. Lies are "parasitic upon" truths. If we did not take it for granted that most of what people tell us is true, then we could not communicate efficiently—or even lie well! For what makes deception possible is that it occurs within an expected pattern of non-deceptive communication. Without the expected pattern, not only would deception be impossible, but communication of any sort would be. Third, our shared use of language is a constitutive feature of our humanity. If we could not communicate, we would not be fully human. We are *homo loquens*, hominids communicating in speech. We are more than that, of course, but we are at least that—even if some of us for physical or social reasons cannot communicate as well as others. It is this theory of language in action—of communicative praxis—which provides a way to retain the boons of modernity while counteracting its banes.

A number of contemporary Roman Catholic writers have used the theory of communicative action in theology. Johann Baptist Metz, Francis Schüssler Fiorenza, Paul Lakeland, Edmund Arens and others have been deeply influenced by Habermas. Perhaps more than others, Helmut Peukert has pushed Habermasian theory into a theological direction (as Karl-Otto Apel has brought out its ethical aspects more clearly). Peukert "masterfully" (Habermas 1992:236) employs an "immanent critique" to attempt to show that Habermas's ethical and political theory based in his analysis of language is necessarily incomplete without an explicit reference to God's saving power.

Peukert's basic insight is that without a religious commitment, the theory of communicative action winds up with an aporia, an insoluble problem at its heart. Peukert begins by accepting Habermas's claim that basic assertions in a discipline are established not by their "correspondence to reality" or by the power or position of those who assert them, but by the consensus of the practitioners of the discipline. A theory in physics, for instance, is deemed acceptable not because it somehow matches reality (although it may) nor because the lab at which it was developed is prestigious, but because the community of physicists reaches a consensus about its probability. An experimental claim about subatomic particles is accepted if the experiment which gave rise to the claim is replicable by another scientific lab. In effect, that second lab's work "stands in" for the whole community of physicists because the experiment could, in principle, be replicated by anyone with the right training and equipment. A claim about the origins of the universe is deemed unacceptable if it fails to square with the known facts about the universe or fails to explain them elegantly—a consensus judgment that is often slow in developing among astrophysicists. Habermas takes an unusual step for a European philosopher when he follows the American pragmatist C. S. Pierce in finding that "consensus" is the measure of what is acceptable as "true" (also compare Kuhn).

But then the question arises: by "what criteria can it be decided that a consensus is a true consensus?" (Peukert 1984:193). No external criteria are sufficient, because any criteria for judging the reliability of a consensus also need to be validated. And how would one do that but by arguing a position and reaching a consensus? But how would one decide that that was a true consensus? The trick is to find a way to avoid an infinite regress of arguments about criteria for consensus. Peukert, following Pierce and Habermas, argues for the principle that a conversation "in which validity claims are decided upon argumentatively cannot in principle be limited" (187) will do the trick. A conversation in principle open to all who can participate would "stand in" for and, in fact, be (as in physics) the way in which criteria would ultimately be practically warranted.

To avoid infinite regress, anyone who is committed to saying that what we accept as true or right is bound to accepting an unlimited conversation as the normative way to establish criteria. An unlimited conversation is thus what Habermas calls an "ideal speech situation" in which all people are in principle able to participate. This situation is obviously not real—an actual unlimited conversation does not occur, at least this side of the grave. But if one accepts the argument that one justifies one's claims by argument and achieving consensus of those who can participate in the conversation, then one must accept the implication that full justification requires at least a conversation potentially unlimited, open to all, even if it is not "real" yet. Just as a physicist's predictions about subatomic particles is potentially open to checking by all the members of the discipline, although actually checked only by a few, so a universal ethical or political claim must be potentially open to checking by all people, even if it is only actually checked by a few. In short, if you make a claim to empirical truth or moral rightness, you are implicitly committed to warranting that claim in an ideal speech situation.

However, in our society, people are debilitated from participating in the discursive redemption of claims which concern them. Voices from the margins of the local society, voices from the dominated cultures which the "first world" exploits, and voices from those who are disempowered in other ways are silenced. Even today in a representative democracy, poor neighborhoods have industry foisted upon them against their wishes and without regard for the disruption such industry will cause. Moneyed interests with powerful voices coordinate and steer our social policies and their implementation. Those who control the "tools" for making the system run smoothly use those tools to drown out the voices of others or to promote their own interests—as when a giant corporation like U.S. Sugar provides 90 percent of the support for a campaign supporting a tax-limitation initiative in the State of Florida, because passing the initiative would make it highly unlikely that a proposed tax on sugar producers, earmarked to clean up the contamination in the Everglades produced especially by sugar plantations, could be passed (Tallahassee *Democrat* 4/21/94). The power of lobbyists to influence legislation in favor of interest groups they represent without regard to the commonweal, especially in state legislatures, is a prime symptom of the systematic colonization of the lifeworld. In other words, in those very political institutions established for the discursive validation of claims, where representatives of all the people gather to "stand in" for the people who will be affected by their decisions, there are the voices of the people silenced, drowned out by the rich and powerful.

Hence, as your very use of language commits you to discursive valida-tion, and it is presently impossible because the system has colonized the lifeworld, you are also implicitly committed to undertake innovative ac-tions, actions which change the conventions that silence the voices which should be heard. We are implicitly committed to changing the patterns wherein money and power drown out human interests. You—we all—are obliged to work to enable all people to participate in the conversation, to have their voices heard. To redeem the implicit commitments we make in communicating with one another, commitments to truth and sincerity as seen above, we must finally acknowledge that we are in solidarity not merely with those who are like us, but with all people. We are committed to a universal solidarity, for we are all finally bound to one another as a universal community searching to establish what is true and what is right. In sum, if anyone is committed to establishing truth, that person *ipso facto* must be committed to universal solidarity in which the validation of those claims would be fully possible and thus to instantiating the unlimited conversation in which a consensus on what is true and what is right can be properly established, without the silencing of any human voice.

However, Peukert shows that the theory of communicative action develops an insoluble dilemma. He brings this out brilliantly by showing the present significance of a dispute between earlier critical theorists Walter Benjamin and Max Horkheimer over the issue of our relationship with the dead. Either the universal solidarity to which we are committed when we engage in the act of communicating is temporally universal or it is not. If it is not temporally universal, then it is not truly universal. The "ideal speech situation" is a mere illusion, for there are always excluded those of the past and those of the future. To be truly universal, our solidarity must encompass the past and the future. But the past is dead, and "humans who have tried to act out of solidarity, those to whom we owe our own life possibilities, have been annihilated" (Peukert 1984:211). We cannot have solidarity with them. Whatever happiness which we have now is based on whatever justice and solidarity which the past achieved. But the dead martyrs, heroes, soldiers, and laborers who have worked for the reality of this better life deserve our solidarity, unless we pitilessly erase them and the debt we owe them from our memory—unless, that is, we engage in deceit, a violation of our fundamental commitments as *homines loquentes*. Peukert writes:

> If the unconsciousness of world history is the presupposition of living happily, then is not the life of those human beings in this future inhuman? According to our previous analysis, unconditioned and universal solidarity with others was seen as the constitutive condition of one's own being human. How can one retain the memory of the conclusive, irretrievable loss of the victims of the historical process, to whom one owes one's entire happiness, and still be happy, still find one's identity? If for the sake of one's own happiness and one's own identity this memory is banished from consciousness, is this not tantamount to the betrayal of the very solidarity by which alone one is able to discover oneself.
>
> Anamnestic solidarity marks, then, the most extreme paradox of a historically and communicatively acting entity; one's own existence becomes a self-contradiction by means of the solidarity to which it is

indebted. The condition of its possibility becomes its destruction. The idea of "perfect justice" can only then become a nightmare (Peukert 1984:209).

This is the central paradox of the theory of communicative action: to enjoy what we have, we must both deny and affirm our interactive solidarity with those who are gone. If we obliterate our debt to them, we fail to affirm our own humanity; but if we acknowledge our debt to them, we must realize the impossibility of justice and happiness. The fact has been established that "the other has ultimately been annihilated in his innocence and that one benefits from his annihilation. To simply direct one's solidarity to others and finally to the future generation does not resolve this inner contradiction" (Peukert 1984:233). We owe a debt we can never pay; we must be in solidarity with those who can never be present; we are trapped in a paradox.

The only escape is a religious affirmation. Peukert, writing from the Christian tradition claims:

Temporal, communicative action in solidarity unto death anticipates a reality about which it is asserted first of all by one's own practical performance that it can and does actually save others. The performance of one's own existence in communicative action is then factually the assertion, in this action itself, of a reality that does not simply allow others to become an already superseded fact of the past (Peukert 1984:234).

In other words, to avoid the paradox, one must find that the "reality disclosed in communicative action, asserted as the saving reality for others and at the same time as the reality that through this salvation of the other makes possible one's own temporal existence unto death, must be called 'God'" (Peukert 1984:235).

We can avoid the paradox and be in solidarity with the dead if and only if the dead live in God. In short, the only way to validate without paradox the theory of communicative praxis of Jürgen Habermas is to accept the reality of God who saves.

Peukert provides a summary of the Creed of the Judeo-Christian tradition by giving a powerfully moving account of the history in which we are enmeshed, a history of solidarity:

The original profession of faith of Judaism is that of liberation from the slavery of Egypt. This experience is intensified during the period of exile and finally in the fight against the Seleucid empire in the second century, b.c.e. The latter was a totalitarian system that not only practiced external repression, but also tried to control the consciences of individuals. The apocalyptic [vision] originates as an answer to this exterminating power of the state. In an ever more radical way, God is confessed as the one who, intervening eschatologically robs this untamable power of its force. God deprives this eschatological animal, with its continually reappearing new heads, of its ability to exterminate human beings, and in a way that extends even beyond the grave: God is the saving power whose range of action does not end at the threshold of death. God can call even the dead to life and make up for past injustice. The knowledge of God includes the knowledge that a communal existence is possible, an existence that is not dominated by the mechanisms of power accumulation.

Viewed historically, Jesus is the one who decisively changes this apocalyptical understanding of history. For him also, of course, God is the one who in an eschatological intervention ultimately transforms the world through its completion. But the evil nexus has already been broken ("I watched Satan fall from the sky like lightning," Luke 10:18). God has begun to reign in unconditioned goodness and to restore creation. It is not now only possible, but necessary, indeed a matter of course, that one should realize this prevenient goodness of God practically: in the unconditioned affirmation of the other, even the one who may be an enemy. For this person, too, has been affirmed unconditionally. The execution of Jesus becomes the starting point for the experience and the confession that this is also true for his own person: that precisely in his death, he is saved and that, from now on, an intersubjective mode of conduct has become possible for all, in which we progress toward God as the saving reality even in death. Intersubjectivity is qualified in a new way; God's dominion means the abandonment of the domination of human beings over each other (Peukert 1992:57).

The confidence that God saves makes possible, then, not merely a hope that calls the dead to life, but even a political practice of openness and vulnerability in which one participates in making real the prevenient goodness of God. Only when we understand the liberating power of God can we grasp the commitments and practices which must involve us:

[T]he integrity and inviolable dignity of human beings; human rights in the wider social context in addition to the codified basic rights and the rights to political participation; justice that is more than the equal treatment of unequals, but that seeks to make individual integrity really possible; forms of discourse that enable the voiceless to speak; innovative conciliatory action that opens up the possibility for peace; and a solidarity which also includes the dead and the generations to come (Peukert 1992:62).

The practice of universal anticipatory and anamnestic solidarity, the solidarity finally demanded by the theory of communicative action, is possible without paradox only if there is a God who calls the dead to life so we can anticipatorily be in solidarity with them. Habermas (1992:237), not surprisingly, rejects Peukert's view, saying Peukert argues for a "theological foundation" for the theory of communicative action. But designating Peukert's work as "foundational" shows that Habermas has missed the point. He has confused the place commitment to God's saving power has in Peukert's work with the place it had in modern theology. God is not the foundation for a system, but the only power that can resolve an insoluble dilemma within the system-without-God. To Catholic ears, Peukert sounds remarkably as if he is invoking not the god of the gaps, but the communion of saints.

Although this theory sounds remarkably abstract and philosophical, it need not be. Edmund Arens has argued that this sort of practice can be found in Jesus' practice as portrayed in the gospels:

> In recollecting the exposition of the basic structure of communicative action, of the communicative structure of the Gospels as well as the communicative praxis of Jesus, his Apostles and disciples, we can understand faith as a communicative practice. . . . The propositional content of Christian faith is in its heart the person and praxis of Jesus as well as God's action in and on him (Arens 1992:130; my translation).

Arens argues that faith in Jesus is not merely cognitive, emotional, or volitional, but active. To believe in Jesus *is* to follow in his communicative praxis: his actions, his teaching, his death and resurrection. "Orthopraxis means to do the truth. The truth which Jesus Christ is is to be done in Christopraxis" (Arens 1992:117). Jesus' apostles and disciples carry on this Christopraxis in the community of the church and thus continue to make present the reign of God. The full range of this Christopraxis is authentic discipleship (Arens 1992:147; compare Tilley 1985). Insofar as the community of the church fails to be a community of Christopraxis, it needs to be reformed. But the community of the Church can always be called to its senses to reform itself, for it carries a dangerous memory which can interrupt "business as usual" when "business as usual" is a deformed set of practices.

Yet two fundamental problems bedevil this approach to retaining the boons of modernity. The first is that in the modern world—and the emerging postmodern world—power is an omnipresent force. When people refuse to conform to the norms of society, they are either forced to conform or to be punished. Power inevitably is used to enforce the "mainstream" social goals and to suppress the voices and the practices of those who dissent. The mode of suppression is not necessarily violent or carceral, although contemporary American ideology valorizes the odd notion that the problem of crime in the lifeworld is to be resolved by the systemic use of power which increases the number of people forced to live unproductive lives in prisons. Like it or not, homogenization of culture and flattening of difference is a result of seeking efficiency and productivity in every aspect of life. Like it or not, all the developed world (and much of the "third world") drinks Coca-Cola (or Pepsi-Cola), eats McDonald's hamburgers, and discusses human rights in terms defined by Western, post-Christian, liberal, democratic ideology which rubs out the differences from other discourses about justice that valorize goals other than life, liberty, and the pursuit of happiness—goals like solidarity in this life and the next. The global communications system means the loss of many distinctive languages and dialects, for the most local languages are useless in a global communications network. Many linguists see this as a tragic loss (*Chronicle of Higher Education:* 4/18/94). Kenneth Surin (1990:67-100) has shown just how this social, economic, and political homogenization and degradation is paralleled in much modern theology as well. In short, the very process of "potentially universal" dialogue which Habermas advocates to overcome the colonization of the (Western, Euro-American) lifeworld by the system (of money power) *is itself* a colonization of other lifeworlds by a (hidden? Western?) system which demands that all the voices speak a commensurable, fully translatable, universal language—which inevitably is a language that erases real and essentially contested differences in the concepts which are constituted in and constitute differing lifeworlds.

Second, there is also an aporia in Peukert's thought. It is the problem of evil. In order to affirm that the dead are not merely the jetsam of history, he has to offer a redemptive theodicy, an explanation of why and how the apparent evil of the annihilation of the innocent is not ultimately evil. Since he offers no explanation, but only a defense of the possibility that there might be an explanation, he shows to his audience that it is as permissible to take his position as to take other positions. However, he does not show that his position is superior to others since it, too, does not explain a central anomaly; and (if Tilley 1991 is correct) he cannot explain that central anomaly without creating even worse problems.

Perhaps these problems can be overcome in practice, but they seem insoluble in theory. The "critical theoretical" system proposed by Habermas and influential on theological discourse remains plagued with a devastating theoretical anomaly. Yet perhaps such theoretical anomalies don't plague all sorts of constructive postmodern theory. Indeed, the communalism advocated by David Ray Griffin, starting from a totally different philosophical basis, seems to avoid them. We turn to Griffin's work in Chapter 2.

Chapter 2

David Ray Griffin and Constructive
Postmodern Communalism

with Craig Westman

Postmodern thought is ecological through and through, and provides the philosophical and theological grounding for the lasting insights popularized by the ecological movement.

—David Ray Griffin

David Ray Griffin works in the context of Whiteheadian process philosophy. He has been constructing a postmodern theology which directly addresses both of the problems Lakeland sees in modern society: the valorization of the individual and his [sic] use of technical reason, and the destruction of the environment. Griffin's vision defines itself over against the modern individualistic dualism that allows humans to exploit nature mechanistically through setting the exploiting self apart from exploitable nature.

Griffin's use of the term "postmodern" is uniquely his own. He recognizes that it is quite different from its dominant use in artistic, literary, and deconstructive philosophical circles.

That type of postmodernism should really be called *ultra*modernism, or *most*modernism, because it results from taking some of the presuppositions of modernity to their logical conclusions. In contrast with this relativistic, nihilistic, deconstructive postmodernism, I speak of a constructive, reconstructive, or revisionary postmodernism, in which many of the presuppositions of modernity are challenged and revised (1990a:6-7).

That the "ultramodernists" would reject this characterization of their relationship to modernity (as we shall see in the next parts) is irrelevant. Here Griffin defines his own project "oppositionally," just as Kort suggests theologians do, in order to make its central and distinctive shape clear.

Griffin defines his "postmodernism" over against three other forms: deconstruction, liberationist, and restorationist (Griffin, Beardslee, and Holland 1989:3). Griffin seeks "a new unity of scientific, ethical, aesthetic, and religious intuitions. It rejects not science as such but only that scientism in which the data of the modern natural sciences are alone allowed to contribute to the construction of our worldview..." (Griffin, Beardslee, and Holland 1989:xii-xiii). Mark C. Taylor (discussed in Chapter 5) is an obvious example of deconstruction which exemplifies the worst of "mostmodernism." Griffin's primary examples of liberationists, are North American, Protestant, male theologians Harvey Cox and Cornel West. Restorationist theologies idealize premodern and antimodern modes of thought. As they try to recover intact a world that can be present only in the memory of God, their longings for premodernity are beyond the purview of our work.

Concern with the "global ecological crisis" permeates his agenda and serves to focus Griffin's differences with "modernism" (1993:6). His ecological emphasis can be found even in his earliest works in which he argues against the "modern Christian" emphasis on individualism. Instead, Griffin claims:

> [T]he "social gospel" emphasis of Christianity must become an "ecological gospel" emphasis, since the "society" for which God is concerned includes the totality of beings, especially the totality of living beings.... [T]he "others" should not be understood as limited to other human beings, but as including God and nature as well (1973:240-41).

This theme continues from his first book through his most recent work wherein he portrays modernity in terms similar to critical theory,

> in terms of the drive to dominate nature for human benefit, a drive that found justification in the anthropocentric dualism of the early modern worldview and found expression in modern economics and technology. A political leader with a postmodern vision would be one who has broken free from this self-destructive outlook, who has come to see humanity as *one among millions of species that have a right to flourish* [emphasis added], and who sees that the human economy must, for the sake of the human race as well as other species, fit harmoniously within nature's economy. A postmodern president would lead America and thereby the world to realize that the ecological crisis is the greatest challenge ever faced by the human race (1993:6-7).

Unlike modern theologies, a postmodern theology must be concerned with the crisis of nature as well as the crises in the lifeworld. The havoc wreaked on natural beauty and the destruction of our global habitat are modern trends which postmodernism must oppose.

In calling for a global postmodern change, Griffin narrates the story of modernity. Griffin seeks to illustrate what led to his ecological postmodernism. But he shows an intellectualist bias, for his narrative highlights not the social formations of the modern world (as Habermas does), but rather attributes the degradation to a set of philosophical ideas. He writes:

In its seventeenth-century founders, except for Hobbes, this mechanistic view of nature was part of a dualistic worldview, in which the human soul was in effect treated as supernatural. In fact, these scientist-philosophers could remove all nonquantitative qualities from nature precisely because they could lodge them in the soul. But in the following centuries, more and more thinkers followed Hobbes's lead and rejected dualism in favor of complete materialism. . . . The rejection of this dualism meant that not only all quality but also all soul was banished from reality. Soul was said to be epiphenomenal at most, an ineffectual by-product of purely material mechanisms which control the world (1990a:240).

In the first stage of this movement that came to constitute the "modern" worldview, nature was disenchanted. In the second stage, the world was desouled. This is the metaphysical catastrophe that lies behind the present threat of physical catastrophe.

Griffin finds we need to recover a "sense of the sacred depths of our souls and of the world as a whole and our bondedness to it. . ." (1990a:240-41). As the basic cause is ideational, so the cure is a better idea. Whether this diagnosis and prescription is plausible remains to be seen.

Griffin advocates a global ecological vision of "community" which allows the divine to establish a "harmony with ourselves and all of creation" (1973:246). Griffin's communalism originated while he was a graduate student in the turbulent 1960s. He became concerned with ecological issues about 1969 while teaching theology at the University of Dayton. He began to devote "considerable attention to a process theology of nature, becoming convinced that anthropocentrism and dualism are errors that must be rooted out if we are to survive" (Griffin and Smith 1989:4). He came to see "process theology as providing a good basis for a social (and ecological) gospel . . . a more just and survivable way of life, on this planet" (3).

In the mid to late 1970s, with the influence of Eastern religious philosophies and the natural sciences (physics and biology), Griffin's ecological agenda began to grow: "I became more convinced than ever of both the possibility and the necessity of a postmodern worldview (although I was not yet using the word) based primarily upon a synthesis of Whiteheadian philosophy and the best of the more recent thinking in these and other areas" (5). While on a research leave in 1980-81 at Cambridge University "the final stimulus to make the contrast between modernity and postmodernity" came to Griffin. It was here at Cambridge that Griffin became convinced of the "need to relate talk of nature, human nature, and divine action to contemporary sciences and philosophical reflection thereon" (5).

> I came to see Whitehead's philosophy, especially when its support for these influences is emphasized, to be a twentieth-century recrudescence of that Renaissance worldview which spawned modern science only to be rejected in the name of reactionary theological and sociological interests. My sense of the Whiteheadian philosophy as a *postmodern* world view thereby increased, along with my interest in stressing its distinctively postmodern features. In 1983, I started the Center for a Postmodern World in Santa Barbara (6-7; emphasis added).

The founding of this Center for a Postmodern World by Griffin has resulted in a series of books published by SUNY Press on Constructive Postmodern Thought. The series offers analyses of modernity, critiques of eliminative postmodernism, and "an elaboration of the process philosophy and theology of Whitehead and Hartshorne as the best foundation for a postmodern worldview, and finally, the application of this panentheism and similar views to the problems of the modern world" (Thomas 1992:209-10).

Whiteheadian process thought is central to Griffin's work. It provides a "world-view capable of sustaining a sense of the meaning and importance of life, and an ethical stance adequate to the needs of the present and future situation of the world, with its hunger, diminishing resources, and potential ecological disaster" (1985:130). Within Whitehead's philosophy is a vision of the world as an interactive community. "Process Theology calls for still further extension of the sense of participation. The whole of nature participates in us and we in it" (Cobb and Griffin 1976:155). This community of nature theme is derived from the works of Whitehead whom they quote as follows:

> There is a unity in the universe, enjoying value and (by its immanence) sharing value. For example, take the subtle beauty of a flower in some isolated glade of a primeval forest. No animal has ever had the subtlety of experience to enjoy its full beauty. And yet this beauty is a grand fact in the universe. When we survey nature and think however flitting and superficial has been the animal enjoyment of its wonders, and when we realize how incapable the separate cells and pulsations of each flower are of enjoying the total effect—then our sense of the value of the details for the totality dawns upon our consciousness.

This is the intuition of holiness, the intuition of the sacred, which is at the foundation of all religion (1976:150-51).

One is immediately struck by the romantic language Whitehead uses. Whitehead with his "primeval forest" calls for a return to a view of nature as "an inclusive unity" common in the nineteenth century.

Ecological emphases carry over into Griffin's philosophy of science. He uses Whiteheadian process philosophy to oppose modern science's "mechanistic vision" which attempts to reduce the "functioning of organisms in terms of their elementary constituents" (1985:137). As Griffin notes:

The tension between fate and freedom is only one aspect of the dichotomy between the sciences and the humanities. As Prigogine stresses, the dichotomy of the temporal and nontemporal is at the root of a more general opposition between humanity and nature. . . . The idea that the world of nature is a passive realm, devoid of aesthetic qualities and intrinsic value, has led to a devaluation of these values in modern life. Hence, the issue of the ultimate status of time is part of the overall problem of modern thought, which has, among other things, contributed significantly to the ecological crisis of our time (1985:29).

In Griffin's metaphysics, not only human entities, but all entities, are free. Thus, for Griffin's vision, modern thought's loss of an inherent value in nature is devastatingly significant. This denial of the (minimal and limited) freedom and creativity in and of the natural world has led to an "ecological crisis" characterized by the possibility of the nuclear annihilation of all valuing and valued entities on this planet. In hopes of rectifying this "ecological crisis" Griffin calls for a return "in a sense to one aspect of pre-modern naturalism, in which matter was seen as active and self-organizing" (1985:16). The human individual can no longer be viewed in isolation apart from the community of nature. Properly understood, the human person is a "hierarchy" of living cells. As Griffin notes in Whiteheadian terminology:

[T]here is a hierarchy involved in all compound individuals. The atom is already a hierarchical society, since it is not merely an aggregate of subatomic parts. Rather, inclusive of these parts there is a series of atomic occasions of experience that make the atom into an integrated whole. Molecules can likewise be thought to be unified by molecular occasions of experience. The same can be thought to be true of macromolecules, viruses, etc. The living cell is dominated by living occasions of experience. Finally, the multicelled animal is not just a democracy of cells, but has a dominating member, the series of experiences constituting the soul. . . . However, there is another kind of hierarchy of societies in Whitehead. Whitehead suggests that all compound individuals (discussed above) are specialized societies (developed to foster more intense experience) within more general forms of social order (1985:148, 150).

In order to avoid ecological destruction, humanity needs to envision itself as Whitehead's philosophy does: as part of nature. Griffin attempts to demonstrate that since "the human mind is now considered a genuine part of nature, . . . [this] means that the categories needed to describe it should be generalized to other natural unities" (1977:100). What this entails is not only a more interactive concern for the physical environment, but also a turning inward to the self as a center of value.

Since human experience *is* natural, and "since it is that part of nature one knows most intimately, it provides the best starting point for finding principles that can be generalized to all actual entities" (1985:124). This turning inward is only strategic. Griffin also reflectively turns outward to the environment itself: an environment in which even nature with its "subhuman actualities can be conceived in terms of the primary elements in human experience" (1985:126). The world is truly an ordered "multiplicity of actual things which are genuinely related" (1985:127) by mutually constituting each other. This is possible in Whiteheadian thought because nature cannot be understood materialistically. This view breaks with modern scientific thought of nature as an inert and passive realm. Nature is composed of active and feeling entities, not passive things. This vision implies the rightness of redirecting modern science into a postmodern, ecologically sensitive context. Griffin calls for a re-investment of nature with viable meaning: a meaning eclipsed in modern science's materialistic and reductionist ways of understanding the biosphere (1985:ii). As nature provides the key for understanding humans, so humans provide the key for understanding nature. But then the scientific study of nature and humanity must be nonreductionist, nonmaterialist, and nondualist.

One result of Griffin's integration of philosophy of science into process thought is to provide room for social science under the rubric of *panexperientialism*, "in which feeling and intrinsic value are attributed to all individuals comprising nature" (1989b:5). This is Griffin's ontological basis for his "naturalistic theism or affirmation of a cosmic soul as a natural reality interacting with the world as part of the natural process" (Thomas 1992:212). In this world nothing is totally passive, nothing purely active. Everything is in some way creative. Thus, creativity is the ultimate verifiable reality, "which is embodied by all individuals, from God to electrons" (Griffin 1989b:5). Griffin also argues that panexperientialism

overcomes the bifurcation between the natural and the social sciences. Human beings, on the one hand, are declared to be fully natural, exemplifying the same principles as the rest of nature. All natural things, on the other hand, are said to be social. Reality is, to use Hartshorne's term, "social process." . . . *Natural laws have already been elevated to sociological laws*. . . . Panexperientialism can thereby help us overcome the increasing intellectual fragmentation of modernity by moving toward a postmodern integration of our cultural interests. The pluriversity could again become a university, in which courses in physics, biology, psychology, sociology, economics, ethics, and aesthetics would help students achieve an integrated view of themselves and the universe (1989a:14-15).

As Griffin notes, such a universal postmodern outlook would be all-encompassing. Given the problems of silencing different voices, as noted in our discussion of Habermasian universalism above, this tendency may raise more problems than it can solve.

Griffin concludes his work by bringing out the distinctively postmodern aspects of Whitehead's and Hartshorne's metaphysics, arguing that a "widespread appropriation of postmodern theism at a deep level by our culture would do much to overcome our penchant for imperialism and nuclearism" (1989b:145). But postmodern theism is nothing but Whiteheadian panentheism "according to which God is in all things and all things are in God" (1990b:2).

Modern individualism denies the reality of internal relations. Instead of entities mutually constituting each other, the worldview derived from modern science sees independent things only externally related to each other. Lack of communal relations, was the result of

the modern worldview [which] was *dualistic*, distinguishing the human soul radically from "nature," and *supernaturalistic*, thinking of nature and human souls as having been created *ex nihilo* by an omnipotent deity, who imposed motion and order on nature and implanted moral, religious, and aesthetic values in the human soul. ... In the later half of the eighteenth century, God and the soul began disappearing, leaving *atheistic materialism* as the dominate outlook of the scientific community and eventually of the majority of the cultural elite. . . . With this development, not only was nature disenchanted— stripped of all purpose, interiority, enjoyment, and "magic" (events involving action at a distance), but also the world as a whole was disenchanted—stripped of all purpose, meaning, and objective values (1990a:5).

Griffin has also used Jungian archetypal psychology to help to return "soul and divinity to the world" (1990a:vii). The world-soul is "a truly divine reality, that all-encompassing soul in which we live, move, and have our being . . . the divine soul of the world" (1990a:246). Griffin claims that both Jung and Whitehead are "postmodern" in their worldviews, in that they reject the tenets of "the modern worldview, yet without returning to a premodern approach. They retain the formal commitment of modernity to rational empiricism, but they reject some of the substantive presuppositions of modernity" (1990a:6).

Griffin explores the notion of a spiritually oriented community, attacking modern science's creation of a destructive dualism in the individual (1988:3,5). Griffin sees that the modern worldview gives society little hope of dealing with the destructiveness of modernity apart from a "cataclysmic revolution" (1988:14). In contrast Griffin sees his postmodern perspective as offering "the more hopeful vision that, through the emergence of a new worldview and concomitant spirituality, . . . the course of our world can be radically changed without cataclysmic revolution" (1988:14). Owen Thomas summed up Griffin's agenda as follows:

> Griffin describes postmodern spirituality as emphasizing internal relations, organicism, human self-determination, a new respect for the past (a new conservatism or transformative traditionalism), a naturalistic panentheism, experience of norms, and a post-patriarchal vision. He describes the direction of the thinking of postmodern social theorists as communitarian. . . . Postmodern society will also be characterized by pluralistic religious values in public life, a steady-state economy, plus the continuation of the good features of modernity such as progress, liberty, and equality (1992:214).

What Thomas neglects to inform his readers is that Griffin's envisioned community is a rather romantic vision in which we are called to "imagine what we could do if we became religiously committed to a human society of liberty, equality, and community, with 'community' understood as the whole biotic community" (1988:23). Griffin's imagined society is one of an expanded naturalism, in which "pluralistic religious values" are ecologically centered. As Griffin further notes, "the possibilities are beyond imagination, because we would be employing all the scientific and technological knowledge garnered during the modern period for postmodern purposes, and therefore for the long-term good of the planet as a whole" (1988: 23).

The place of the individual in the human and ecological community requires a world centered on ecological concerns. We quote at length to give the flavor of his meditation:

> Postmodern thought is ecological through and through, and provides the philosophical and theological grounding for the lasting insights popularized by the ecological movement. If it, in fact, becomes the basis for the new paradigm of our culture, future generations of citizens will *grow up* with an ecological consciousness in which the value of all things is respected and the interconnectedness of all things is recognized. The awareness that we must walk gently through the

world, using only what we need, preserving the ecological balance for our neighbors and future generations, will be "common sense."

This ethic will be as basic to the religion of these postmodern humans as the drive to acquire possessions and dominate nature has been to the citizens of the modern world. World citizens with such an attitude will have a much better chance of living in peace with themselves and each other.... The task is to combine forces to develop a new *worldview* that their contemporaries and especially the rising generation will find convincing and also begin spelling out the *new ethic*, the new way of ordering our individual, communal, national, and international relations, so as to provide realistic hope that it will lead to a better form of life. The Center for a Postmodern World came into being to promote this effort.

If this effort succeeds, so that postmodern thought of this sort becomes the foundation of the postmodern paradigm (just as substance thought of Descartes, Newton, and others became the foundation of the modern paradigm), the human beings of future generations will not regard relations based upon coercive power as the "natural" and only "realistic" way to get things done; they will not regard nature as a "disenchanted" realm which is not akin to us and whose only value lies in its being a "natural resource" for us; their *real* religion will not consist in the drive to dominate nature and acquire material goods; they will not believe that human satisfaction comes primarily through money and things it buys, and hence will not believe that economic considerations should be paramount in our public life; and they will not envisage the world as comprising autonomous atoms, and hence will not assume that problems can be solved in a piecemeal fashion, nor that the good of one individual or community can be attained in isolation from the good of all. They will have a sense of the Divine as permeating all things and as working persuasively in each part for the good of the whole. Their religious drive to imitate deity will lead them to make cooperative persuasion their chief modus operandi and habitually to look for ways to mesh their good with the good of the whole (1988:152-53).

Griffin's unified vision of reality is set in the near future. The sacred interconnections of all entities on the planet is vision, however, that requires "a postmodern politics" (1988:23) to be realized.

Griffin recognizes that if his vision is to come to pass that a "new style of leadership, grounded in a new vision of the world" is needed for the "approaching millennium" (1993:4). It will be leadership grounded in a "Green Spirituality" of sacredness (1992:19-20). "A postmodern president would lead America and thereby the world to realize that the ecological crisis is the greatest challenge ever faced by the human race" (1993:6,7). With recent advancements on the ecological front, it would seem that

Griffin's agenda is coming more into the fore for the American populace. Griffin also has begun to address concrete individual threats of modernity to life on the planet:

What is the biggest of all stories? It is that one of the millions of species of life on our planet has now, in our century, developed the power to threaten not only its own existence but also that of most of the other species of life on our planet. This has never happened before. From a cosmic standpoint, it has to be the biggest story not only of our time, but of the adventure of life on planet Earth itself (1993: 70).

Griffin not only addresses the nuclear threat of this age, but also the ozone hole, global warming, the modern industrial system, and modern economics. Griffin then offers concrete solutions to these ecological threats: energy efficiency, energy supply (solar energy), (mass) transportation, and curtailing deforestation. Griffin addresses modern militarization and notes how battles are "destructive of land and forests—as a visit to Vietnam makes clear." Griffin describes the detrimental effects of toxic chemicals and the equally hindering effects of overpopulation on earth's resources. And while Griffin insists that his facts show "that the global environmental crisis is extremely serious, the good news is that the ideas and the technological means for responding to the crisis in an adequate way are already at hand"(1993:94).

But is this a postmodern view? In one sense, it would be churlish to deny Griffin his label. But Griffin's vision and style are finally much more characteristic of a modern neo-romantic communal vision than of postmodern forms of thought. Like the romantics, Griffin valorizes nature and urges humans to live in harmony with their environment. Like the romantics, he values the local community but becomes profoundly vague when writing of what Habermas calls the colonization of the lifeworld by the system. Like the romantics, Griffin rejects rationalism's reduction of perception to mere sensation, of nature to mechanism, and of God to irrelevance to the world. Like the romantics, his writing is rather optimistic, especially compared to the "mostmodernists" he opposes. Like the romantics, his politics is not practical, but visionary. But if politics is the art of the practical, then such an approach, while inspiring, is deficient because impractical. The issue is not to develop a vision, but how to put reform into practice. For Griffin, as a postmodern neo-romantic communalist, states that we

must hope . . . that some presidents will arise from among us who do have "the vision thing" and are willing and able to use the "White House effect" to realize this vision—a postmodern vision of humanity living in harmony, for God's sake, with the rest of nature (1993:98).

But is vision enough? Can it be a "foundation" for change? Can it be the basis for a universal culture in a pluralistic world? The world that results from modernity may be one far too vicious to allow such a vision either to be a foundation for a political agenda or to be a realistic spirituality. In short, as rationality and romanticism seem to be a dialectic within the modern world of the enlightenment, is Griffin postmodern or does he continue the modern dialectic of rationalism and romanticism?

The answer to this question becomes clear when we examine Griffin's vision. His vision requires a substantial revision of each of the world's religious traditions. In effect, he is requiring that they become translated into (or at least translatable into) the categories of process panentheism, the philosophical discourse of Alfred North Whitehead. But this valorization of process thought as an all-inclusive system runs into problems analogous to Habermas's ideal speech situation. Just as all had to speak a commensurable language or set of languages to speak in that situation, so all valid religious visions must fit in a world in which nature is enchanted with the sacred. This leveling of differences into identity is just the repressive fault that many "dissolute" postmodernists see as a vicious flaw in modernism. As soon as a vision becomes all-inclusive, it becomes repressive of difference; and Griffin's vision is all-inclusive.

In the end, Griffin's postmodernism is a new and inspiring variety of modern, romantic communalism. But whether it has the power to transform a culture where the lifeworld has been colonized by the system is finally dubious. It provides an alternative vision, but it is difficult to see how it can be more than visionary, given the breadth and depth of the colonization. Unlike theologians considered in Part 4 below, Griffin doesn't show us how to put this theory into practice.

Yet how else are we to proceed, if we would not use the systemic power of coercion, to change the world? Key to both Habermasian and process agendas is deliberative discourse. In his attempts to develop a theology in and for a postmodern world, David Tracy also supports discourse, but a discourse which does not necessarily have a universal foundation, but one which includes ambiguity and plurality. We turn to his work in Chapter 3.

Chapter 3

Revisionist Theology and Reinterpreting Classics for Present Practice

with John Edwards

We can continue to give ourselves over to the great hope of Western reason, including the hope for adequate interpretation. But that hope is now a more modest one as a result of the discovery of the plurality of both language and knowledge and the ambiguities of all histories, including the history of reason itself.

—David Tracy

Theological "revisionism" is the position of David Tracy. Tracy, arguably the most prominent Roman Catholic theologian working in the U.S. today, has produced dozens of books and articles on a dizzying variety of theological and cultural topics. More than other "revisionists," including Schubert Ogden, Gordon Kaufmann, and David Griffin, Tracy is in dialogue with the radical postmodern writers (see 1987c and 1990, *passim*). Tracy was born in 1939 in Yonkers, New York. He is a Roman Catholic priest who received his doctorate from the Pontifical Gregorian University in 1964. After teaching at several Catholic colleges and universities both in the U.S. and abroad, in 1969 he joined the faculty of the Divinity School at the University of Chicago. This location has proven very important in his development, as it has brought him into contact with leading thinkers in various fields of religious studies, including Mircea Eliade, Paul Ricoeur *et al.* Moreover, as Charles W. Allen notes, "there is an obvious link between [the revisionists] and the University of Chicago Divinity School" (Allen 1990:389).

Central and distinctive to Tracy's theology is correlation as a theological method:

> ... insofar as philosophy and theology are reflective and correlational disciplines, they attempt, in properly general terms, to correlate critically an interpretation of the tradition and an interpretation of the contemporary situation (Tracy 1989b:550).

"Tradition" is understood here as the whole history of Christian theological development; the "contemporary situation" is regarded as involving all present realities of human existence beyond the sphere of the religious tradition being explored, in Tracy's case, the Christian. Tracy elsewhere describes the "contemporary situation" as the realm of "common human experience and language" (Tracy 1975:43). This formulation has opened Tracy to the charge of being a modern, liberal foundationalist in his theology.

Tracy admits the derivation of this concept of correlation from the work of Paul Tillich, though he claims that his notion is nuanced differently from Tillich's. Tillich states his version of correlation as follows in volume 1 of his *Systematic Theology*, "A theological system is supposed to satisfy two basic needs: the statement of the truth of the Christian message and the interpretation of this truth for every new generation" (Tillich 1951:3). Tracy responds:

> In sum, Paul Tillich's position continues to seem peculiarly helpful: for his expression of the proper ideal of contemporary theology; for his insistence that only an investigation of both "situation" and "message" can hope to fulfill this ideal; and for his articulation of the need for some general model of correlation as the proper response to this need (Tracy 1975:45-46).

Along with Tillich, Tracy cites concepts derived from modern theologians like Bultmann ("the 'kerygma' ") and Ogden ("the 'Christian witness of faith' ") as informing his understanding of "the tradition," and insights from Bultmann ("the 'contemporary scientific world view' ") and Lonergan ("a full-fledged 'historical consciousness' ") as sources for his idea of "common human experience" (Tracy 1975:44).

Once the data from both of these sources are collected, the process of correlation must itself begin. This process "demands logically that a critical comparison of the Christian 'answer' [to the questions raised by the human predicament] with all other 'answers' be initiated" (Tracy 1975:46). In phrasing his methodological program in this way, he is revising the Tillichian version of the correlational method, which, according to Tracy, sought its "answers" to the "questions" posed by the contemporary situation only in the tradition, not looking to the contemporary situation itself for answers (Tracy 1975:46). Tracy's version involves recognizing that both sources raise questions and can provide answers, which then must be correlated in the theological enterprise.

Correlation is not Tracy's *recommendation* for a way of doing theology; rather, it is what all theologians unavoidably *do*. The results of correlation differ, of course, from school to school. Tracy writes:

> Even Barthians correlate—if usually through a *Nein* to the situation. Even left-wing Hegelians among political and liberation theologians correlate—if often through an exposure of a confrontational, radical nonidentity of reason or the biblical message to see societal distortions in the present situation. Even those "liberal" theologians of culture who lack Tillich's own fine postliberal dialectical sense for the presence of negations correlate—if usually through a too-sanguine assumption of the identity or radical teleological similarity between the "highest values" of Christianity and the reigning liberal culture. All theologians, in fact, employ some method of correlation (Tracy 1985:261-262).

This passage indicates that Tracy's revisionist proposal is not a radical departure from previous or prevailing trends in Christian thought. In fact, he notes, forms of religious thought which do not utilize some form of the correlational method, such as fundamentalism, are not properly "theologies" at all, but ideologies which merely repeat that which has gone before rather than reaching new insights to be incorporated into a living tradition (Tracy 1981:99).

Tracy indicates that it is this method which defines what he calls the "revisionist model" for contemporary theology (Tracy 1975:32). He regards it as "the only hope for a way forward for theological method" (Tracy 1989b:556). Nonetheless, he recognizes the danger of complacency even within the correlational method and affirms the need for theologians of the revisionist type to "be continually open to critique and revision" (Tracy 1989b:556). Otherwise, stagnation may result.

Flowing from Tracy's assertion of the need for theological correlation is his claim that theology is a public discourse. Theology has, as a matter of fact, three publics: society, academy, and church (Tracy 1981:5). The public in which and for which the theologian works influences, and may determine, the shape of the theologian's work. Tracy writes:

> Sometimes that influence will prove so powerful that it will effectively determine the theology. More often a social location will provide "elective affinities" for a particular emphasis in theology, including the emphasis on what will count as a genuinely theological statement (Tracy 1981:5).

Tracy's focus on the role of social location in determining theological emphases is a good reflection of the correlational method itself. For in the development of any theology, the contemporary situation is largely a function of the public being addressed.

Tracy deals with the differences in "publics" at some length. To summarize, it can be observed that the public of *society* involves the realms of technoeconomic structure, polity, and culture, each of which has its own terms of internal discourse and its own relation to theology; that the public of the *academy* exists as a realm in which theology is carried out with reference to established rules of order utilized by researchers in the whole variety of academic disciplines; and that the public of the *church* is in some ways the determining locus for all theological discourse, regardless of the public primarily addressed by any particular theologian, and which seems necessarily to have not only sociological but also theological significance for the discipline (Tracy 1981:6-28). Commitment to one of the publics, always in the context of the general reality that the theologian is responsible for addressing all three, involves immersion in the canons of evidence, argumentation, and discourse peculiar to that public. As a result of these commitments, theology as a whole takes on the character of public discourse; as Tracy notes, "Insofar as theologians must render explicit the major claims and counterclaims of each of the three publics, they aid the cause of clarity for the wider public" (Tracy 1981:29).

Tracy's division of the theological public into church, society, and academy is mirrored by his distinction of three types of theology, one fitting each public: systematic, practical, and fundamental, respectively (Tracy 1981:51-58). Tracy describes himself as a fundamental theologian, addressing himself primarily to the academy, but not ignoring society and church as well (Tracy 1981:51). Fundamental theology is characterized by an attempt to articulate the truth-claims of theology in language that conforms to the canons of argumentation valorized in the context of academic discourse, specifically in terms derived from a particular philosophical method (Tracy 1981:62-63). Tracy sees fundamental theology not merely as a necessity in a situation of pluralism and secularism, but also as warranted by important strands of the Christian tradition itself and particularly by the Christian doctrine of God, with its notions of "creation and the universal salvific will of God" (Tracy 1981:63).

Systematic theology is that theology whose primary public is the public of the church, though naturally the church must be included in the wider set of addressees of every theologian. This discipline is defined in appropriately Tillichian terms as "the reinterpretation of the tradition for the present situation" (Tracy 1981:64). It is thus perhaps the clearest example of the correlational method, though Tracy seems to suggest that it is less likely to fulfill this role than is fundamental theology (Tracy 1981:81).

Practical theology is, obviously enough, the theology of praxis, whereby the correct course of action true to the tradition, in any given instance, is determined. Tracy defines it as "the mutually critical correlation of the interpreted theory and praxis of the Christian fact and the interpreted theory and praxis of the contemporary situation" (Tracy 1983:76). This definition fits practical theology into the general correlational program of Tracy's revisionist paradigm. But as we shall see in Part 4, this notion of praxis is significantly different from that of liberation theologians' accounts, especially that of Gustavo Gutiérrez. For Tracy, theory guides praxis more than praxis gives rise to theory.

Practical theology has been a developing interest for Tracy, and he has given it more attention over the last few years. He wishes to cast practical theology in a more "fundamental" light, arguing for its grounding in the correlational method and emphasizing its theoretical aspects. Tracy has been criticized by liberation theologians, themselves clear representatives of a practical theology (see Hawks 1990), and his interest in the link between theory and practice can be seen as in part a response to these criticisms. However, he claims that a "failure to take account of this inevitable presence of theory in all praxis occasions a failure to note how praxis criteria actually relate to critical theory as theory's sublation, not its simple negation" (Tracy 1983:62). A liberationist would acknowledge the presence of theory constructing the perception of conditions in which people act, but would note that developing "criteria of or for praxis" is a theoretical and critical, not a practical and strategic action.

The significance of Tracy's response is crucial. In it he distances himself from the most "practical" of liberation theologies by making theory in some sense prior to praxis. Praxis is the "sublation" of theory, that is, the outcome of a dialectic between tradition and situation mediated by the working of the theologian. The differences between Tracy's practical theology and liberation theology are technical, but very important.

The claim that theology is and must be a public discourse is of particular interest in the North American context, which has no established church or religious body and claims to affirm a pluralism of religious options. How, one might ask, can theology specific to one religious tradition (i.e., the Christian) claim to be truly "public" in such a society? As Tracy notes, "theology attempts to speak its word about Ultimate Reality in fidelity to the sometimes conflicting demands and criteria of its three publics, not simply to one of them" (Tracy 1989a:193). Van Harvey has described the situation of academic theology in America as one of "intellectual marginality," a marginality championed by secularists, but denied by some practicing theologians, yet nonetheless a present reality (Harvey 1989:172).

The problems of pluralism are clearly central for the development of a critical revisionist theology. In seeking a solution, Tracy turns to language that a postliberal theology like that of George Lindbeck (see Chapter 7, below) would find to be completely modern, not postmodern. It seems to be a form of modern liberal "experiential-expressivism" (Lindbeck 1984:16). Tracy writes:

Like strictly metaphysical questions, the enduring questions of religion must be logically odd questions, because they are about the most
fundamental presuppositions, the most basic beliefs, of all our knowing, willing, and acting. Like strictly metaphysical questions, religious
questions must be on the nature of Ultimate Reality. Unlike metaphysical questions, however, religious inquiry seeks the meaning and
truth of Ultimate Reality not only as it is in itself, but as it is related to
us (Tracy 1989a:197).

Religions seem, then, to be various expressions based in particular
experiences of a universal Ultimate. It is this postulation of an Ultimate One
behind the many expressions which characterizes the liberal tradition
which began with German theologian F. D. E. Schleiermacher.

The mechanism that allows such transcendental categories to become
accessible to immanent human thinking and knowing, and thus a mechanism by which we can understand the role of theology as public discourse
in a pluralist society, provides the third major theme in Tracy's thought: the
category of the religious classic.

For Tracy, a classic is a person, text, rite, symbol, or event in which "we
recognize nothing less than the disclosure of a reality we cannot but name
truth" (Tracy 1981:108). It is important, Tracy argues, that the category be
limited neither to particular genres (a person or a ritual can be as much a
classic, in this sense, as can a text) nor to expressions of culture deemed
"classical" by an elitist critical agenda (Tracy 1981:108). Just as people
encounter classics in art, music, or film and experience, understand, and
judge them differently, so the encounter with religious classics is undeni-
ably plural: "The wider community of readers, living and dead, must
continue to be heard as all return to the struggle of finding some appropriate response (from some initial sense of import to a formed judgment) to
[a] possibly classic text" (Tracy 1981:116).

Tracy advocates a "model of dialogue" (Tracy 1981:120) as the approach
a reader (or other subject of the experience of a classic) must take fully to
engage and understand the import of the classic in question. As he goes on
to note,

The present theory of interpretation, therefore, with its model of
dialogue focussed primarily upon the response of the reader to the
classic, does allow for, indeed encourages, a responsible pluralism of
readings based on a recognition of the plurality in text and reader alike
(Tracy 1981:124).

Here, then, seems to be the solution to the problem of public theology in
a pluralist society. "The religious classics are testimonies to the responses
of the religions to those questions [about the nature of, and our relation to,
Ultimate Reality]" (Tracy 1989a:197). If the theologian recognizes, or indeed

valorizes, a pluralism both of classics and interpretations, then the recognized canons of discourse, involving argumentation, debate, and discussion, can remain inviolate. "Insofar as one defends argument and conversation," Tracy writes, "one defends a public realm. . . . Consensus is not a failing but the hope of the public realm" (Tracy 1989a:202). In this Tracy clearly parallels Jürgen Habermas: claims are to be decided as they would be in an ideal speech situation.

Tracy's revisionist theology seems to fit very comfortably into the realm of the postmodern. In his first major work, *Blessed Rage for Order*, the typical postmodern rejection of modern options is visible. The work begins with a survey of prevailing modernist paradigms for theological discourse, which are rejected by Tracy in favor of his revisionist scheme. Classic orthodox theology fails because of its "inability to make intrinsic (i.e., inner-theological) use of other scholarly disciplines," which Tracy relates not only to an "inability to come to terms with the cognitive, ethical, and existential counter-claims of modernity," but also to a narrowly individualistic and propositional construal of the nature of religious beliefs (Tracy 1975:25). Though not clearly specified by Tracy (at least not in this context), individualism and propositional positivism are key components of the modernist idiom. To this extent, therefore, "orthodox" theology represents a modernist paradigm to be rejected or overcome.

Modernist liberal theology posits Christian belief in the face of secularization. Tracy is less clear here in delineating the weaknesses of the paradigm, though he seems to suggest that primary among them is a kind of schizophrenia:

> The liberal theologian finds himself committed not marginally but fundamentally to the values of the modern experiment. He [sic] cannot but find himself open to the challenge which those values, when applied by modern cognitive disciplines, pose for the classical claims of traditional Christianity to truth and to value (Tracy 1975:26).

The modern liberal theologian, then, is an alienated theologian, to use Van Harvey's term.

Neo-orthodoxy, Tracy's third model, attempts to overcome the weaknesses of its liberal parent by affirming the liberal paradigm in understanding the human situation, but rejecting it as an interpretation of the specifically Christian experience. Neo-orthodoxy "argued that only an explicit recognition of the unique gift of faith in the Word of God could provide an adequate foundation for a truly Christian theology" (Tracy 1975:28). In this case, Tracy cites what might be called a failure of will as the key factor in his rejection of neo-orthodoxy: "the neo-orthodox seemed unwilling at some inevitable final moment to follow to a truly critical conclusion the task which they themselves initiated" (Tracy 1975:29). Insofar as postliberal theology like George Lindbeck's is an instantiation of neo-orthodoxy, it should also fall to Tracy's claim. But as we shall see in Chapter 7, its own mode of correlation is clearly revisionist, in Tracy's categorization, in that it recognizes the problems and prospects of the present situation, but doubts the need for or possibility of achieving a consensus like that of an ideal speech situation for validating theological claims.

The fourth model outlined by Tracy is the radical model, which he also rejects. In radicalism, with its rejection of theism in the interest of affirming the secular, Tracy detects the obvious weakness: "can one really continue the enterprise of Christian theology if there is no meaningful way to affirm the reality of God?" (Tracy 1975:32). Presumably, he would answer this question in the negative. Indeed, the whole question of whether radical theology truly is radically postmodern is the subject for Part 2, below.

While it is unclear that Tracy has cleared the board of other options as fully as he thinks, he does here oppositionally place (in Kort's sense) his own paradigm. Tracy clarifies his own postmodern, revisionist paradigm in opposition to strands of modern—and postmodern—theology. Within the revisionist paradigm is another element which is deeply suggestive of a postmodern consciousness: the affirmation of pluralism and ambiguity as positive features of the human religious enterprise. Tracy describes this feature of postmodernism as "that radical plurality and a heightened sense of ambiguity, so typical of all postmodern movements of thought with their refusal of premature closure and their focus upon the categories of the 'different' and the 'other'. . ." (Tracy 1989b:550).

Plural readings of the religious classics, plural traditions, and the pluralism of American society have been discussed above. In *Plurality and Ambiguity*, Tracy analyzes these issues in great detail. Interpretation of the received "classics" forms the starting point for the theological enterprise; as Tracy indicates, "To understand is to interpret" (Tracy 1987c:9). No theologian can claim to be less than an interpreter. "To give an interpretation is to make a claim," Tracy adds; and making a claim in a pluralistic context entails a responsibility to argue for and defend that claim (Tracy 1987c:25).

Tracy's understanding of plurality and ambiguity as they relate to the realm of religious thought is not limited to purely intellectual concerns. He is also well aware of the postmodern emphasis on power as a function of discourse:

> Any religion, whether past or present, in a position of power surely demonstrates that religious movements, like secular ones, are open to corruption. The impacted memories of religious fanaticism and its demonic history of effects upon all cultures are memories that cannot be erased. Whoever comes to speak in favor of religion and its possibilities of enlightenment and emancipation does not come with clean

hands nor with a clear conscience. If interpreters of religion come with any pretense to purity, they should not be listened to (Tracy 1987c:85).

Unlike many modern theologies which ignore the practical issues of how institutions have the power to shape practices and beliefs, Tracy recognizes the dark side of Christian history (and that of other religions).

An important postmodern feature of Tracy's work is his rejection of classic modernist individualism in favor of an approach emphasizing collectivity and consensus. As noted above, Tracy's vision of American society revolves around discussion and debate, with consensus as a goal. The privatization of religion which can be seen in much of the modernist agenda is rejected by Tracy in his quest for publicness in theological discourse (Tracy 1985:6). This is very much in line with the thought of postmodern critical theorists such as Jürgen Habermas, a connection which Tracy notes (Tracy 1985:73-75). The "conversation" advocated by Tracy is a reaction against the whole stream of enlightenment/modernist epistemology, which saw facts as arranged in a "field" before the neutral, lone observer, whose duty it was to collect the facts and decipher their meaning. A conversational model stresses the always-dialogic relationship not merely between seekers themselves, but also between seekers and the data they seek.

Despite his postmodern interests, however, Tracy's work also continues to exhibit modernist trends. Perhaps key among these is his continuation of the modern theological apologetic: the defense of Christianity's rightful place against the formidable counterclaims of other modern systems of inquiry, such as science. George Lindbeck casts Tracy as thoroughly modern, not postmodern. Tracy is an experiential-expressivist. In Lindbeck's view this means that Tracy "maintain[s] a kind of privacy in the origins of experience and language" which is no longer tenable and which contrasts with the stated "publicness" of Tracy's theological agenda (Lindbeck 1984:38). What is Lindbeck's problem with the experiential-expressivist option? It continues the (purportedly) dead-end liberal tradition begun by Schleiermacher and is thus firmly planted in the modern (Lindbeck 1984:16). More to the point,

> Because this core experience [the so-called experience of the Ultimate] is said to be common to a wide diversity of religions, it is difficult or impossible to specify its distinctive features, and yet unless this is done, the assertion of commonality becomes logically and empirically vacuous (Lindbeck 1984:32).

The implications of this assertion for the present issue are clear. If Tracy is an experiential-expressivist, then his theology is based on a loosely identified "core experience" to which religious symbol systems, and preeminently religious classics, refer with varying degrees of success. This ties his theology firmly to an apologetic method, for Christianity must be defended, in the public realm, as the most accurate, or at least *an* accurate, response to and representation of the essentials of this core experience.

In any case, regardless of the truth in the accusations, Tracy does carry both typically modernist and postmodern concerns. The very fact that he sees himself primarily as a fundamental theologian, whose efforts must be directed primarily toward the academy and must therefore fulfill academic demands for argument and verification (Tracy 1981:56), indicates that some apologetic will be in order for his theology, an apologetic which will fix him, at least in part, in the "state of siege" mentality of modernist, post-Enlightenment Christianity.

Tracy's concern for publicness and conversation seems committed to the universal commensurability of concepts that Habermas's work requires. Tracy notes that fundamental theology, like the other types of theology, "is concerned to speak a truth about God that can, in principle, be heard by all" (Tracy 1981:81). Insofar as this is a universalizing principle, Tracy's work is open to a critique analogous to that leveled against the Habermasians.

Yet Tracy's concept of the "classic" and its truth-revealing possibilities distances his work from classic modern views. Modernity presumes that all knowledge was to be found in quantifiable expressions of mathematics or natural science, or perhaps in the convoluted syllogisms of rationalist philosophy. Art, poetry, and other expressive media were thought to be at best ornaments for the cultivated life, or at worst distracting fluff without the ability to make genuine contributions to human intellectual development. Religious narrative was most scathingly attacked as worthless myth and primitive, failed "science." Thus, religious narrative, sacred story, "myth" in the neutral academic sense, was banished from the arena of serious discourse, to languish in the basement of human achievement.

Tracy's emphasis on the classic represents one attempt among many in the postmodern era to give such narratives new importance. Tracy sees the classic as the root of theology, particularly of systematic theology; the job of the systematic theologian is to interpret religious classics (Tracy 1981:130). This is to be done, as one might expect, with a view toward correlating this interpretation with an interpretation of the contemporary situation, because this hermeneutical approach (rooted in the philosophical work of Paul Ricoeur and Hans-Georg Gadamer) renders systematic theology's interpretation of the classics public (Tracy 1981:133). Moreover, the systematic enterprise has implications for praxis as well. As Tracy notes:

When Christian self-understanding is tempted to de-politicize its self-understanding and praxis anew, Christians need only reflect on Exodus as the paradigm which should inform and transform the highly personal but not individualist Christian self-understanding in

the reality of the death and resurrection of Jesus Christ (Tracy
1987b:119).

Exodus is a "classic" in the Tracian sense, and as such it arrives at the
postmodern doorstep with a history of "plurality and ambiguity" in its
interpretations (Tracy 1987b:121). In a statement which reveals the postmodern character of Tracy's commitment to narrative, he writes:

> We can continue to give ourselves over to the great hope of Western
> reason, including the hope for adequate interpretation. But that hope
> is now a more modest one as a result of the discovery of the *plurality
> of both language and knowledge and the ambiguities of all histories,* includ-
> ing the history of reason itself (Tracy 1987b:121-22).

In light of the "plurality and ambiguity" so strongly affirmed in the
above quotation, Tracy has been concerned with the diversity of religions
and active in Buddhist-Christian dialogues. It is difficult to separate this
issue from Tracy's theology more generally, because almost the whole of
his career has, in some sense, been devoted to the theological implications
of religious plurality. From *Blessed Rage for Order* to *The Analogical Imagination* to *Plurality and Ambiguity,* Tracy has focused on the diversity of theological options within the Christian tradition, as well as the plurality of
intellectual epistemological options available in Western society and culture as a whole. In 1990, however, Tracy published *Dialogue with the Other:
The Inter-Religious Dialogue,* which is his first book-length attempt to deal
with global pluralism and non-Christian religions. A short work, *Dialogue
with the Other* is a refined, nuanced program for dealing with extra-Christian diversity, drawing on insights from Sigmund Freud, William James,
and Mircea Eliade, among others, to construct a theologically grounded
method for interreligious dialogue. That text, however, will be considered
in the context of Chapter 11, where we highlight the ways theologians
address religious diversity.

David Tracy, then, with his revisionist model for postmodern theology—
his emphasis on the correlation between the plural and ambiguous received
tradition and the apparently shared experience of contemporary humanity—has produced a subtle and highly individual "middle way" for understanding the diversity of today's religious world, and by emphasizing these
themes in a prolific and influential career (which, one hopes, is yet far from
over), he has brought his approach before a wide scholarly audience.

Yet the same sort of question comes up for Tracy as for the Habermasians
and the process theologians: can discourse do the work it must do to
neutralize the acids of modernity and to provide a "postmodern vision"?
In one sense, it is fitting and just to laud plurality in religious classics, in
religious interpretations, in religious communities. It is similarly right to

delight in the fecund ambiguity of the world. But *how* is discursive redemption of our claims to solve our problems?

Kort's insight must be extended. Not only do individual theologians define their positions oppositionally, but traditions do so too. Christianity distinguished itself oppositionally from other "philosophies" like Judaism, neo-Platonism, stoicism, epicureanism, and paganism in the ancient world. Orthodoxy is defined oppositionally over against whatever heresies arise. Indeed, the history of Catholic theology could be written as a history of defining heresy and opposing it orthodoxly, as Kurtz does for the turn of the century heresy of modernism and the growth of Catholic integralism. How is it possible to be "concerned to speak a truth about God that can, in principle, be heard by all" (Tracy 1981:81) without presuming that basic oppositions can be overcome? For if we do define ourselves oppositionally, then overcoming such oppositions may well be robbing people of their hard-won diverse identities.

Of course, Tracy would respond that that is just the point: a revisionist theology requires the revisioning of identity, but a revisioning that is faithful to traditions. One must be able to put the old wine of tradition in the new bottle of the contemporary situation—which includes mutual recognition of dialogue and interaction. But if opposition *is* of the essence of a tradition, perhaps the tradition of Islam, then a Tracian dialogue demands the rejection of a constitutive tradition and, bluntly, the loss of self-identity.

But how could this be done? What does one do with those who refuse to play the game of interreligious dialogue? Either one has to concede that there are some who cannot, even in principle, hear the word of God because their identity keeps them from it. Or one has to use the systemic power of coercion, whether the more subtle power of propaganda and Westernization noted by Surin (1990) or the more obvious power of forcing them into the game or letting their traditions die as they are starved out of the game.

And finally starvation—spiritual and physical—is the issue. We live in a world of limited resources. When one's children starve spiritually and physically, dialogue may be a luxury which cannot be afforded. What the constructive postmodernists seem to miss is the depth of oppositions in the world created by modernity. Edith Wyschogrod finds that parts of the modern life-world are really death-worlds (Wyschogrod 1985:25). In a situation in which one's identity is being undermined by irenic and universalizing opposition or in which the future of one's family, tribe, or nation is being overwhelmed by either the homogenized vision of a world without difference or by the soldiers of one's enemies (whether they carry rifles or briefcases), why would it be rational for a person constituted in the particularity of a society, constituted by the particular language he or she speaks as *homo loquens*, constituted to cherish a distinctive vision, to dissolve that distinctive particularity in either a universal discursive situation or a romantic Western optimism based in a utopian vision or in a dialogue whose purpose is to let the world of God be heard, in principle, where the word of God is alien?

The critics of modernity would argue that the constructive postmodernists have carried with them far too much modern baggage. Moreover, they must presume a world in which the only real problem is the distribution of the resources which support the life-world, not a real scarcity of resources necessary to sustain a rich and varied life-world. Is there reason to think that a romantic vision or a potentially universal discussion will provide a way to counteract the rapid depletion of limited resources? It hasn't happened yet, and given the systemic power invested in the rich (as suggested above about U.S. Sugar's political activity) is there any reason to think that our present liberal democratic arrangements will bring it about? Celebration of diversity is possible only when one's own basic needs are met—including the needs of identity. But as so much of the world does not have its needs met and can see that the liberal democratic path to the future holds little promise for developing an ecologically satisfying and sustainable world, why should it join in the celebration?

In light of these deep problems which attend the extension of the boons of modernity to the marginalized, perhaps another approach is needed. Perhaps we need not to extend the modern project, but to dissolve it in the hopes that in so doing room for "something else," something unavowable, might appear. But considering the boons and banes of that sort of approach is the task for Part 2.

PART 2

POSTMODERN DISSOLUTIONS

What are these churches if they are not the tombs and sepulchers of God?
—Friedrich Nietzsche

The postmodern theologians discussed in Part 1 constructed their theologies under a vision which seeks to extend the gains of authentic modernism to those who have been bypassed, abandoned and marginalized. The task before us, in their view, is to complete the unfinished modern project. In contrast, the postmodernisms of the theorists in this part seek to overthrow alienating and debilitating patterns in modernity. In the most general terms, the task is to make room for the possibility of a space wherein the marginal can reveal the gaps, fissures, and cancers in the heart of modernity and can, possibly, provide something else.

Not all theologians whose work is "deconstructive" would accept the title "postmodernist." Thomas J. J. Altizer, whose work is discussed in Chapter 4, is one. Yet Altizer's *Gospel of Christian Atheism* (1966) seems to be a quintessential postmodern work. His work is an important stimulus to postmodernist thinkers. Moreover, he is also a primary partner in the postmodernists' theological (or a/theological) conversations. Thus he fits with present company. Yet, as we shall see, Altizer's radical metaphysics of presence contrasts sharply with his discourse partners' denial of presence and affirmation of *différance*. Whether that means his radical voice is not "postmodern" is another question.

Mark C. Taylor, the William R. Kenan, Jr., Professor of Religion at Williams College in Williamstown, Massachusetts, is the most obvious example of an author explicitly engaged in such deconstructive religious thought or a/theology. His racy and unique textual performances mark postmodernist theology as a virtuoso discourse in the American academy.

This deconstructive postmodernism is sometimes pejoratively labeled eliminative "ultramodernism, in that its eliminations result from carrying modern premises to their logical conclusions" (Griffin 1989b:x). Such "ultramodernism" seeks to undermine the foundations of the Enlightenment's concrete political and social structures and of the modernist theories which support them. Yet these deconstructionists use the Enlightenment's methods of atomization, dissociation, and rampant (if not universal) skepticism. It is not merely the premises of modernity which the deconstructionists valorize but also the methods of modernity. These modernist premises and methods paradoxically have led to the very structures and theories these postmodernists attack—possibly using those premises and methods.

Edith Wyschogrod has sought to confront the blindnesses in both modernism and postmodernism by providing a concrete vision of "another way." This Columbia-trained professor of religion who taught for many years at Queens College in New York and now holds a chair in religion at Rice University uses life narratives, "specifically those of saints, defined in terms that both overlap and overturn traditional normative stipulations and that defy the structure of moral theory" (1990a:xiii) to overcome the inadequacies of contemporary moral theory.

This strand of postmodernism seems extremely alien to much Christian (and other) theology. This is due to its apparent failure to be accessible to or significant for theological reflection done with and for any ecclesial community. Taylor's a/theology carries an implied an/ecclesiology—a bypassing or denying the communities called church. Yet these experiments in writing may have an important contribution to make to theologies still deeply in touch with religious communities. This is Joseph O'Leary's argument.

O'Leary works from a Catholic background while attacking metaphysics as intensely and deftly as any other postmodern thinker. Even if postmodernists would reject his "use" of their work as abuse, he has highlighted the possible contributions of deconstructive work to more constructive theologies still favored in actively religious communities:

> In the last analysis the deconstruction of tradition is the effect of a change in the consciousness of the Christian community, a change which it articulates and confirms. It is the reappropriation of the tradition in light of a change in the Church's self-understanding. This theological enterprise is sustained by a movement in the church at large and thus has everything to gain from remaining in close contact and dialogue with that movement. The damaging marginality which was the lot of Pascal, Kierkegaard and the [turn-of-the-century Roman Catholic] Modernists need not be that of the contemporary theological deconstructionist, for the crisis of metaphysical theology has now become a public one and the Church as a whole is thrown back on the necessity of adopting a prophetic style of teaching and acting (O'Leary 1985:145).

The "normal" life and theology of the church has been repeatedly interrupted in our postmodern era. The Second Vatican Council upset Tridentine triumphalism, juridicism, and clericalism. The voices of women have interrupted (but not dethroned) patriarchy. The resistance of the laity has defanged much official teaching on sexuality and reproduction. *Communidades de base* have broken the parochialism of ecclesial structures. While it is hard to imagine what an explicitly Catholic or Presbyterian or Lutheran or Baptist deconstructionist theology would look like, O'Leary reminds us that Catholics and Presbyterians and Lutherans and Baptists can learn from deconstructionist theologies and should at least have an eliminative moment within their own work.

Chapter 4

Thomas J. J. Altizer and the Death of God

with Bruce Richey

God has actually died in Christ . . . this death is both a historical and a cosmic event . . . a final and irrevocable event.

—Thomas Altizer

Thomas J. J. Altizer articulated his radical "death of God" theology beginning some three decades ago. The throng of critics who attacked him then neglected the fact that he was restating what the nineteenth-century masters of suspicion had discovered: The transcendent God of Christendom had vanished from "enlightened" society.

Public uproar over radical theology has waned. Even now conservative theologians simply gloss over the event as though it were an ephemeral fad in a turbulent decade. But even more radical theologies, atheologies, and reductions have "infected" the academy—many of them in dialogue with and inspired by Altizer's writings. And Altizer himself continues to write a theology still radical.

Thomas Jonathan Jackson Altizer, named after a well-known historic figure and distant relative, General Thomas Jonathan "Stonewall" Jackson, was born on September 28, 1927. He received a doctorate from the University of Chicago. From 1956-1968 he taught at Emory University. His publication of *The Gospel of Christian Atheism* (1966) and other writings made him very controversial and in 1968—a year he even received death threats (interview with Altizer by Bruce Richey, November 20, 1993)—he moved to SUNY Stony Brook, where he still teaches.

In the summer of 1956, after reading an essay by Eric Heller on Nietzsche for the seventh time, he suddenly was struck with the awareness that God was really dead. What this meant for Altizer then was that the traditional

Christian God had perished from the secularized consciousness of contemporary humanity. Later he would reinterpret this as an actual historical event, not merely a cultural one. But the death of God has remained the focal point of his theological inquiries.

Altizer has been consistently drawn to the problems and opportunities for religious thought posed by the increasing secularization of Western society. Modernity has led to a deep sense of alienation in the human spirit, an encounter with nothingness and meaninglessness. His response has been to construct a radical theology of the kenotic immanence of God. In Mark C. Taylor's words, Altizer "is obsessed with presence," which is the modern analogue of the postmodernists' being "haunted by absence" (Taylor 1984b:570).

Altizer's thought often seems perplexing, even incoherent. But a key to understanding Altizer is the concept of *coincidentia oppositorum*. However it may appear here and now, ultimately absence *is* presence, Spirit *is* matter, beginnings *are* endings, finite *is* infinite. The constant in Altizer's evolving vision is the reconciliation of opposites in the Ultimate, even the reconciliations of East and West, of theism and atheism.

In his early work, Altizer sought to understand and interpret the "nihilism" of the Theravada Buddhist tradition in comparison and contrast with Western religiosity: "To realize the nothingness that lies within is the portal through which to realize the Nothing that lies beyond all things, for finally the Nothing within and the Nothing without are one" (1961:173). Altizer stressed that both oriental mysticism and more familiar biblical eschatology shared a commitment to such an "awareness of the world [which] is either suspended or dissolved as a means of making possible a total immersion in the religious Reality" (1961:174). Further, the experiential encounter with the sacred cannot be grasped in language. It is so ultimate that "the mystical nature of this experience necessitates the negation or dissolution of all other experiences whatsoever" (1961:175). Many contemporary Western religious traditions have lost real touch with their mystical roots. Western consciousness, attending increasingly to secular or profane existence, thereby precluded any genuine participation in the holy or sacred Reality. And insofar as western humanity understands itself as purely autonomous and secular subjects, God remains alien (1961:198). The loss of the ultimate experience and of its negation of other experiences alienates us from God.

Modern Christian theology has emphasized God as wholly Other. In so doing, it has dug an unbridgeable chasm between the sacred "Other" and human experience. Contemporary consciousness itself has been "thrust into the void of nothingness," issuing forth in a deep sense of estrangement (1961:190). But the archaic religious encounter with the "Other" hints at a solution:

> There can be no question that the nihilistic foundations of Buddhist mysticism have become profoundly meaningful to modern Western

man, and it should be clear that this is because nihilism in various forms has so decisively affected modern thought and feeling (1961:176).

. . . just as the Buddhist comes to know samsara as Nirvana, the Christian must come to know the Nothing as the hither side of God (199).

In these early writings, Altizer had not yet fully conceived of the implications such a proposal might have in the context of the practical atheism of the West.

Altizer acknowledged that the Western theological tradition had spawned a seemingly irreversible secularization. Yet he thought that the profanity of Western consciousness could be overtaken and absorbed by sacred Reality. He focused on the "uniqueness" of the Christian message and bemoaned the consequent effect of a religiosity which rationalized and concretized the name of God:

And here lies the genuine uniqueness of Christianity. Only when Christianity postulates God as Being qua *being* does Christianity assume a form that is radically distinguished from the other higher religions of the world. Thereby faith rests upon a submission to *being* that makes impossible the realization of God as the Wholly Other. ... The inevitable result of this process has been that the name and power of God have been eclipsed even in the modern religious consciousness, for modern man can know only the death of God. . . . [But] [o]nly through repentance—a turning away from the values of the world— can the man of prophetic faith know the reality of God (1961:194-5, emphasis added).

Because contemporary secular humanity participates in profane existence, it is in a strategic position to affirm the Nothing it encounters as "Wholly Other" and thereby paradoxically to participate in religious Reality.

Both profane or secular experiences and religious experiences at their base encounter the Nothingness of God. The former relates to the Nothing of religious Reality. The latter attends to nothingness in the world (1961:196). Altizer attempted to dispel the vertiginous effect of these locutions by construing them as the opposite poles of a single dialectical movement. But the result was a semi-gnostic description of the sacred-profane continuum. The emphasis on the "world-denying" force of religious experience realized the negation of the radically profane (samsara) in its absorption by the radically sacred (Nirvana). Although Altizer (1990c) called this early work "an extraordinarily bad book," he also affirmed its main thesis that there exists "an essential and a historical correlation" between Oriental mysticism and biblical eschatology.

Altizer continued in comparative religious study while incorporating more material from literary and psychoanalytic disciplines. He sought an accessible and effectual "symbol" which might intelligibly convey the dialectical relationship of profane and sacred realities. He contended that Mircea Eliade contributed the greatest insight to understanding archaic religious experience (1963). That insight revealed how primitive religion practiced or attempted a reunification with the primordial Nothing through myth and ritual. In primitive religion profane and sacred elements "coincided," and so formed the universal basis of all religious phenomena. In *Genesis & Apocalypse*, Altizer acknowledged his continuing debt to Eliade's thought by saying, "I continue to be persuaded that Eliade is the purest religious thinker of our century, and that his phenomenological understanding of the . . . eternal return is a genuine theological understanding of that original Nothing . . ." (1990a:11).

There is an important shift in Altizer's early thought. What had appeared as a "world-denying" dialectic (1961) was inverted (1963). He came to emphasize the "world-affirming" aspect of religious experience. In a homiletic tone, he called the reader to accept the radically profane existence which is the root "substance" of human temporality. A rationalized concept of God as "Wholly Other" had served to separate the sacred from the profane. Christianity's central and distinctive doctrine of the Incarnation on the other hand undermines such a concept of eternal transcendence. Incarnation means that the sacred is apprehended as coming into the profane world of time. The sacred is not *wholly* Other. Echoing Nietzsche's vision, Altizer concludes the book, "No longer can we dream that the path to the sacred is *backwards,* nor can we live in the vain hope that the true path is only *forwards:* the Center is everywhere, eternity begins in every Now" (1963: 200).

Altizer now seems to dismiss his earlier commitment to an Eternal Return evidenced among the "higher" religions (especially Buddhism) wherein the Nothingness of God is found to be the hither side of the "Wholly Other." But this is only partially correct. Mahayana Buddhist equation of Samsara (absorption in the Other) and Nirvana (ultimate Nothingness) still points the way to a fundamental dialectical appropriation of opposites, specifically of those opposite notions which are constitutive of traditional Christian theology (1985:2). Buddhist meditation amounts to a "homologous" conceptual framework for apprehending the *coincidentia oppositorum* which comprise the range of "objects" attended to in all religious experience.

Whereas his orientation toward comparison yielded a presumably basic pattern or function in religion, Altizer's attention to the distinctive eschatological character of earliest Christianity found therein a more accurate dialectical complement to the eternal return of other religions. Such a dialectic genuinely accounted for historical movement. As the result of an early study of nineteenth-century biblical scholarship and in particular that of Schweitzer, Altizer came to believe that "apocalypse" provided the emblematic force needed to hold together a viable Christian dialectic. Eschatological vision, which was the direct repository of prophetic or apocalyptic Judaism, disclosed a way out of the impasse inherent in modern existentialist theologies. It saw the kingdom of God manifested in the *hic et nunc* of profane existence, and called for a radical affirmation of contemporaneity vís-a-vís the vain hope of ever touching the "Otherness" of the traditional deity. Altizer appropriated Nietzschean terminology to identify apocalyptic vision as the vehicle through which one beholds the eternal recurrence of being. This "archeoteleological" bent gave Altizer the ammunition he needed to assault the modern theologies which conceived of history and nature as merely profane, the inviolable other of a transcendent God.

Altizer sought the "ground" of religious experience in religious practice, i.e., ritual and myth. These present what is common, even universal, in the human composition of the particular religions. Yet he also emphasized what is unique in (early) Christianity. The way of "negativity" and a thorough-going eschatology equally inform and definitely undergird his later theological writings. But the master image in Altizer's thought which provides their general structure is the Hegelian dialectic.

Oddly, Altizer's earlier works contain little explicit description of Hegelian philosophy, although they betray Hegel's overwhelming contribution to his thinking. The following paragraph captures the essence of Altizer's purpose for appropriating Hegelian dialectic:

Dialectical thinking and vision not only attempt to negate and transcend an established or given world of consciousness and society; they also attempt to annul or dissolve all those polarities and antinomies which alienate and isolate all individual centers of experience. Whether we turn to ancient or modern expressions of a dialectical way, we discover that it seeks out the lost or hidden ground of suffering and illusion. Spurning every partial or temporary assuagement of illusion and pain, it is in quest of the goal of total redemption or freedom. Accordingly, a dialectical way seeks to dissolve or reverse all those laws and categories which sanction and uphold an established mode of life. Wherever they have appeared, dialectical thinking and vision have been revolutionary, for they have assaulted the most deeply embedded principles and values of their world. There is no path for us into the meaning of a contemporary dialectical vision unless we are prepared to question our most deeply cherished convictions. Furthermore, we must also be prepared not only to question but also to abandon our established modes of thinking and analysis. There can be no doubt that this is a difficult if not impossible task for the nonrevolutionary thinker. Yet, at bottom, the task has already been accomplished—and accomplished, in its foundations, in the nineteenth century. Our task is only to appropriate this revolutionary accomplishment, and to appropriate it in such a way as to make it meaningful and real in our world (1970:10).

Altizer argued that Hegel's account of the reality of Spirit (which is defined as Being attempting to know itself) contains his "deepest understanding of negativity" (1972:109). In a telling comment on the reality of Spirit or *Geist*, Altizer quotes Hegel's view that "True reality is merely this process of reinstating self-identity, of reflecting into its own self in and from its other, and is not an original and primal unity as such, not an immediate unity as such. It is the process of its own becoming, the circle which presupposes its end as its purpose, and has its end for its beginning. . ." (1972:108). Put succinctly and perhaps too simply, *Geist* eternally learns about itself through its own differentiation. That negation is symbolized in the image of the *kenosis* of eternal Being. As Altizer observes, Hegelian dialectical identification of Identity and Difference, of Subject and Object, of Being (*Sein-an-sich*) and Self-Consciousness (*Sein-für-sich*), is finally only meaningful by "means of understanding negation as *kenosis*." Indeed, Hegel himself used Christian mythic language to describe such ultimate emptying of Being, though only as a temporary recourse awaiting a purer reformulation (1972:109).

Altizer contended that such a kenotic understanding of Spirit points to a deeper understanding of negativity as embodied in Christ. The dialectic produces a *coincidentia oppositorum* between the finite and the infinite *without* reverting to a sort of primordial synthetic reality. Earlier Hegel showed that opposites forged a union or unity with each other; Altizer is now particularly keen in adding that "transcendence is neither otherness nor the transcendence of something," for if the finite exists in the Other of itself as infinite passes beyond itself, then transcendence is really immanence (1972:113).

Altizer's concern with comparative religions and his immersion in the philosophy of Hegel and the poetry of William Blake situate the most famous theme of Altizer's work, the "death of God." It also spawns other similar imaginative themes which Altizer emphasizes in other works, e.g., "the self-embodiment of God," "primal Speech negating an original Silence which now exists as the unsaid," "divine kenosis," and the "genesis of God negating primordial Nothingness."

Altizer, unlike other radical theologians or even Nietzsche, takes the "death of God" as referring literally to an actual historic event: "The radical Christian proclaims that God has actually died in Christ, that this death is both a historical and a cosmic event, and, as such, it is a final and irrevocable event, which cannot be reversed by a subsequent religious or cosmic movement" (1966:103).

It must be actual because humanity is inescapably embodied in history. For the sacred to coincide with the profane, God must enter into our existence, our time, our history. Insofar as Christianity has understood God to be transcendent and therefore removed from the immanent world in which we live, a *coincidentia oppositorum* could not occur. But out of this negativity shone forth a horrific revelation bespeaking the true gospel: God is dead. The ultimate gift of all, God's sacrificing transcendent divine life separate from the world—in effect, divine suicide—secured a coinherence or coincidence of all opposites: the profane is sacred, the immanent is transcendent. On account of such divine emptying, theology must recant orthodoxy, by negating and reversing all doctrines which keep opposites apart.

The death of God is the pivotal point in history. It bridges the sacred and the profane, transforming each into its other. In traditional language, God was in Christ reconciling the world to himself—totally. Here is the *coincidentia oppositorum* in its fullness. It is more than the ancient heresy of patripassionism, that God the Father died on the cross. Altizer proclaims the ultimate and total self-donation.

But the radical character of this original Christian apocalyptic message became domesticated as the result of its fusion with Hellenism. Jesus spoke of the kingdom of God as subsisting in our midst. Such a radical proposal negated and reversed institutionalized forms of religion. It also superseded other forms of religion which attempted to reverse the *coincidentia* by returning to a primordial Eternal absolutely separate from the temporal. Genuine redemption could not make any sense in the dualisms that dominated Christianity. Nonetheless, the gospel of Christian atheism was not altogether obscured. It surfaced occasionally in the writing of prophetic visionaries throughout the ages and remained a covert challenge in the *kenosis* hymn in Philippians 2.

For Altizer, the true gospel is told through the imagination of historical consciousness. Since opposites have merged in the fashion discussed by Hegel, human consciousness is nothing other than the hither side of divine consciousness. As Altizer puts the matter in numerous passages:

> ... the only God about whom we can speak is the God who is manifest in consciousness and real in experience. Therefore the God we can name is the God who is actualized or realized in history, the God whom our history has given us. Apart from our history, God is not only unrealized but unreal: hence any attempt to transcend history in speaking about God must culminate in total silence. ... [But] the God whom we have been given has "named" himself in us, and named himself in such a manner that we cannot dissociate his identity from our own (1970:36-37).

A kenotic or self-emptying center is now passing into a full and final actuality, and as that actuality realizes itself in our midst, a pure negativity becomes both our innermost and our outermost identity, a total identity and a total presence which even now is becoming all in all (1980:96-97).

If we employ the paradigm of the origin, the evolution and the ending of the individuality and interiority of consciousness, we will find a way into the historical and organic identity of our epic tradition, and one that will offer the possibility of understanding that tradition as an organic whole (1985:11).

This last passage links divine consciousness and human imagination explicitly. For with the death of God comes the death of self—that which we formerly believed in Western consciousness to be autonomous identity or selfhood. Absolute interiority and individuality are negated and upset by the continual infusion or movement of Being in human consciousness. Consequently, all historical imagination is a reflection on *becoming*. The theological imagination reflects on the *divine* becoming. But that imagination cannot be equated with sacred scripture or doctrine or theology. Altizer's "canon" is radically open: Dante, Milton, Blake, and Joyce (not to mention Hegel and Kierkegaard) write revelatory imaginative texts.

Dante's purgatory and Milton's description of the twin sons Jesus and Satan suggest an apocalyptic resolution whereby formerly opposed antagonists clash to create a new heaven. Although Milton wrote primarily of absolute polarity and Dante of a utopian harmonization, reading them together reveals that the imagination can see a prefallen world as the final end. In Altizer's words, "At the birth of modernity, and of a revolutionary modernity, those deep and primal powers could dwell and exist in a precarious harmony" (1985:15). In short, genesis *is* apocalypse; beginning and ending coincide.

Blake was the first modern seer, in Altizer's estimation, to realize the death of God as a *redemptive* act (1985:189). Blake's *Jerusalem* narrates a final and irreversible *kenosis* which anticipates an apocalyptic finality. The cataclysm in William Blake's imagination, of Albion's vicarious loss of selfhood—of his own satanic deceitfulness, and of the otherness of God—in Jesus' death consummates an apocalyptic *coincidentia*. The death of God makes possible the overcoming of opposites.

But the epic writer who figures most prominently in Altizer's view is James Joyce. His apocalyptic writings "unite and conjoin" mythology and history, enabling myth to pass into "our time" (1985:210). Indeed, Joyce's own development as a visionary reenacts three stages of historical evolution beyond the premodern era. Beginning with his *Portrait of the Artist as a Young Man*, Joyce appears consumed as an artist in "immediate relation to himself," but progresses in *Ulysses* as he struggles to work out a "mediate relation to himself and others" (211-212). However, the Joyce of *Finnegan's Wake* heralds the end of modernity, because he seeks to understand his "immediate relation not only to others but to all others whatsoever" (212).

His character H.C.E. ("Here Comes Everybody") embodies the generative coincidence of two unlikely parents. H.C.E.'s fall, condemnation, and crucifixion issues forth in a cosmic resurrection. Thus death signals a *felix culpa*—a theme derived from ancient Easter liturgies—ushering in a new apocalypse, one in which the "universe is converted into an entirely new stuff. . ." (245). Altizer's comments on the epic recall his early theology.

> Nothing is more fundamental to this cosmic and apocalyptic metamorphosis than a radically new integration of mind and matter, of body and soul, as body or matter finally becomes indistinguishable from both the center and the depths of mind and consciousness. Accordingly, a real presence that once was real in the moment of consecration and thereafter now becomes real in a cosmic and universal epiphany. That epiphany heralds *the termination of history itself*, thereby inaugurating a new world, a world realizing the "eucharistic essence of existence itself" (1985:245; emphasis added).

Altizer's radical theology here deepens. In the wake of the death of God and the death of the self, history also closes.

The suggestion is peculiarly heuristic. A newcomer to Altizer's writing might question whether it is meant literally. It would certainly be impossible to judge its truth, given our temporality. If we are bound to live in history, how could we figure out if history closes?

Taken another way, however, the "termination of history" suggests that a former epoch *in history* which is typified by a particular consciousness has ended. A new period, a new history or world, a transformed consciousness, begins. Even taken in this sense, accurate assessment would be slow in coming, since a demonstration of its pervasiveness among all "consciousnesses" would certainly be left unfinished.

But if we read the passage in the context of the broader corpus of Altizer's writing, a more sober meaning discloses itself. He often speaks of a "dawning" of consciousness and a continual movement of spirit into flesh ever maintaining, but never completing, a *coincidentia oppositorum*. Few have ever grasped this vision. Nevertheless, a transformation has happened and has effected an ending which can never be again, but that ending is paradoxically a beginning or genesis, the recurring result of the negation of every "it was." Apocalypse conceived as God's death engenders an eternal recurrence, an unending genesis. To continue in Nietzsche's language: *In jedem nunc beginnt Sein* ("Being begins in every now.").

Consistent with his method of negation and reversal, Altizer mixes metaphor and straightforward language when he writes of the collapsing of all dichotomies. The outcome is, in his words, a "parabolic" vision or speech which the hearer (or reader) beholds directly (1980:10ff). With this in mind, we can attend to a critical excerpt on historical ending:

If there is a *coincidentia oppositorum* between absolute beginning and absolute ending, it lies wholly in the once-for-all finality of each event, and if each finality is the opposite of the other, each is also necessary and essential to the other, for an actual beginning must finally end, just as an actual ending is an ending of an actual beginning.

Our deepest seers have known such [apocalypse] as grace, and so [have] known it both in the ancient and the modern worlds, for at no other point is there a deeper coincidence between postmodern and the ancient worlds. But now such grace is actually and historically present, and present in the final ending of history, an ending which is not only ending of every center of consciousness, but also and even therefore the ending of horizon or world. . . . the ending of everything except ending itself (1990c:107-109).

In other words, history *qua* process presses forward. But both attempts to return to a past (for an actual beginning which ends) and to seek a finality in the future (for ending does not itself end) fail. History itself—whether past or future—cannot provide a resolution for the issues of the present. Thus, history is a closed book.

As early as *The Gospel of Christian Atheism,* Altizer put forth this dialectic in distinctively theological terms:

. . . neither the Incarnation [like apocalpyse] nor the crucifixion [like genesis] can here be understood as isolated and once-for-all events; rather, they must be conceived as primary expressions of a forward-moving and eschatological process of redemption, a process embodying a progressive movement of Spirit into flesh. At no point in this process does the incarnate Word or Spirit assume a final and definitive form, just as God himself can never be wholly or simply identified with any given revelatory event or epiphany, if only because the divine process undergoes a *continual* metamorphosis. . . (1966:104; emphasis added).

In short, the *coincidentia oppositorum* is never achieved, but is always in process, even if especially realized in the kenotic death of God.

Given Altizer's debt to modern authors of the nineteenth century, the question is whether Altizer's theology, however radical, continues the patterns of modernity. Or by visualizing the "end of history" does he thereby forecast a "post"-age?

Altizer himself refuses to describe current theology as "postmodern." He claims that

. . . the simple truth is that a fully modern theology has not yet been written or conceived, so that there cannot yet be a postmodern theology, but only a renewed medieval, or patristic, or pagan theology, even if such renewal forecloses all possibility of either a truly imaginative or a genuinely philosophical ground (1993:2).

But it is clear from the context that he has in mind those "conservative" theologians who distance themselves from "deeply modern" traditions (e.g., Lindbeck). Nonetheless, Altizer speaks of a need for theology to become "fully modern," not postmodern.

Of course, Altizer insists that any theology must account for the "death of God." Secular atheism is our situation. It is the product of historical consciousness engendered by Western religious traditions. Modern theology failed to discard an old dualism, e.g., of natural and supernatural, even in its most serious attempts to be dialectic, and therefore perpetuated "bad faith" in a distant God (e.g., Altizer 1970:33-34).

Given Christianity's mystical base, it follows for Altizer that faith must be nihilistic. Faith negates, upends, reverses previous dichotomies. Theology, then, must be a radical practice which dissolves opposites that efface and oppress human consciousness and faithful imagination. On this count, then, Altizer seems to resonate with genealogical postmodernists' orientation toward dissolution. Using Hegelian method, Altizer's identification of Subject-Object, Transcendence-Immanence, Christ-Antichrist, faith-*Weltanschauung*, figurative-literal, all betray a deconstruction of oppositions.

Altizer issued a mandate for modern Christian theology to restore its original eschatological orientation. Insofar as Altizer's apocalypticism is conceived as being radically teleological in the sense of being "progressive," it fails to instantiate a deconstructive postmodernism. As Mark C. Taylor put it, Altizer has a "nostalgia" for "total presence." Altizer's thought is "archeoteleological" thus evincing an emphatically forward-moving eschatology. Taylor writes, "The enjoyment of this 'total and immediate presence' is 'total grace.' The self-embodiment of God originally enacted in the words of Jesus becomes fully actual and real in the speech-silence of the modern world. Modernity is the *end* of history—the *hic et nunc* of *parousia*" (Taylor 1984b:580). Or, *genesis* is *apocalypse*.

In a similar vein, Aichele finds that Altizer may express a postmodern concern for immanence and the marginality of a deconstructed distinction between fantasy and "the real," but his attempt to "recover the eschatological identity" of Jesus betrays a modernist's metaphysical framework. Employing the work of Tzvetan Todorov, Aichele describes postmodern literature as conveying a "fantastic choice" to a reader: to take a chance to assume a role as "implied reader" in the "implied dialog" of the piece whereby and wherein one withholds judgment on the text. One is instead transferred into its "narrative reality" (1991:325). Similarly, a key passage in Altizer's *Total Presence* details the relationship between "parabolic speech" and its "hearer" who is said to participate in the deconstruction of text, wherein both meaning and identity beyond the text are dissolved in the parable's re/enactment (Altizer 1980:3-13). Aichele argues that Altizer's vivid and radically dissolving imagery is a strikingly postmodern language, as postmodern themes go. Nonetheless, he finds that Altizer is not fully postmodern. The "fantastic imagery and conceptual reversals are little more than embellishments" Altizer encloses within a modernist historical framework (Aichele 1991: 331).

Other evidence within Altizer's writing, however, reveals an acute appreciation for postmodern linguistics. Murphy and McClendon demonstrated how Altizer via his assessment of Joyce moves *beyond* a strictly modern view of language to embrace the richness of its multiple uses (1989:210). If postmodern linguistics involves "destructuring" texts in deference to inter- and intra-textuality, Altizer's regard for the indistinguishable fusion of epic and scripture and for the negation of narrative structure is postmodern (1985:214-215;239).

Altizer seems to straddle two strands of postmodernism (though perhaps uncomfortably): an eliminative or dissolute one and a revisionist tradition (compare Griffin 1989b:29-62). The radicality of his on-going project of "the transgressive negation of doctrine" coincides with a postmodernism of dissolution or elimination. But if it is true that modernity is characterized by a "flight from authority" (Stout 1981), Altizer's propensity toward a rigorous anti-authoritarianism seems quintessentially modern. His radical, transgressive program of negation and reversal of all past doctrine immediately demonstrates his subversive tendency. Another telling feature of Altizer's anti-authoritarianism is his recent refusal to adhere to accepted or expected practice of scholarly documentation. He sees such a practice as a substitute for past appeals to "authority," which the death of God nullified once and for all (1990:13-15).

Altizer also rejects modern attempts to establish an epistemic foundation for religious beliefs. He denies autonomous and privileged knowledge to the Subject (no innate ideas), opposes any elevation of any text (no scripture), and negates the possibility of external encroachment on consciousness by a sovereign other (no revelation). On this score, he appears radically anti-foundationalist. And yet there may be one last vestige of modernist epistemology. From one angle, Altizer remains dedicated to the modern quest for certainty. Not only is nihilistic method (like Cartesian doubt) a prelude to definite *affirmation*, but the absolute permanency of dialectic movement in Altizer's view constructs a solid and irrevocable pattern for interpreting or reinterpreting all apprehension of polarity. In a revealing passage, Altizer comments on the movement of the negation of divine silence into parabolic speech, which enacts and is enacted by hearing, as an "ending [which] evokes and embodies an actuality which is indubitable, and not only indubitable but overwhelming to its hearers as well" (1980:10). Further, parabolic speech establishes "identity and meaning incarnate here and now: thus enabling awareness of total presence" (10). Such vision betrays an interest for certitude. Taylor's recognition that Altizer has a "nostalgia" for total presence suggests that the *coincidentia oppositorum* itself needs a postmodern deconstruction.

Altizer has a fascination for archaic religion and primitive mystical experience. In the latter he uncovered a nihilistic path toward an encounter with the eternal or sacred. As an initial movement toward recovering that which is lost, mysticism's nihilation is comparable to the pristine Christian message. A late passage conveys this:

> Christianity, even as all religious ways, names death as the way to life, and knows a ritual passage through death as the way to an actual realization of life. Of course, this way is a universal way, and perhaps it is most powerfully present in ritual, and above all in that pure or archaic ritual which is uncontaminated by modernization, a ritual wherein resurrection is wholly illusory and unreal apart from its manifestation and realization as crucifixion (1980:92).

Similarly, Altizer valorizes Jesus' message of the immanence of the kingdom of God. He captures the mystique of Jesus' apocalyptic proclamation and reinterprets it for the modern world.

Yet Altizer also wrote of all religions' interest in positing a *coincidentia*, a union of sacred and profane realities. The upshot of his investigations led him to believe all religions seek a redemption of "opposites." Yet he fails to be consistent with the dialectic or reversal of doctrine. Insofar as he calls for the radical negation and reversal or inversion of all previously established forms of religion and doctrine, but simultaneously upholds a standard calling for the reinstatement of a "primitive" Christian message, Altizer unwittingly reveals his inconsistency. In other words, he subverts his own conscious interest to negate the past in all its forms.

Altizer's real distinction is that his thought evokes a uniquely construed fusion of Nietzschean nihilism and radical apocalypticism; and insofar as it does, his Christian atheism may foreclose its enduring. Indeed, it seems to be superseded by the even more radical a/theology of Mark C. Taylor. Quite conceivably, Christian atheism could die with Altizer. Whether its demise is nigh, Christian atheism will long be remembered as a radically modern theology, one which signalled the dawn of a new age, a postmodern age. Or perhaps Altizer proleptically reveals that most paradoxical coincidence of opposites: the modern *is* postmodern!

Chapter 5

The A/theology of Mark C. Taylor

with Tami England

> *. . . everything is profoundly cracked.*
> —Georges Bataille

> *Only the hand that erases can write the true thing.*
> —Meister Eckhart

If the contemporary era is in fact a "post-age," we are in a paradox out of time. In this era or non-era, a history beyond history, Mark C. Taylor engages in deconstructing theology and forging a "Postmodern A/theology." Yet, for the Harvard-trained Taylor, "[i]n the space-time of writing, every age is a post-age" (Taylor 1986:34; see Taylor 1984b:583). Every time is ambiguous and ambivalent, so it is practically impossible to characterize any time positively. Rather, we know the present, if at all, by its *difference* from the past. Taylor deconstructs the foundations of the Western theological tradition, but he does not want to end up with pure *nihilism*. Instead, he seeks an affirmation of some kind—an a/theology.

Taylor remains a thinker who is extremely difficult to "place." Clearly he rejects Altizer's atheism wherein the *coincidentia oppositiorum* is radically present; Taylor writes of absence. But as we often express frustration at the inability to recognize someone by saying, "I've seen that person somewhere before, but I just can't place her right now," so with Taylor. Can we place him? He is certainly a disfiguring and playful maverick who refuses to be penned in by inherited dichotomies. Perhaps the best clue is that his writing represents a twentieth-century radicalization of the writing of apophatic mysticism. The way of many mystics is to write interminably to say that God can neither be what they say nor what they omit. Like those mystics, perhaps Taylor writes incessantly and playfully about that of which no one can write in an effort to open a place for a way beyond.

Taylor describes the / of his a/theology as a "permeable membrane [that] forms a border where fixed boundaries disintegrate. Along this boundless boundary the traditional polarities between which Western theology has been suspended are inverted and subverted" (Taylor 1984a:12-13). Taylor can only talk about this "marginally." Since / never "is" absolutely or determinedly, one must describe it in the negative, i.e., by writing what it is not, what it is between and beyond. However, since Taylor is making an affirmation about this /, we need to discover what can be liminally affirmed of/along this "edge." The real question, however, is whether Taylor succeeds in turning the loss of modern foundations—God, Self, History, and Book—into a gain, even a "marginal" one.

Taylor's early work centered on Hegel and Kierkegaard. He claimed that "most of the major issues in twentieth-century theology and philosophy of religion were defined by these two philosophers" (*Contemporary Authors* 1990:447). His work has seemed to oscillate between these two thinkers. In *Journeys to Selfhood* he discussed Hegel and Kierkegaard's views of self and concluded that

> Hegel's dialectical vision offers a more satisfying perspective from which to comprehend the nature of the self and the dynamics of personal and corporate history. . . . Hegel's conception of selfhood is, in fact, implicit in its opposite—Kierkegaardian spirit (Taylor 1980:272).

In later works he asked, "What is beyond Hegel? What is beyond absolute knowledge?" Yet Taylor claimed that Kierkegaard's criticism of Hegel's "speculative notion of identity, and his analysis of the temporality of the individual" is devastating. Nothing that can be known is beyond Hegel, and that nothing is of prime importance. "Kierkegaard anticipates many of the most important insights of poststructuralism" (Taylor 1986:14). Nothing that can be constructed is beyond structuralism, and that nothing is of prime importance.

After moving back and forth between all-encompassing "both/and" of Hegel and the stridently incisive "either/or" of Kierkegaard, Taylor has tried to find a position between/beyond the two by adapting the work of Jacques Derrida. Derrida takes up the question of what remains after Hegel, the question of

> how to think otherwise than being by thinking a difference that is not reducible to identity. . . . [I]n relation to Hegel's System, Derrida maintains: "As for what 'begins' then—'beyond' absolute knowl-edge—*unheard-of* thoughts are required. . . . In the openness of this question we *no longer know*." This does not mean that we know

nothing but that we are beyond absolute knowledge (and its ethical, aesthetic, or religious system) (Taylor 1988:26-27).

Taylor endorses this deconstructive approach and believes that a space can be found between extremes, beyond the system. Beyond the deconstruction of polarities there remains room for religious reflection in a postmodern era (*Contemporary Authors* 1990:447).

If any specific theme in Taylor's work is key, it is the theme of the margin between the poles of the Western tradition. All of Taylor's work moves toward and on this margin, trying to discover what is not, the "nothing" beyond the oppositions of Hegel and Kierkegaard, at structuralist and poststructuralist. In his latest work Taylor goes beyond the Hegelian "both/and" of universal affirmation and the Kierkegaardian "either/or" of particular faithfulness to valorize a *"neither/nor."* While Hegel and Kierkegaard, structuralist and poststructuralist, universal and particular seem to take up all the space that is possible to be, Taylor says, in effect, "neither the one nor the other." Something else is neither of them nor in them, but beyond and between them all.

Others have used similar images: Heidegger "defines" "nothing" as "the complete negation of the totality of beings" and says that people must

allow space for beings as a whole . . . [and that] we release ourselves into the nothing, which is to say, that we liberate ourselves from those idols [foundations or constructions for Taylor] everyone has and to which he is wont to go clinging (Krell 1977:100).

Even though the Heideggerian "nothing" is different from Taylor's "margin," Heidegger illustrates the need for people to deny the *things* that bind them and to accept and to find fulfillment in negation as Taylor does.

A better clue is found in the Middle Way in Madhyamika Buddhism founded by Nagarjuna. This school believes that there are three levels of truth. The ultimate is the "intermediate" which corresponds to "the voidness or emptiness of reality, the ultimate identity of samsara and nirvana, and the necessity of making relative all mental or linguistic constructions in order to attain release" (Fenton et al. 1988:151). Taylor says:

if viewed in terms of "co-dependent origination" (pratitya samutpada), sunyata [emptiness] approaches "the non-original origin" that I have reinterpreted in terms of the divine milieu. Within this milieu, the erasure of the self-in-itself recalls the dissolution of illusory svabhava (Wyschogrod 1986:553).

This "middle way" corresponds to Taylor's "margin along" which the polarities of Western thought oscillate. He calls it (possibly with a bow to Teilhard de Chardin) the "divine milieu."

In *Erring: A Postmodern A/theology* Taylor addresses those who are "[s]us-pended between the loss of old certainties and the discovery of new beliefs, these marginal people constantly live on the border that both joins and separates belief and unbelief" (Taylor 1984a:5). He wants to illustrate the possibility of living within a world of opposites, that is in the margin between opposites. Even though there are no foundations or certainties, there is still room for religious reflection through and in the marginal "space." Embracing this place "in between" affirms the negation of abso-lutes and affirms absolute relativity. If "moderns" are struggling along the edge between polarities, perhaps, "postmoderns" should dive into the marginal space.

Taylor finds four interdependent foundational notions in traditional Western theology. These are not nearly as stable or certain as they have been thought to be. In the first half of *Erring* he deconstructs them: God, self, history, and the book. The modern death of God entails the death of self. Nietzsche's Zarathustra was right: we have killed God. God is irrelevant to the everyday world in which we truly live and move and have our being. Secularization is the cultural death of God, the absence of a divine founda-tion for society. Moderns without God must remain within the master-slave dialectic. They seek to be dominant, for that is the only way to establish their self-identity. When one can no longer participate in divine power, the self can be sustained only by its own power. Within this system the self searches for "individual identity and to secure personal property. . . . The temporality of the subject, however, subverts the identity, propriety, pres-ence, and property of selfhood. This subversion effectively dispossesses the subject" (Taylor 1984a:14). In modernity not only is the foundation of everything in God lost, so is the identity of a substantial self lost in the fleeing temporality of history. Time, fate, and death undermine security and identity: we moderns, with no other Power to sustain us, always lose our selves to those irresistable forces which overpower our power.

Time and history are relative, not absolute. All time is "out of time," so with the death of God and the self, history as a grand narrative ends. Since history and all relationships are relative, the words and things are bound together. Yet that tie is temporary and conventional. We forget the fact that *we* have tied our signifiers to what they signify. As our signifiers slip their moorings, so the meanings of our words cannot be stable or absolutely representative of the things which once gave them anchorage. Hence, there can be no canon of texts, no finality to the story. History's tale is not told and cannot be told, for the passage of time undermines history. Hence, any book that has a sense of an ending must be closed, for it willfully asserts what is not and cannot be—an absolute perspective from which to view the incessant march of the whole of history. Taylor proclaims the closure of the book as such, especially the Book which begins with Genesis as the divine foundation and closes with the Apocalypse as the divine consummation.

Deconstructing the God-self-history-book of modernity creates an emptiness. But this hole in the fabric of Western life and thought is a space beyond them. In the "space" of the second half of *Erring* Taylor creates an a/theology in which God becomes writing, self becomes trace, history becomes erring, and book becomes text. A/theology is *neither* completely deconstructive *nor* constructive, "it might be defined as something like a nonnegative negative theology that nonetheless is not positive. A/theology pursues or, more precisely, is pursued by an alterity that neither exists nor does not exist but is beyond both Being and Nonbeing" (Taylor 1992:316). It is suspended between traditional poles of Western theology, accepting neither one nor the other.

In a/theology, strict alterity, difference and opposition do not exist. Writing-trace-erring-text becomes an intermingling matrix of notions in an eternal interplay. Writing is the divine milieu. "Writing is the interplay of presence/absence and identity/difference that overturns the polar opposites of classical theology . . . Along this middle way, writing of God repeatedly appears as the unending dissemination of the word" (Taylor 1984a:15). Writing, for Taylor, is a way to approach the mystery of the space between, the space created by the deconstruction of God-self-history-book.

In this space, the "self" realizes it cannot and "need" not possess or "own" identity. This frees the self to desire, a theme even more explicitly taken up by Edith Wyschogrod, as we shall see. Taylor places "free-floating desire," which is the trace of what was constructed as the modern self, in the following:

> While need pursues a particular object that the subject assumes will fill the hole, close the gap, or heal the wound that rends, desire, which is not directed toward anything specific, remains free-floating. This hovering desire points to the necessary incompletion of the trace (Taylor 1984a:147).

One gives up the race for domination, for self-identity, for self-stability, for self-mastery. In doing so self becomes trace. The trace is not definite or finite or full. It simply accepts the space and lives without certainty or stability or mastery. It is neither master nor slave.

Since whatever is left of history is "out of time," it is wandering, it is "erring." The errant path we walk is without limits and without definite plot or storyline. Now the trace errs and writes the divine milieu while embracing "mazing grace," i.e., the loss of limits and boundaries and the discovering of endless connections. In this loss of certainty, knowledge and truth are relative. The closure of the book which defined a path creates a place for an open text, a text with meanings always not yet defined. Readers become writers, writers become readers, texts affect other texts. If meaning is found in between, it is found between texts, or through intertextuality, beyond all of the boundless interpretations and interrelations in the writing of the divine milieu:

The fascination of the drama lies in neither one nor the other of the binary opposites, but in their ceaseless interplay. The ritual marks "the eternal return" of a play that promises no final act, no resolution, no conclusion. The masks, in other words, mask a margin, a limen, that can never be unmasked, "as though we are in some Nietzschean world where behind every mask there are only more masks" (Wyschogrod 1986:548-549).

This boundlessness means mazing grace is neither absent nor present. It is never cut off by boundaries, but always in and through the permeable membrane of the space of a/theology.

The margin "recurs" (eternally?) throughout Taylor's work. In "The Anachronism of A/theology" he explores the margin "out of time" and relates the mean between Hegel and Kierkegaard to that between Barth and Altizer. He wants to explore what lies beyond traditional philosophy and theology. Using the myth of Chronus, Taylor illustrates how "Time," the Son of Father Heaven and Mother Earth, is suspended between the opposites. He writes:

[P]erhaps we can figure the disruptive, nonsynthetic third by refiguring the anachronism of time. . . I would like to suggest that to think this mean is, in effect, to reexamine the *difference* between Hegel and Kierkegaard by rethinking Hegelian identity and Kierkegaardian alterity in and through Derridean *différance* (Taylor 1988:24).

Between Hegel and Kierkegaard, between identity and otherness, Taylor discovers with Derrida a different difference and an other other. Instead of the "both/and" of Hegel and the "either/or" of Kierkegaard, they posit a third dialectic of "neither/nor" that is an anachronism, a dialectic which is out of time along the margin in and of the divine milieu.

Much twentieth-century theology has been plagued with the formation of opposites. Karl Barth's negation of immanence is an affirmation of transcendence. Altizer's negation of transcendence is a negation of Barth's negation and is an affirmation of the coincidence of opposites. For Barth the kingdom of God is elsewhere and for Altizer, the kingdom of God is already here. "What *neither* Barth *nor* Altizer confronts is the possibility of the impossibility of the presence of the Kingdom—here or elsewhere, now or then. Consequently, neither thinks the negative radically enough" (Taylor 1992:316-317; emphasis added).

"It is possible to relate Altizer's critique of Barth as a reversal of Kierkegaard's critique of Hegel" (Taylor 1988:28). Altizerian immanence reminds one of Hegelian identity and Barthian transcendence recalls Kierkegaardian alterity. For Taylor, the "neither/nor" between the philosophers is the "impossibility" between the theologians. The "nondialectical third" of which Taylor writes is neither alterity nor identity, transcendence nor immanence, then nor now.

Taylor sees middle ground in Maurice Blanchot's work. Blanchot opposes Altizer's view of complete and actual presence. Taylor and Blanchot "approach the present by way of the detour through past and future" (Taylor 1988:30). The present *is* never fully present. The present *was* never fully present. The present never *will be* fully present. Hence, among other things, there are neither true origins nor true endings. Everything is developing. All is codependent origination. There always must be a lack, a gap. Time is "un-re-present-able." For Taylor, this negation is neither Barth's negation nor Altizer's negation of Barth's negation. The *pas* which Taylor takes from Blanchot is outside of time as such—it is an anachronism. This "unrepresentable" gap is another image of the unnameable margin of a/theology (Taylor 1988:30-31). Identity is impossible.

Blanchot's literary criticism reveals aspects of Taylor's view of writing as divine milieu:

> Bearing everything toward that which exceeds the all . . . beyond the totality . . . on the margins of the universe . . . outside the laws . . . outside the possible . . . mirror of perfect nothingness . . . the origin of that which has no origin . . . The "I" of the text . . . is also art . . . [A]rt can be interpreted as *"la recherche du temps perdu"* (Silverman 1990:20-21).

Since writing can be neither fully past nor present, it can not be original or absolutely representable. The writer explores the boundaries of space and time, reinscribing the past which was never truly present—the nonoriginal origin. Writing for Blanchot (and Taylor) is always reinscription, "an endless repetition of traces." It searches and re-searches for the unrepresentable gap in time, to which and by which it is bound. Writing is an incision, a wound. Writing uses words to cut to the quick and expose that neither traditional limits nor foundations of language can stand fast. The fissure between traditional and cultural poles occurs *"in and as* art." Taylor says that for Blanchot *literature* is the privileged vehicle for the journey to and in the space where, for Taylor, writing-trace-erring-text eternally play together (Silverman 1990:20-32) after the displacement of the illusory limits of God-self-history-book.

In art, as in a/theology, Taylor sees room for religious reflection in "a/theoesthetics." Even though there may not be a direct identification of religion with aesthetics, as in theoesthetics, Taylor sees an a/theoesthetics emerging in art and architecture that is "disfiguring." These "artists and architects . . . strive to figure the unfigurable in a disfiguring that is *neither* modern *nor* modernist postmodern" (Taylor 1992: 316; emphasis added). This "disfiguring" is done in the space between the figure and the unfigurable, affirmation and negation. Disfiguring characterizes a/theoesthetics, like erring does a/theology—as the "nonnegative negative" which is even-so not positive.

"While theoesthetics defines the parameters of modern theology, a/theoesthetics creates the possibility of a postmodern a/theology" (Taylor 1992:316). Both are at play and like comics on a stage, are what they *spiel*. A/theology involves resisting religious, social, cultural, and historical structures that have traditionally been binding. It is not a complete negation, but neither negation nor affirmation. Taylor's "neither/nor," suspended between Hegel and Kierkegaard, between Altizer and Barth, reveals that the Kingdom is neither present nor coming, and that the dream of future salvation must be let go as must that of present salvation.

But this letting go, this accepting "neither the one nor the other," is not completely negative. It reveals a different way of thinking religion as a "double movement," neither strictly negative nor strictly positive:

> The unsettling call for resistance approaches from the proximate distance of an Other I can never know. One of the improper "names" of this unnameable Other, I have suggested, is "altarity." To think the unthinkable Other, erroneously named altarity, it is necessary to unthink all we have thought with the name "God" . . . [T]raditional religious and philosophical concepts must be disfigured by refiguring the disfiguring of postmodern art and architecture. Altarity can be rendered—if at all—only in a text that is rent. The wounded word is the bleeding trace in and through which altarity approaches by withdrawing and withdraws by approaching. Fragments within fragments are not unified or synthesized but come together by being held apart in their differences. The text woven from these traces is an *allograph*, which, in its failure—in its gaps and fissures, its faults and lacks—inscribes an Other it cannot represent. Though never present, the unrepresentable is unavoidable. It is the unsaid in all saying that undoes all we do (Taylor 1992:318-319).

This notion that is between and beyond the many poles of the twentieth century is envisioned in many ways: as unnameable, unknowable, impossible, unrepresentable, out of time, anachronistic, Other, altarity, *différance*, space, a permeable membrane, wound, fissure, tear, gap, lack, fault, third, margin, et cetera. It is associated with writing, divine milieu, trace, erring, mazing grace, text, literature, art, and a/theoesthetics which reveal the possibility of a/theology which is suspended over all of these things and between all "modern" irreconcilable oppositions (altarity and identity, transcendence and immanence, past and present, signified and signifier, to point out a few). For Taylor, postmodernism allows the rethinking and unthinking of all modern concepts. By opening oneself to and embracing the absence of foundations, one combats repression. The struggle is a never-ending and never-beginning one that unrecognizably disfigures, but also leaves one attached to neither one pole nor the other in the modern pattern of figuring it all out.

Taylor "appears to present a paradigm case of postmodern thought" (Murphy and McClendon 1989:211). Taylor's deconstruction reaches far into the concepts that have defined how we perceive and talk about our world. For Taylor, the structures of the modern world are repressive because they are boundaries. The notion in postmodern a/theology of the divine milieu is liberating because it is suspended between and beyond the confines of modernity. It is unbounded, and thus "free."

Quintessentially postmodern, he rejects philosophy of the subject and modern individualism. Descartes ushered in the modern period by only relying on the "rational" and indubitable. Descartes's quest for certainty and establishment of the Cartesian mind as a separate and autonomous Self are concepts that Taylor refuses. Descartes thinks in terms of opposites, such as, dubitable and indubitable, extension and self, and body and mind. Cartesian dualism is the kind of philosophy Taylor seeks to go beyond. Neither soul nor body is essential; something beyond them both is crucial.

For Taylor the individual is made up of his or her relations. Yet he does not focus on a sense of community as do some other postmoderns. However, in the sense that every relationship is communal and the individual has no separate identity, there is more of an emphasis on the other than on the individual. Edith Wyschogrod, however, develops this theme more extensively. In his denial of a substantial self, of a hierarchy of meaning, of a "best" intepretation, of the stability of signification, Taylor clearly has postmodern traits: For him, there are no absolute answers, no solutions, but only endless erring.

Taylor does not wittingly preserve any modern ideals, but he does accept without question the death of God. But for him, instead of freeing the Self to be itself, the death of God further entraps the self. Taylor wants to get out beyond Nietzsche's master-slave dialectic, because it is, for him, an exercise seeking to settle irreconcilable differences. This settlement traps people into striving for the illusions of domination. The only way to have an identity in the modern world without God is to be an enslaving master of others. If one accepts Taylor's notion that embracing the negation sets one free, then Taylor has succeeded in inverting or subverting what many see as the "tragedy" of the death of God. If one does not think that he escapes nihilism and skepticism, then the self remains entrapped in a world of nothing, and now knows that there is nothing—God nor self.

Murphy and McClendon call Taylor "arch-modern." Instead of playing down the role of the individual for the sake of the community, they find no real restoration of community and an even further "*atomization*" of the individual. "Metaphysically, this is a modern move, already present as limit in Hume's bundle theory of the self" (1989:211). Taylor does not successfully escape modern individualism, but arrives at an intensive atomism. Like

Griffin, Murphy and McClendon find that Taylor buys into the premises and projects of modernity, and takes them to their extreme end.

Murphy and McClendon also view Taylor's concept of language as an "extreme version of something essentially modern." The quintessential modernists, the logical positivists, divided language into two types: cognitively meaningful and merely expressive. The former has truth value, the latter is literally nonsense, even if valued nonsense. Murphy and McClendon see Taylor's affirmation of meaning as relative and his rejection of original authorship as extending modern expressivism.

> Old modern expressivism now appears a more moderate position along the way toward a meaninglessness—a view, we may recall, also indicated by some "modern" existentialists . . . Taylor's skeptical conclusion, drawn from the insupportability of a correspondence theory of truth, is even less novel; it is simply and typically modern (Murphy and McClendon 1989:212).

But is Taylor "simply and typically" modern? Perhaps. But then so would be the Wittgenstein of the *Tractatus*, another writer who used the premises and procedures of modernity to show that what modernity cannot speak of, what must be passed over in silence, is what can be shown when all modern speaking is finished. Taylor seeks to use "ultramodern" language to write of that which cannot be written, to show what is beyond modern writing.

Taylor's concept of time keeps him from saying that he can recapture the past. For him, one can not simply return, because the past is never completely present and is never completely past. There is a sense of "eternal recurrence." He does use several of Augustine's ideas, sees non-scientific sources such as myths as useful, and does in a certain sense imply a "re-turn" to the communal.

Taylor points out that Augustine was the first to capture the full scope of the subjectivity of time. Augustine realized that the past, present and future are not the correct three modes of time, but instead—"a present of things past, a present of things present, and a present of things future" (Taylor 1984a:43). He recognized the complexity of the present and how it reflects the complexity of the self. Augustine's autobiography illustrates, for Taylor, how self-realization and self-presentation are bound to narrative.

> The relationship between narrativity and meaning is so close as to suggest that absence of the former leads to the lack of latter. Conversely, meaning emerges when episodes are narrated so as to form a plot . . . [which] requires an identifiable center. . . . In view of the imaginative coherence of autobiography the centered self appears to be more a literary creation than a literal fact (Taylor 1984a:45).

In *Erring* Taylor also points out that Augustine used typological interpretation. For this type of interpretation there is always something more beyond the symbol than it seems on the surface. Interpretation and "decipherment" is essential to understanding, to opening up the symbol, to presenting what was absent, to "speaking the unspoken" (Taylor 1984a:56-57). Taylor uses Augustine to illustrate the development of his theory of the breakdown of time, self, language, and history as traditional thought.

Taylor, like premoderns but unlike typical moderns, sees myths and stories as useful. Taylor uses the myths of Chronus, of Ariadne's thread, and of Abraham and Isaac to flesh out his thinking. Although he, of course, does not view them literally, he finds them allegorical and recognizes value in them. Even if they do not have a definite meaning as premoderns believed, and are not scientific or "rational" as moderns demand, Taylor finds significance in their interpretations.

Taylor's notion of community is more complicated than it seems. As Ted Peters has charted it, in the premodern period there is a sense of "continuity between self and world"; and in the postmodern there is a sense of "continuity between the personal and cosmic wholeness." Taylor's view, that every individual is composed by relations with others, does make room for a community which is neither particular nor universal. Everything is interrelated as interrelation. But he would not find Truth in self or world as the premoderns do. Premodernity defined the world and its inhabitants' places in it by their structures and boundaries beyond question. For Taylor the postmodern world exists in a divine milieu, suspended between traditional ideas of oppositions like self and world.

Taylor deserves thanks for addressing the "space" that contemporary people experience but do not understand. He does not want to leave people in a world without religious reflection, in world of complete nihilism. He attempts to be somewhat "constructive" in his deconstruction when he posits his postmodern a/theology. But, does he deny some things that are undeniable? Does he succeed in escaping complete skepticism? Does he leave us a world in which we *can* "err"?

Taylor writes *Erring* for "marginal people" who are struggling between belief and unbelief. He is correct in saying that modern people are alienated. Whether this is due to the structures of capitalism more than to dualistic thought is debatable. But because Descartes saw the mind, the rational, and the indubitable as superior and as what people should live by, his dualism separates people from their experience. Like the banes of modernity cited by Habermas and Griffin, reductionist rationalism separates and differentiates people so they must dominate the world or be dominated by it.

In the Prelude to *Erring*, Taylor cites Walker Percy's novel *The Moviegoer* and uses Binx as an example of a person on the margin. Binx says, "To become aware of the possibility of the search is to be onto something. . . . Not to be onto something is to be in despair. . . . The search always ends in despair" (Percy 1961:17-18). The search, for Taylor, is the journey along the divine milieu which always re-turns and re-curs, and so is never-ending. There are never any easy answers for Binx or Taylor. The opposites and difference of modernity are misleading. Life is never fixed. The search is what keeps us alive. As long as we keep on, we don't end in despair.

Embracing the negation is how, for Taylor, one can escape complete nihilism, Binx's despair. But is Taylor's deconstruction also an affirmation, as he says it is? And, if so, what does he affirm? Taylor addresses this question in terms of accepting that the Kingdom is neither here nor coming, that is, accepting the impossibility of salvation. He says,

> the denial of utopia can become utopian and the loss of the dream of salvation can become a salvation. The impossibility of reconciliation means that there is no resurrexit here or elsewhere, nor in the future. The door is closed, closed tightly; there is no upper room (Taylor 1992:317).

Taylor says that he escapes the modern dialectic, and so implies that his anti-polar philosophy does not become a pole, i.e., the opposite of polar philosophy. However, the last sentence in the above quotation is definitive. Here it is difficult to see "room" for "erring." Here he gives in to modernity. Here he loses touch with the apophatic tradition which keeps doors neither open nor closed. In a world of erring, how can a door be tightly closed and the room on the other side denied? In making this claim, Taylor moors his thought at the fragile pier of modernity. He leaves the ocean of erring, the divine milieu beyond all humanly constructed harbors. For the true post-modernist, this door must be neither open nor closed, the room neither entered nor left, salvation neither given nor taken. There must be something else beyond and between all our constructed images. At this crucial point, Taylor, like a modernist, has said what a postmodernist finds cannot be said: we have reached an end. We *are* in despair.

Taylor does recognize our relationships and our erring as part of being human. He also knows that there are no answers and that the journey is what *living* is all about. But if the door *is* shut, then we are not wandering and erring, we are lost and hopeless. Binx says that at times he feels invisible and that "[t]here is a danger of slipping clear out of space and time. . . . The danger is of becoming no one nowhere" (Percy 1961:72,79). Binx is right, this is the danger, and in the end, Taylor's apophatic discourse turns to an affirmation of nihilism—a total turn for one who errs without end in the milieu which is neither wilderness nor path.

Chapter 6

Edith Wyschogrod and Saintly Narratives

with H. Frederick Felice

The postmodern saintly life . . . is a plea for boldness and risk . . . for a new
altruism in an age grown cynical and hardened to catastrophe.
                                        —Edith Wyschogrod

Numerous writers have pointed out the aporias, i.e., the holes, the contradictions, the blind spots, in modern thought. Some have gone forward in an apophatic pattern as Taylor has. Wyschogrod, however, uses saintly narratives to resolve problems insoluble in contemporary modern and postmodern moral theory. One might add that she also works to overcome the inadequacies of "normal" theology by her "edifying" work. In short, a form of hagiographic narrative makes possible the creation of a space in which modern dichotomies and postmodern aporias can be overcome and the voice of the Other can resound.

Wyschogrod's early research centered around the work of the French philosopher Emmanuel Levinas, especially his work on dialogical relationships and the concept of the "Face." Edward Farley's summary of this strand of Levinas's view is elegant and insightful:

> [An] emphasis in the literature of the interpersonal focuses not on the act or posture (recognition, empathy, availability) in which the other is present but on the mystery of personal encounter and dialogue. This is the line from Martin Buber to Emmanuel Levinas. . . . [T]heir fascination is not with the specific acts that yield the reality of the other but with the mystery of that yielding itself, the mystery of the thou. This is the theme of Buber's semi-poetic *I and Thou* and also the theme of the "face" (*visage*) in Levinas. Face articulates neither physiognomy

(the plane of sensibility) nor acts which emotionally feel the other. It is the "infinitely strange" and mysterious presence of something which contests my projecting meanings of it, an unforeseeable depth which can evoke the act of murder but which cannot be cognitively mastered. . . .

What actually occurs when human beings share emotions or engage in dialogue. Levinas, Marcel and others contend that something happens in human being-together which is not just negotiating agendas or calculating how self-interests might be met. Something is going on that is irreducible to the negotiations of power and status. Levinas's thesis is somewhat startling. When we experience the face of the other, or when the face occurs in conjunction with being-together, we experience a summons, an invocation (Marcel), a claim, a call to commitment and responsibility. *This primordial summons is the basis of the values in the normative culture: the normative culture is not the basis of the summons.* . . . The summons from the other is something that evokes a response in which compassion and obligation converge (Farley 1990:39-40,41; emphasis added).

That Wyschogrod continues to owe a debt to Levinas will be seen throughout this section.

Wyschogrod's earliest book (1974) anticipated positions she develops in her more recent work. Her comments on death show both continuity and development in her work. Wyschogrod early on quotes Heidegger as saying "No one can take the other's dying away from him" (1974:108). She later alters this to: "Although we can often substitute for one another, no one can stand in for another's dying" (1985:170). In her most recent book, she moves further:

I cannot die for another in the sense that my dying will take the place of the other's death because at some time the Other must die for herself/himself.

What is omitted from Heidegger's account, however, is that the force of the relation to my own death derives from an awareness of *the time that is left,* the gap between my life now and the event that is my dying and yet to come. This is true even if the length of time I have left is indeterminable. When my death is thought of in this way as the always dwindling time that is left to me rather than as the coming to an end of my life, then the death of the Other and my death become *commensurable.* This is because all along the way, each has a certain quantum of time left. The other's death and mine are now integrated into a common framework that each of us has a certain portion of time still outstanding (1990a:64).

This notion of commensurability is crucial. If one sees this commensurability, one can stand in for another. One cannot die *in place of* another, but one can die *for* another. One can give another a welcome reprieve (Wyschogrod 1985:170). That is the lesson of, among others, Saint Maximillian Kolbe who *did* take another's place in a death line and enabled the other to have more time to live. These reflections on death reveal continuity and development in Wyschogrod's work. Indeed, an intertextual reading of her writings is immensely illuminating.

But who is this "other" in Wyschogrod's view? As with Levinas, Wyschogrod refuses to reduce the "other" to an other self: "for Levinas the other is never an alter ego but the one whom we are not" (1974:50). Wyschogrod later seeks to avoid any danger of reducing the other to oneself and the denial of the other's difference. Only if the other remains an other (who is not taken as a mirror of oneself) can one respond to another and be called out of oneself (1990a:33-34).

Ordinarily one might think of the age of man-made mass death, especially in the wars and concentration camps of the twentieth century, as either the end of modernity or the beginning of the postmodern. Wyschogrod sees the era of man-made mass death as the "bridge" or "chasm" between modernity and postmodernism. *Spirit in Ashes* relates the era of man-made mass death to the modern world. Wyschogrod takes World War I as the beginning of the age of man-made mass death, but rejects the notion that the phenomenon of man-made mass death, specifically the concentration camps and atomic weapons of World War II, is based within the matrix of modern technological thought. Technology is saved, she claims, in that its language is still based on what she refers to as the "life-world." Science is linked to the physicality of the world as an abstraction from it: "The world of immediate qualitative experience grounds the constructed idealities of science. Without it they would hang free of any meaningful context and would lose their spheres of origin and applicability" (1985:24). The death-world utilized the products of science in its destructiveness. But that outcome was not a necessary consequence of modern technology.

Nonetheless, the two worlds, the modern world of science and technology and the interruptive world of man-made mass death constitute two distinct, though easily conflated, worlds:

> [W]hile the death-world trades on technological society, it would be a misunderstanding to consider it as part of that society or, conversely, to imagine technological society as a "universal concentration camp" from which all human freedom is absent. Although alienated from the life-world, technological society depends on it for its continued existence, but the death-world is wrenched almost free of the life-world: its aim is simply death. At present technological society and the death-world exist side by side. If the death-world were the only world, the resulting monolith would spell the end of all life and so the end of the technological society as well (1985:25).

The death-world is parasitic on modernity. But it is not yet postmodern, because murder—the practice which paradoxically gives life to the death-world—requires killers to use the technology to perform murderous acts supporting a community of terror. The death-world is a bizarre mixing of the rationality inherent in the post-enlightenment technological era, and the self-destroying elements that will metamorphose into the postmodern world. It is also a world which figures the postmodern by giving good reason for postmodern cynicism and despair. In Levinasian terms, it is a world of facelessness, in which no other is recognized.

Yet the modern is displaced (not replaced, not surpassed, not over-thrown) by postmodernity. Wyschogrod finds that postmodernism is a constellation with six key characteristics including "differentiality," a tactic which undercuts standard modern accounts which presume stable identi-ties; "double coding," placing and noticing ambiguity within our dis-courses; theoretical "eclecticism"; "alterity," recognizing the otherness of the other; "empowerment," even of an Nietzschean type of will to power; and "materialism," often explicit, sometimes veiled (1990a:xvi-xxi). But the question is whether, in this postmodern world where whirl seems king, an ethic can be found. Wyschogrod writes:

> A postmodern ethic must look not to some opposite of ethics but elsewhere, to life narratives, specifically those of saints, defined in terms that both overlap and overturn traditional normative stipula-tions and that defy the normative structure of moral theory (Wy-schogrod 1990a:xiii).

If it seems odd to try to inscribe saintliness as a postmodern ethic, Michael Gareffa notes that "postmodernism is nothing if not a montage, fragmentation and 'borrowings,' " so it should be not be surprising that a postmodern writer would borrow and import saintliness into the whirl (Gareffa 1991:583).

Wyschogrod's approach is neither to revise saintly narratives nor to place a modern/postmodern filter over the narratives already written to shape the way the reader sees the subject of the hagiographic narrative. Rather, she places a filter *under* the bowl of hagiographic narratives, applies a hearty shake, and examines whatever passes through the postmodern sieve. "Postmodern thinking invites the engagement of strategies drawn from various quarters and whose deployment issues in new ways of thinking and acting" (Wyschogrod 1990a:xv). So, what is it that is about saintliness that is borrowed by postmodernism? The answer to that ques-tion is found within Wyschogrod's redefinition of sanctity. The definition she gives, however, is rather tricky.

> I shall . . . define the saint—the subject of hagiographic narrative—*as one whose adult life in its entirety is devoted to the alleviation of sorrow (the*

psychological suffering) and pain (the physical suffering) that afflicts other persons without distinction of rank or group or, alternatively, that afflicts the sentient beings, whatever the cost to the saint in pain or sorrow (34).

This definition is tricky because the *unitalicized* part is the crucial part of the definition! A saint cannot be a person whose life is an incomplete narrative, but must be the subject of a narrative whose ending is determined ("adult life in its entirety"). Moreover, the saint is a subject of a *narrative;* and while all lives may prefigure narratives, the Wyschogrodian saint is the subject of a configured and complete narrative. The significance of this will appear below, but in brief it seemingly implies that there can be no living saints, no clearly saintly acts, no saintly actualities.

Later Wyschogrod describes the saint as "a radical altruist, one who is dedicated to the alleviation of the suffering of others irrespective of the cost to herself/himself" (58). The postmodern slant appears most clearly when Wyschogrod describes the saint as "the one who is totally at the disposal of the other, and lives this exposure as response to the other by stripping the self of its egoity or formal unity" (98). The totality and costliness of sanctity is highlighted throughout her work.

The saint, then, is the perfect Levinasian "self." Wyschogrod's descriptions of the saint develop her earlier description of a self authentically able to engage in social interaction. In "Man-Made Mass Death: Challenging Paradigms of Selfhood," she follows Levinas in claiming:

The constitution of such a self entails assuming the standpoint of the other, the self becoming other not only to the other but also to itself. Social existence is required ab initio, for only by taking the view of another can something objective be constituted and the individual attain the functional unity of a self (Wyschogrod 1983b:20).

All selves are social, whether or not individuals realize it. The self must become neither the other nor identical with its past. The functional unity is an emergent, not a previously given, unity. Like the premodern self, but unlike the modern self-secure self, the postmodern self emerges only as a social self. That people so often fail to become a self-in-community and resort to the will to power to establish their selves suggests how often we take the other as an alter ego and fail really to assume the position of an *other.* We confront the other as a mirror of ourself, not as an other.

The other, or Other, is often a silenced victim, "the one who as a result of exclusion from some community lacks the power to speak" (Wyschogrod 1990b:171-172). The saint, according to Wyschogrod, speaks and acts for the Other and thus gives him or her voice in the community. The saint is drawn to the other. What makes a person a saint more than anything else is her "motivation." But such motivation empowers the saint by an overpowering desire:

The topographical markers of alterity can be read by anyone—the crumpled body as a signifier of pain, the expressionless face as a signifier of depression—but for saints the Other's destitution is a vortex, a centripetal force, as it were, into which saintly desire on the Other's behalf is drawn. The more fissured the life of the Other, the greater the other's lack, the weightier its claim upon the saintly self. Saints are person-differentiating, but it is lack and not proximity that is encrypted in the body or "group body" of the Other that decides who receives preference. Thus [they] . . . are "in the trace of alterity" and "speak" in the imperative (Wyschogrod 1990a:242).

Saints' desires draw their selves out and they are *consumed* by the needs of the other. What emerges is a new "self," not self-secured or created by a will to power, but selflessly centered on the other.

Wyschogrod's saints seem not to be embodied. This non-corporeality, implicit in the definition noted above, is reemphasized by Wyschogrod's questioning an observer's ability to know the motivation behind a potentially saintly act. Since one can never be sure that radical altruism, rather than patronization or codependency, was the driving force of a saintly act or saintly life, the saint remains necessarily insecure, mysterious: "it can never be established that there was a saint or proved that the primacy of the Other is the source of action" (1990b:149). Wyschogrod alleviates this criterial problem by denying the reality of a living saint and by affirming that only in narratives, complete narratives, can saintliness truly appear. Although suffering bodies play a great role in her text, the suffering seems to remain textual.

Once a saint's life is written in a narrative with an ending, readers can relate to the saint as the other-outside-the-text relates to the one-inscribed-in-the-text. Since they can know the "whole story," they can assure themselves with the power of third person omniscience that altruism is the motivation behind action(s) of a person "whose adult life in its entirety" was placed in the service of the other. Saints, in short, are not real people, but fictions created in a narrative.

If one accepts Wyschogrod's theory, it seems difficult, perhaps impossible, to imagine nonfictional saints. Almost all her examples of saints are drawn not from classic hagiography intended to narrate an edifying truth about an actual life in the real world, but from modern and postmodern texts which make no pretence to being about an actual embodied person. Even some of the traditional saints she cites in passing, like Saint Mary of Egypt, who had been a prostitute, do not fit her definition of a saint. Saints, then, seem to be fictions for Wyschogrod.

But this narrativity and fictionality is evidently not a worry for Wyschogrod. Her purpose in writing is clearly conveyed in the first part of her final paragraph of *Saints and Postmodernism:*

The postmodern saintly life as a new path in ethics is not a proposal to revert to an older hagiographic discourse, least of all to hide behind its metaphysical presuppositions. It is instead a plea for boldness and risk, for an effort to develop a new altruism in an age grown cynical and hardened to catastrophe: war, genocide, the threat of worldwide ecological collapse, sporadic and unpredictable eruptions of urban violence, the use of torture, the emergence of new diseases. In an epoch grown weary not only of its calamities but of its ecstasies, of its collective political fantasies that destroyed millions of lives, and of its chemically induced stupors and joys, the postmodern saint shows the traces of these disasters. . . . Borrowing the compassionate strands of the world's religious traditions, the absurdist gestures of recent modernist art and literature, and modern technologies, saints try to fashion lives of compassion and generosity (1990a:257).

But how do the fictions of saints' lives not only ring true but come true? Do the saints fashion such lives or do the narrators of saintliness create narratives of compassion and generosity?

In analyzing the moral theory of Nicholas Rescher, especially with regard to altruism, Wyschogrod finds that his theory subverts itself because it relies on altruism as displayed in unnamed and unrecognized saintliness to measure the legitimacy of social theories. "It is, to use postmodern language, the saint's response to the Other—not, as Lyotard puts it, the grand meta-narratives of theory—that addresses me and mandates benevolence in everyday life" (1990a:243). But not only does saintliness measure moral theory, as Levinas holds, but moral theory cannot convey the practice or the power of saintliness to a "reader." Theory is not enough. Saints' lives can inspire practice. Thus, it might be said that the theories come true when readers put them into practice.

And here Wyschogrod's attempts to utilize saintly narratives to overcome the aporias in modern moral theory seem to come to a grinding halt. As Wyschogrod put it:

[I]t may be useful to consider in a preliminary way some criticisms, not of any specific moral theory, but of moral theory generally as an instrument for gaining insight into what moral lives are or how they might be pursued. One difficulty connected with moral theory is the gap between the theory (even when it is theory about practice) and life (1990a:3).

The saintly narrative helps bridge that gap. But the saint is a character of complete extravagance. To appreciate a saint is not necessarily to emulate one. So how does this narrative of a life or a display of saintly practice *resolve* theoretical issues? How could a person emulate a saint? Why would one do so? Without answers to these such questions, *how* a narrative might

Wyschogrod's and James's points about the creative and evocative power of saints are correct, but they also are inconsistent with Wyschogrod's account of saintliness. It is not necessarily the narrative which changes lives. It may be the very person we encounter who is (for all anyone can tell) a saint, which is the powerful catalyst of change. The question is how these transformations of lives highlighted in these two quotations can occur.

The saint offers something better and more effective than moral theory. He or she offers a life for the patterning of future lives. The saint offers an example of devotion to the needs of the Other as the basis for his or her sainthood, and thus a moral life. This fits with another more typical definition of sainthood. Lawrence S. Cunningham defined a saint as "anyone who was so grasped by a religious vision that the person's life was radically changed and that changed life then served (or serves) as a model for others" (Cunningham 1983:207). And in general, Ricoeur's concept of refiguration or the practice of mimesis3, which goes beyond mere repetitive imitation and is in fact creative imitation (Ricoeur 1988:passim), provides a satisfactory practical solution to this very practical problem. Basically, transformation is refiguration as an effect of reading a narrative or responding to a person. It is taking the saintly path as one's own.

But even if the "how" question can be resolved, the "why" question remains. We can see how a saint lives. Why emulate this saintly practice, that saintly life? In Wyschogrod's view, these lives are the norms of moral and social theory, so no theoretical answer is possible for such a question. It is a question beyond theory. It is a question external to the narration of lives. Yet saints can "transfigure" others. They are "regenerative." And perhaps there is no clear answer to this question, beyond saying that just as the question "why be moral?" is a question beyond the boundaries of moral theory and unanswerable by any moral or social theory, so the question "why be saintly?" is a question beyond the boundaries of saintly narrative and unanswerable, save in terms that are finally not real answers: saints have "intrinsic authority" and "impressiveness."

But the price is so high! Saints give their lives for the other. They are "radical altruists." They may well, momentarily considered, be dupes. Why take this risk? Wyschogrod's view is that the other's need compels them, implying that the question is unanswerable.

Adapting Ricoeur's discussion of narrative identity, we can perhaps go beyond this "unanswerable" question. This may be very hard ground, but it is possible that it is not yet the "hard rock" which turns our conceptual shovel and halts our theorizing dig. It is possible to say that the impressiveness of the saint displays one way of having character:

The circular relation between what we may call a "character"—which may be that of an individual as well as that of a people—and the narratives that both express and shape this character, illustrates in a

marvelous way the circle referred to at the beginning of our description of threefold mimesis. The third mimetic relation of narrative
[refiguring] leads back to the first relation [prefiguring] by way of the
second relation [configuring]. . . . At the end of our inquiry into the
refiguration of time by narrative we can affirm without hesitation that
this circle is a wholesome one. The first mimetic relation refers, in the
case of an individual, to the semantics of desire, which only includes
those prenarrative features attached to the demand constitutive of
human desire. The third mimetic relation is defined by the narrative
identity of an individual or a people, stemming from the endless
rectification of a previous narrative by a subsequent one, and from the
chain of refigurations that results from this. In a word, narrative
identity is the poetic resolution of the hermeneutic circle (1988:248).

In the present context, Ricoeur's poetic resolution in the quotation is a
practical resolution. It involves a praxis which instantiates a character. That
character is not necessarily a finished character, but an evolving one.
Adapting the insights of James and Cunningham, then, we can say that for
each tradition, the saint is the one who provides a model of rectification.
Why be a saint? Why try to act as a saint *of that tradition* would? Why
emulate her or his reconfiguration of the past with a new reconfiguration
of our own? Why engage in a religious form of mimesis3? The answer is: if
we desire to keep the chain of refigurations going, that is, to keep the
community which carries that tradition alive, we will have to learn how to
be saintly, to express in some way the best of the character of our tradition.
The saint evokes our desire, not only in the exalted sense of total dedication
to the Other and to others (the height of sanctity), but also in the less exalted
way of instantiating, in our own ways, as well as possible, the ever-evolving
character of the tradition we inhabit. And some might even add that the
saint is a sacrament of the power of the Ultimate Other.

If this is on target, then a disconnection of saintliness from concrete and
actual traditions undermines the possibility of even understanding why
one might ask or answer the "why be a saint?" question. For the answer to
the "why" question is simple: "to carry on." If one does not desire to carry
on, if one's response to an other or reading of a text does not evoke the desire
to embody the character of the tradition, then the "why" question receives
the opposite answer: don't continue the chain of refigurations because it is
not a tradition worth carrying on: let it die, do not try to resuscitate the dead.
Rather, open the door for ludic nihilism, the godot for whom we wait, or
the prefiguring beginning of a new tradition in which to dwell, a new
tradition to figure our desires.

Although Wyschogrod tries to disconnect sainthood from the traditions
which generate specific saints, she finally fails to disconnect saints from
actual communities. She discriminates among traditions which instantiate
a life-world worth dwelling in and traditions which instantiate a death-

world. In other words, some communities and their traditions are so impressive that their actions do and should evoke the desire that they do carry on. Wyschogrod uses an example in one of her descriptions of saintly action by citing the rescue of Jews in World War II by the French Protestants—reformed and anabaptist—in the town of Chambon (1990a:183). Wyschogrod describes the actions of these people as saintly in the sense that they risk themselves to help those in need. As such, the community at Chambon appears to be a collection of saintly acting individuals. But the life of individuals in that community and the community itself is not yet over. How can they be identified as saints on Wyschogrod's theory?

Wyschogrod provides resources to answer this question in her discourse on memory and time. She defines time, almost poetically, as a "ceaseless succession to a next" (91). This definition allows for interesting play off a Cartesian sense of the self: I think, therefore I am; I think again, therefore I am again; I have thought, therefore I was; I will probably think tomorrow, therefore I will probably be. In such seemingly silly verbal acts, we have posited the now, the next, the past and the future. But, when positing the "I have thought, therefore I was" statement, one is actually positing "I think now that I thought then, therefore I am and I was." Memory is a present function. Memory is not a doorway from the present into the past. Rather it repositions the past in the form of memory, into the present in the form of thought. To remember is to refigure—a creative process that never ends while still we live.

This continuous repositing and recreation of memory in the present is not unlike the continuous recreation of the self by the saint as he or she comes into contact with the ever changing needs of the Other. This may alleviate the problem of the fictionalization of "historical" saints. Since memory is not a constant but must be refigured to be available now, a fictionalization of history into a viable hagiographic narrative does not necessarily conflict with the reality of the original any more than a memory of the original would. Wyschogrod uses the concepts of repentance, apology, and forgiveness to show a revisionary view of the past and memory. Her idea is that "repentance, apology, pardon, and forgiveness are phenomena that erase the past while maintaining time's irreversibility" (109)—a point explored more fully in light of the fact that the past can never be undone in *The Evils of Theodicy* (Tilley 1991:201-214). Time does not reverse itself for the function of memory, but one can alter the reception of the past as it appears in the now through repentance, apology, etc. Hence, actual people can be *refigured* as saints by active exercise of memory of them.

If the answer to the question "why be a saint?" is "to carry on a tradition," then can we recognize traditions worth carrying on without resort to some moral theory to provide standards? After all, many feminists might find that Wyschogrod's picture of saints as self-donating merely valorizes the historic subjection of women who have been denied any identity save in what women can give to and for another (typically men and children).

Wyschogrod's invocation of saintliness was intended to solve problems in moral theory, so moral theory is in no position to provide standards. Yet Wyschogrod's previous work with the concepts of communities may help provide an unexpected path to answering the question of "carrying on."

In "Man-Made Mass Death: Shifting Concepts of Community," she defines three types of communities as they appear in the age of the awareness of the death event: communities of memory, of terror, and of the unavowable.

> Communities of memory are often identified with archaic forms of life because such communities see themselves as reviving or continuing past modes of association and belief. In the epoch of the death event, social existence founded on nostalgia reflects an attempt to resist the depersonalization resulting from technological change, increased bureaucratization and globalized modes of production and change (Wyschogrod 1990b:169).

It is difficult to find a clear example for a community of memory. While there are numerous groups that have chosen to disregard technological progress for the sake of "simpler" existence, such as the Amish or the communalists of the sixties, one cannot determine if the motivation for that life is recognition of the death event.

Wyschogrod describes the community of terror in much the same way as the community of memory except that it

> differs from them (communities of memory) in its stress on the future rather than on the past. The future for communities of memory is interpreted as the recreation of a past age of bliss, but for communities of terror the past must be expunged and a consciousness divested of funded human experience created. . . .
>
> Communities of terror are born when the concept of man overwhelms the concrete plurality of languages. Terror arises because in actual fact, the ideal of humanity resides in one or several persons in whose hands power is concentrated and who dispense material wealth and spiritual culture, life and death (1990b:172,173).

Wyschogrod cites Lyotard's research on language and the French Revolution. Here, as with the Nazis and the Stalinists, we may see an example of a community of terror.

The community of the unavowable recalls Wyschogrod's saints and Chambon. In Chambon, the needs of the other were a defining factor as the community saw the need for the survival of the greater community rather than just the individual.

I take the unavowable community as emerging with the appearance of a new impulse, the desire for the preservation of human existence in the face of the possible extinction of humankind. This impulse flows not from the subject as a consciousness or agent or even from a desiring unconscious but from the moral subject, that dimension of the subject in which the Other takes precedence over the self (1990b:173).

Wyschogrod uses three functions to define the community of the una-vowable: responsibility, passivity, and unworking.

Saintly action manifests itself most clearly in the area of responsibility. Responsibility, as well as unworking and passivity, "flow from the fact of the Other's primacy. Responsibility means that I am primarily accountable *for* the Other rather than *to* moral values, rules or claims about justice" (1990b:174). The member of a community of the unavowable is motivated as the saint is. The manner in which a member of a community acts is also similar to that of the saint. The passivity referred to within the community of the unavowable recalls Wyschogrod's saintly renunciation of power. Passivity is defined by Wyschogrod as the "renunciation of power in social transactions" (Wyschogrod 1990b:174). According to Wyschogrod, though, it is this dismissal of power that authorizes the saint to act in the manner in which he or she does. "Saintly action is connected with the abnegation of power in that the authorization of saintly work derives from the *renuncia-tion* of power" (1990a:57). Wyschogrod's definition of "unwork" as "the placing of my resources . . . at the disposal of another" (1990b:174) involves the dispossession of the self, which is similar to the total alterity of the saint.

It appears that Chambon would fit into the category of the community of the unavowable. The citizens were responsible, passive, and "unwork-ing." But Chambon is also an example of corporate saintly practice. The communities of the unavowable, then, are the communities which produce saints. They are the communities whose traditions are worth carrying on. Rather than being a universalizing account, Wyschogrod's account is open to very particular forms of saintliness in very particular communities which share a distinguishing, but not constitutive, feature or a feature which alone makes them a community: that they are communities of the Unavowable Other.

In her description of a saint, Wyschogrod distinguishes ordinary work, techniques used in an effort to achieve a goal efficiently, from labor, which "as opposed to both work and violence, entails the corporeal involvement of the laborer but minimizes the input of forces extraneous to the laborer" (1990a:84). Saintly labor is "the psychological, social, and corporeal invest-ment of the self's total resources when they are committed to altruistic existence" (1990b:85). Roughly, work is what we pay and are paid for; labor constructs who we are, at best a form of "unwork."

The distinction between work and labor carries great weight for Wy-schogrod. The saint, though, undermines this distinction—one like the socially constructed distinction between praxis and poesis (Milbank 1990:351-359)—by incorporating both "work" and "labor" into his or her new form of action.

> In the case of saintly labor, the totality of the psychological and corporeal resources of the subject are dedicated to the alleviation of suffering expressed in the hand that responds to destitution rather than the hand that is the prototype of cognitive and intellectual functions. Saintly activity reverses the principle of parsimony that governs work and remains labor intensive. Paradoxically the saint's labor may appear effortless because the saint often sees labor as rooted in a source greater than herself/himself (1990a:85).

There is more of a paradox in this definition than just the apparent strenuousness of the saint's actions. Saintly action is corporeally intensive action, but action that still has a goal, the alleviation of the suffering of the other. Wyschogrod states:

> [S]aintly action is orchestrated as labor, the total corporeal and psychological involvement in the needs and interests of others. Saintly work, the achievement of ends in conformity with a plan, should be seen against this backdrop. Saintly labor is not a ghost in the machine that inhabits everyday works of generosity but is simply the psychological, social, and corporeal investment of the self's total resources when they are committed to altruistic existence (1990a:85).

Wyschogrod here seems to attempt to extend saintly action outside the realm of that of the generic individual by making saintly labor imitable. So, while Wyschogrod states that "saintly effort at alleviating suffering is described as necessarily labor intensive" (1990a:86) this does not remove saintly action from the realm of technique and effort, but, instead, shifts that action into a new type of action which is neither "work" nor "labor," but the "unwork" of the easy yoke and light burden.

This argument against the sufficiency of technique also relates back to the structuring of a moral theory around the action of the saint. The saint is bound by neither moral theory nor technique. Moral theory comes after his or her action has been recognized as saintly. Technique is not sufficient as the need of each other will be distinctly different and will thus require the creation of a new mode of action.

Wyschogrod also distinguishes saints from mystics. The saint's and the mystic's actions may appear similar, but the motivations will be distinctly different. The saint is acting out of immediate cognition of the needs of the other, whereas the mystic is obeying what he or she considers to be the impulse of a higher power. While both the mystic and the saint may perform an altruistic action, the mystic will be one step (or more) removed from the immediate need of the other as he or she will be reacting to the transcendent Other rather than out of alterity. The lines between these two categories can easily be blurred as saints, by Wyschogrod's definition, can believe they are acting on behalf of a higher power and thus appear as a mystic, or the mystic can feel he or she is acting on the needs of the other, but doing so with a technique derived from the teachings of a transcendent Other, and thus not reacting directly to the needs of the other, but, instead to the teaching of technique or moral theory.

The significance of this blurring is that the saint can act within his or her culture, even seeming to act on the principles of a religious tradition; Wyschogrod is not positing and cannot posit a "generic sainthood." While the saint would help all others, we should view this in the context of each and every other, and thus the cultural context of the other may be significant. A saint, by accepting an identity centered around the Other, will also be accepting the cultural context of his or her new center. A saint who must address a member of a specific class or culture must recognize those specificities in order to properly address the needs of that Other. A saint, then, could fulfill the needs of an other outside the saint's own native cultural context, but if those needs require that the saint understand the culture of the destitute other, then the saint will work towards that understanding. The actions of a saint within different cultures will reflect those differences.

So what, then, has *Saints and Postmodernism* accomplished? Read in light of Wyschogrod's other works, it becomes a very un/canny text. It seems to place saintliness exclusively into the realm of the hagiographic narratives and thus to distance saintly action from human life over the unbridgeable space of text. But then it gives examples of living saints in Chambon. It seems to make recognition of saintliness impossible as it appears in actual embodied life. But it is open to models and to an easy emendation that allows saintly people to evoke recognition and response. It seems to proffer a generic and traditionless concept of sainthood. But it richly links sainthood to traditions as those lives which make the tradition seem worth carrying on. It seems to collapse into the tasteless relativism of the easiest sort of postmodernity. Yet it provides a profound critique of such relativism not by argument, but by displaying that the community of the unavowable is the only community worth living in, the only community that can produce actual saints in the present because it idolizes neither the past as do communities of memory or the future as do communities of terror. In the whirl of postmodernity, Wyschogrod does not attempt to find a rock to cling to or a port to be sought, but *shows* what cannot be *said* in chaos: orderings can emerge. The task, then, is to see that saintly orderings can emerge and to create them out of the chaos of postmodernity. This is the task of the community of the unavowable.

What Wyschogrod is attempting to do is to create a space for saintliness in the postmodern realm of multiple communities which valorize unreined desires and seek the short and shabby ecstasies which are possible only in the sickness of modernity, the *amnesia* of man-made mass death (1990a:252). Postmodernism is nothing if not a recognition of the self-destructive elements in politics, literature or religion. The eliminative nature of postmodernism seems to create chaos. But Wyschogrod, like Taylor at his apophatic best, tries to show how in self-destruction an orientation can emerge that enables "something else" to appear, a saintly form of "self-destruction" that responds to the other and is thus a way within the whirl to open the door to a wholeness, a holiness, a healthiness (in Latin, *salus*) and thus to salvation. Through and in the whirl there sounds the voice of the Other which can be heard in and through the actions of the saint—who gives the other a voice—and it speaks, today, in the imperative: whoever would find life must lose it.

Epilogue to Part 2

PER OMNIA SAECULA SAECULORUM

These three chapters do not bring us to a conclusion. There can be, finally, no sense of an ending. The radical writers addressed herein can be characterized, but may well claim that any characterization is nothing but caricature. If this be caricature, so be it.

Thomas Altizer, as much as any contemporary theologian, continues or reworks the discourse of the coincidence of opposites. Paradoxically, spirit is flesh, the divine is the human, the transcendent is immanent. Altizer's radical theology of the death of God, of divine kenosis, of total presence partakes in the paradoxes of presence: "Only an apocalyptic genesis could be an inauguration of that [absolute] freedom, a genesis which is a full negation of a primordial plenitude in 'a pure and total *act*" (1993:180). "Hence the dissolution of God is the consummation of the inauguration of the will of God, an inauguration which is an actual genesis, even as an apocalypse is an actual apocalypse" (1993:184). The language of Altizer is not the both-and of Hegel, not the either/or of Kierkegaard, not the neither/nor of Taylor, but the paradoxical presence of opposites, the language of total presence, never partial presence and partial absence. Like Nicholas of Cusa in the fifteenth century, Altizer displays that only if one rejects the law of non-contradiction can one come to the mystical vision of the infinity of being, of the coincidence of opposites. The "theos" which is rejected in Altizer's gospel of Christian atheism, then, is the "theos" which conforms to the law of non-contradiction, a law which need not apply to Infinity.

Mark C. Taylor, in contrast, continues or reworks the discourse of apophatic mysticism. Advocating neither spirit nor flesh, divine nor human, transcendent nor immanent, Taylor's writing of radical absence creates a space for something other—or tries to do so at its best. In opposition to Altizer, Taylor valorizes absence against the oppression of Total Presence. Like the apophatic mystics, Taylor's thought offers the odd hope that neither darkness nor light is ultimate; one cannot say what is ultimate, only, like Meister Eckhart said of the Godhead (*deitas*) beyond God (*deus*) in the fourteenth century, that the ultimate, the divine milieu, is neither this nor that.

Edith Wyschogrod makes room for saints. We have argued here that hers is a truly uncanny text that requires reading through more than reading. This reading exponentially raises the possibility of caricature to new heights for it valorizes, finally, the *communio sanctorum*, but as is necessary in every post-age, a communion or community of solidarity in and with diversity.

Each of these writers finds room for religiosity (if not religious institutions or much of religious traditions) in the interstices of the postmodern age. To do so, we have argued, each creates a discourse which curiously resonates with premodern discourses discarded or forgotten in most of modernity. Where their concerns resonate with ours and where they reveal gracious possibilities present in a fragmented world, we are in their debt. They reveal that the story is not yet over, that other possibilities remain, that the contours of being are not limned even in a post-age.

Yet none of these seems to take postmodernity head-on and argue against its valorization of the nihilism that is said to be the outcome of the concerns and practices of modernity. Postliberal theology, arguably the most conservative of theologies conceived in a post-age, takes postmodernity head-on. Or so Part 3 argues.

POSTLIBERAL THEOLOGY

Theology as grammar.
—Ludwig Wittgenstein

A picture held us captive. And we could not get outside it, for it lay in our language and language seemed to repeat it to us inexorably.
—Ludwig Wittgenstein

Philip R. Shields, in *Logic and Sin in the Writings of Ludwig Wittgenstein*, writes, "From calling the *Tractatus* an 'ethical' work, to prefacing the *Philosophical Remarks* with the wish 'This book is written to the glory of God' Wittgenstein consistently framed his technical writings on logic and philosophy in ethical and religious terms" (1993:1). Given this point, one wonders why it took theologians as long as it did to apply the work of this brilliant twentieth-century philosopher to the problems of theology. Systematic theologians made little use of Wittgenstein's work the first decade after the important *Philosophical Investigations* was published in 1953. Philosophers of religion like D. Z. Phillips had used Wittgenstein's insights sufficiently that in 1967 Kai Nielsen could accuse them of being "Wittgensteinian fideists." Nonetheless, it wasn't until 1984, with the publication of George Lindbeck's *The Nature of Doctrine: Religion and Theology in a Postliberal Age*, that a historical and systematic theologian attempted to develop a theological approach based on Wittgenstein's insights into the nature of language and culture.

Lindbeck's text has become the defining landmark of what has come to be called postliberal theology or "intratextual" theology or the "New Yale" school. The latter nickname emerged because of the congruence of Lindbeck's work with positions taken by his former colleagues at Yale, philosophers of religion Paul Holmer and William A. Christian, Sr., and his late colleague from Yale, biblical theologian Hans Frei (see Comstock 1987).

Other writers, including John Milbank; J. A. DiNoia, O.P.; and Peter Ochs have used or adapted Lindbeck's postliberalism as a way to get "back down to business after so many centuries of modernist hemming and hawing we call epistemology" (Ochs 1990:213). Lindbeck himself characterizes his work as follows: "Intratextual theology redescribes reality within the scriptural framework rather than translating Scripture into extra-scriptural categories. It is the text, so to speak, which absorbs the world rather than the world the text" (1984:118). It is to that work which we can now turn.

Chapter 7

Intratextual Theology in a Postmodern World

with Stuart Kendall

It is the text, so to speak, which absorbs the world rather than the world the text.

—George Lindbeck

The relation of the text to the world is the key for postliberal, intratextual theology. Lindbeck had worked within a general framework, using Wittgenstein's concepts in earlier essays, but it wasn't until *The Nature of Doctrine* that he developed a tightly organized methodological program based on Wittgesteinian ideas.

Primary among them is that of the related concepts of language game and forms of life. Languages are seen as being guided, as is a ball game (Wittgenstein 1958:83), by a system of formal or informal rules. These rules structure the game as it is played or the language as it is used. But language is actually used in specific contexts. One could say that language games are "played" in specific forms of life. "What has to be accepted, the given, is—so one could say—*forms of life*" (Wittgenstein 1958:226). It is difficult to say precisely what a "form of life" is. Dallas High described the significance of the term about as well as possible:

[I]t is our "form of life" which provides the sense and sensibility of our speech. Therefore, to deny or attempt to escape these forms, which is to deny or attempt to escape human life itself, not only brings philosophy to grief, as Wittgenstein argued, but assaults language and breeds a perverse sensibility. . . . Wittgenstein is reminding us that words, symbols, and sentences, woven together with action, finally rest upon the concept of human life in all its social, cultural, or interpersonal forms (1967:101).

One might say that postliberal theology seeks to understand the grammatical rules of the language game that is the central and distinctive characteristic of the Christian forms of life. Or, as Wittgenstein laconically put it, "Theology as grammar" (1958:373).

Lest it be thought that such an approach is necessarily conservative, it must be noted that rules are not always simply given in a preexisting framework. They may emerge as the language game is played and lived out in a form of life. As Wittgenstein put it, "And is there not also the case where we play and make up the rules as we go along? And there is even one where we alter them as we go along" (Wittgenstein 1958:83). As the work of J. W. McClendon (considered below in Chapter 10) shows, the evolution of practices in traditions, like language games in forms of life, rules are not necessarily constricting even if they are rules.

Another central concept is that of family resemblances. "Family resemblance," for Wittgenstein and those who follow him, characterizes a certain form of similarity. The members of a family are similar not because they each and all carry or replicate an essential or distinctive characteristic, but because "we see a complicated network of similarities overlapping and criss-crossing: sometimes overall similarities, sometimes similarities of details." These are like the "various resemblances between members of a family: build, features, colour of eyes, gait, temperament, etc., etc." which overlap in a similar way (Wittgenstein 1958:67). Family resemblances are discerned as similarities in diversity; in contrast, essences or identical characteristics are defining qualities or attributes picked out from accidental differences. Wittgenstein, like other postmodernists, finds the notion of identity not very useful.

In an overt reference to religious matters, Wittgenstein speaks of religion in the following way:

> Is talking essential to religion? I can well imagine a religion in which there are no doctrinal propositions, in which there is no talking. Obviously, the essence of religion cannot have anything to do with the fact that there is talking, or rather: when people talk, then this itself is part of a religious act and not a theory. Thus it also does not matter at all if the words used are true or false or nonsense (Waismann 1979:117).

As in the reconstructed *Lectures and Conversations on Aesthetics, Psychology and Religious Belief* (1966), Wittgenstein saw religious language as growing out of religious practices embedded in religious forms of life, not out of systematic theology. And such practices resemble games—not in a trivial, but in a deep and rich sense.

The lineage from Wittgenstein does not lead directly to the postliberal theologians, but detours (a bit) through the work of the anthropologist Clifford Geertz. Geertz, particularly in *The Interpretation of Cultures*, developed Wittgenstein's linguistic and cultural analysis into a "cultural-symbolic" anthropological approach to cultures in general and to their religious "systems" in particular (1973, especially 87-125). Geertz also recognized that "play" and "games" can be very deep and rich (1973:412-453). Lindbeck uses Geertz's anthropology of religion to develop his own cultural-linguistic approach to the study of Christian doctrine.

Lindbeck, an American Lutheran born in China and educated at Gustavus Adolphus College and Yale University, is Pitkin Professor of Historical Theology (emeritus) at Yale Divinity School. His main interests have been in historical and ecumenical theology from a Lutheran perspective. He was a Protestant observer at Vatican II and edited the reports generated by the Protestant observers (Lindbeck, ed. 1965). This ecumenical work in the service of inter-Christian understanding, as he remarks at the beginning of *The Nature of Doctrine*, led him into the cultural-linguistic approach to theology (7).

But he could not have developed the distinctive account in *The Nature of Doctrine* without the work of Hans Frei. Of the two, Frei emerged first as having something important and interesting to say with his book, *The Eclipse of Biblical Narrative*, published a decade before *The Nature of Doctrine*.

Frei argued that a profound "reversal" took place in the seventeenth century with regard to the way people read the Bible (1974:130). Prior to the seventeenth century, the Bible was used to give shape to the "real world" (the forms of life) in which European people lived. Readers took it upon themselves to fit their own lives and experiences into the reality rendered in and through the Biblical narrative. Then the great reversal took place. By the eighteenth century readers no longer worked to fit their lives into the narrative of the Bible, but rather worked to fit the Biblical stories, through various means of abstraction and/or interpretation, into the "real world" of their own lives (124-154). Frei summarized this new approach as follows:

> The explicative meaning of the narrative texts came to be their ostensive or ideal reference. Their applicative meaning or religious meaningfulness was either a truth of revelation embodied in an indispensable historical event or a universal spiritual truth known independently of the texts but exemplified by them, or, finally, a compromise between the two positions... (124).

To put it gently, the reversal was part and parcel of the Enlightenment's turn to the subject (282-306). To put it more harshly, the reversal is the essence of the myth of modernity, the story that kills stories (Tilley 1985:30-36).

Frei took Schleiermacher's general hermeneutics as representative of the age of romanticism. He charged this influential approach with being subjective, individualist, and psychologistic (318). Between the sixteenth and eighteenth centuries Man [sic], saw fit to find himself [sic] a subject, an individual self with inalienable rights. And man [sic] learned a new way to read the Bible: not as a character in the world structured by the text, but as an individual to whom the text had to speak.

In this cultural milieu, biblical narratives took a back-seat to individual concerns. The Bible came to be read in two ways. First, it could be interpreted as a complex of symbolic structures telling universal stories through abstract means without specific reference to the human world. Second, it could be taken as the source of mere historical references, retaining a kind of literalism without reference beyond history. But neither the "liberal" universalizing approach nor the "proto-fundamentalist" sourcebook approach takes seriously either the shape of the text as a narrative that begins with Genesis and ends with Apocalypse or the way in which the passion narratives identify Christ and should identify Christians. So Frei found that both major modern approaches to the biblical text were unsatisfactory.

Frei argued for a reading of the narratives as narratives, as stories similar to those told in a realistic novel. This approach takes the overarching story for what it is and the smaller narratives within it for what they are: narratives with their own linguistic rules and integrity. Frei called for a return of the key insight of precritical exegesis: to first take the structures of the narratives *as* structures of narratives. His approach sees no need for alleged universal symbolism to be found in the text or historical referents to be designated by the text, save as subsidiary matters, at best. Frei's approach is thoroughly intratextual. As in the quotation from Lindbeck above, it takes the biblical narrative as a story to be dwelt in, not a text to be interpreted to and for people who live outside its narrative and the world of the text.

Lindbeck develops this approach in a systematic direction. He doesn't limit his discussion to narratives or to readings of the Bible, although he claims the Bible is the central document in the Christian traditions. He seeks a methodology for the study of religious traditions as a whole, specifically for studying the doctrines that define a particular religion. He wants to offer those involved in the perpetual ecumenical debate a way out of their impasses on doctrine which will neither compromise anyone's position nor serve as foundation for future confusion and or animosity. With this end in mind, Lindbeck expands Frei's intratextualist approach using Wittgenstein's linguistic analysis and Geertz's cultural anthropology to accommodate the study of religious doctrines.

In Lindbeck's reading, doctrines are communally authoritative rules of discourse, attitude, and action, specifically with regard to those beliefs and practices that are considered essential to the identity or welfare of the group in question (see Lindbeck 1984:18,74). These rules are the centerpiece of what Lindbeck calls a regulative or rule theory of doctrine. Like other "games," the "game" of Christianity can be defined by its rules. As Wittgenstein put it, ". . . isn't chess defined by its rules?" (1958:205). Lindbeck tells us that these rules, which may be formally stated or informally operative (1984:74), are the constants which define the Christian tradition. They retain their meaning through changing conditions. Doctrinal or constitutive rules give a particular community an interpretive framework for understanding whatever there is. They define what he calls an experimental matrix from which cultural achievements flow (1984:34). In other words, doctrinal rules are like the grammar of the religious language game, the central discourse of those who live in a specific religious form of life.

Within Christianity Lindbeck finds that three doctrinal rules give Christainity its identity:

> First, there is the monotheistic principle: there is only one God, the God of Abraham, Isaac, Jacob, and Jesus. Second, there is the principle of historical specificity: the stories of Jesus refer to a genuine human being who was born, lived, and died in a particular time and place. Third, there is the principle of what may be infelicitously called Christological maximalism: every possible importance is to be ascribed to Jesus that is not inconsistent with the first rules. This last rule, it may be noted, follows from the central Christian conviction that Jesus Christ is the highest possible clue (though an often dim and ambiguous one to creaturely and sinful eyes) within the space-time world of human experience to God, i.e., to what is of maximal importance (94).

Lindbeck must not be mistaken to be claiming that these rules are sufficient to generate or guide the Christian "language game" or "form of life." Many more rules, some central and permanent, some peripheral and evanescent, are needed to guide a full set of Christian beliefs and practices. Nonetheless, these rules are necessary for a form of life to be identified or distinguished as fully Christian (96).

Modernity has given prime importance to religious experience, often as a "foundation" for religious faith. In postliberal theology, religious doctrines are related to experience, but not in the way that modern theology has typically conceived that relation. Many modern theologians have argued that certain forms of religious experience are the "ground" for religious practice. Schleiermacher's claim in *The Christian Faith* that religion is based on and in a "feeling [*Gefuhl*] of absolute dependence" (§4) is often taken as the fountainhead for this approach. The cultural-linguistic approach claims that even *having* an experience requires a linguistic framework, so that the experience can't be the *foundation* for such a framework. Identifiable experiences can occur only because one already participates in a form of life. One can have experiences, especially sophisticated and nuanced ones, only because one can use the language appropriate to that form of life (a point that was finally not unknown even to Schleiermacher as Thiel 1991:33-63 shows). Without a language how could any experience even be identified? Rich religious experiences are not, and cannot be, a "foundation" for religious life and language as many liberal Christian theologians have claimed, but emerge *within* the discourse of the community.

Doctrinal rules set the conceptual vocabulary for understanding whatever there is. If the rule or regulative principle for a particular experience does not exist within the community, then the experience cannot occur within that community. For instance, the experience of being appeared to by the Blessed Virgin Mary is an uncommon, but recognized, event for Catholics. But that experience just isn't had by Baptists or Buddhists. It is not part of their cultural linguistic framework. This doesn't mean that such experiences are necessarily impossible for any individual. Far from it. The point is that Marian apparitions simply aren't experiences which fit in with a Baptist or Buddhist form of life or world. A Catholic might find another Catholic's report of such an experience impressive, but a Baptist would be far more likely to find another Baptist's report of such experience weird. There is no rule implicit in Baptist or Buddhist communities to make sense of such an experience. There is no rule within those traditions that would make such an experience possible. Baptists or Buddhists who did claim that the Blessed Virgin appeared to them would be considered very odd, at best. The questions which would be raised would not be about whether the Virgin appeared or not, but how it was that they got such odd notions and whether they could still be Baptists or Buddhists, given they had such odd experiences or had been swayed or infected by such "Catholic" ideas. Doctrinal rules are not merely regulative of what can be said in a community, but constitutive. They allow and disallow particular events to occur in and to the community and its proper members.

Similarly, there are stories told within one community which make no sense in the other. A common Catholic fairy tale involves an unbeliever stealing the communion host, biting it or cutting it, and being sickened or converted (or both) when the host starts to bleed furiously from the wound the unbeliever inflicted on it. Such a fairy tale cannot sensibly be told in a community which does not accept a very strong doctrine of the real presence of Christ in the Eucharistic elements or which is ruled by a doctrine of the Lord's Supper as a symbolic meal. Of course, a Baptist or Buddhist could be told the point of the Catholic story, but would likely find it bizarre, nonsensical, and pointless. Yet a Catholic or high Anglican might come to recognize that it is a fairy tale with a sharp doctrinal and devotional point and "get" the point of the story even while finding it silly.

A community without rules is not a community and hence cannot exist as such. But this is not to say that communities or their rules are static artifacts. Lindbeck finds that change in the community occurs in a dialectical exchange. His own view is worth quoting at length because here he seeks to preempt the challenge that the rule theory of doctrine makes Christianity seem too static (like the static rules of chess):

> Turning now in more detail to the relation of religion and experience, it may be noted that this is not unilateral but dialectical. It is simplistic to say . . . merely that religions produce experiences, for the causality is reciprocal. Patterns of experience alien to a given religion can profoundly influence it. The warrior passions of barbarian Teutons and Japanese occasioned great changes in originally pacifistic Christianity and Buddhism. These religions were pressed into service to sanction the values of militaristic societies and were largely transformed in the process. Yet in providing new legitimations for the ancient patterns, they also altered the latter. Presumably the inner experiences as well as the code of behavior of a Zen samurai or a Christian knight are markedly different from those of their pagan or pre-Buddhist predecessors. Yet, as this illustration shows, in the interplay between "inner" experience and "external" religious and cultural factors, *the latter can be viewed as the leading partners, and it is this option which the cultural and/or linguistic analyst favors* (1984:33-34; emphasis added).

Of course, if such encounters provoked substantial changes in the necessary rules which give one or the other their identity (like the three rules Lindbeck cites as essential to Christianity), then the traditions might well lose or substantially change their identity. Hence, baseball can (even though purists object) admit aluminum bats in lieu of wooden ones and designated hitters who bat but don't play defense and still be baseball; but it cannot admit underhand pitching or a larger ball without becoming another game, i.e., softball. What counts as a substantial change and which rules give identity to a form of life or a game, of course, vary from game to game and tradition to tradition.

These rules go so far as to determine the limits or types of truth claims a particular religion or community can make. Nonetheless, a rule theory of doctrine does not preclude religious believers from making literal truth claims (68). Lindbeck allows for epistemological realism. The same sentence, e.g., "God created the heavens and the earth," can be taken as the content of a first order expression of faith (and thus be true or false) as well as a second order rule governing what can and can't be said within the tradition. The rules forbid a bunt in slow pitch softball, and those who lay down a bunt are "out." But that does not preclude the truth or falsity of the factual claim "that was a bunt" in certain circumstances. The rules forbid ascribing creative power to the devil in Christianity, and those who express their faith dualistically are also violating the rules of Christianity. But as one can argue whether a batter bunted or swung away, so one can argue whether a believer accepts divine creativity; thus "she wasn't bunting" or "God created the world" can be *statements* made by participants in a practice or community which closely reflect the rules guiding statements. Whether the utterances constitute expressions of normative rules or statements of actual belief depends on the context in which and the purposes for which they are uttered.

Lindbeck's cultural-linguistic approach construes each religious tradition as being constituted by different frameworks of rules. Thus different religions will have different rules governing different categories of need depending on the particular needs of each particular religious community. For instance, the Buddhist concept of Nirvana is foreign to Roman Catholicism. Roman Catholicism lacks a rule governing anything like talk of Nirvana, so the experience of Nirvana is incomprehensible to Roman Catholics unless they somehow step outside their community. Roman Catholicism is categorially inadequate to the consideration of the experience of Nirvana; but the Buddhist tradition is conceptually inadequate to prepare one for the experience of the beatific vision of the Blessed Trinity.

That some concepts are conceptually incomprehensible in each tradition allows the cultural-linguistic approach to dub religions "incommensurable." Different religions operate within different regulative or rule systems and thus cannot be compared within a commensurating framework foreign to one or all of them. Rather, they can only be judged independently for their own categorial adequacy. The question is how well the rules of each particular religious tradition function in regard to the needs of the community defined by that tradition. Within a religion, a rule may not function adequately, its grammar may not be in accord with the needs of the community in the area governed by that rule. This is the domain for ecumenical discussion about changing the rules. The job of an ecumenist is to help other people learn to better understand the grammar of their own religion (Lindbeck 1984:61).

Rules can function in several different ways within a religion. It is the job of the theological grammarian to understand the way in which the rules of the particular tradition function. Most functional limitations are contextual. The problems generally have to do with if and how rules apply in a specific context. Some rules only apply at certain times and places, while others are unconditionally necessary to the existence of the community (85ff) and always and everywhere "in force." Such central and distinctive rules give a community its identity; to change them is to change the identity of the community.

For the community defined as Christian, Lindbeck maintains that the narratives of the Bible serve the function of these identity-giving rules. The biblical narratives generate the rules that govern the experience of Christians. The Bible provides the interpretive framework in which Christians live and through which Christians see their reality. Here the influence of Frei is clear.

Basic to Lindbeck's theology is his conception of the law. This relates both to secular law and to the rules or regulative principles that give a specific community its identity. According to Lindbeck, "Socially enforced behavioral rules are necessary for the sake of civilization, but we often talk as if the effort to obey these rules, to become virtuous, to acquire moral merit, was deeply repressive and hypocritical and likely to damage psychic health or personal authenticity" (Lindbeck 1985:3). Here a thinker like Michel Foucault might ask, "Why do people feel the need to claim they are repressed?"

But Lindbeck attacks the problem of "repression" in a different way. He claims that the human condition is to be oppressed or bound by "anxiety." This anxiety is Lindbeck's version of the modern meaning of the term "original sin." It refers to all of our basic insecurities and the bondage we feel in our existence. Lindbeck associates it with existentialists like Sartre and Camus (1985:4; and, oddly, with Heidegger as well). For Lindbeck, faith provides the escape from the burdens and oppression of anxiety. Human freedom, for Lindbeck, is related to faith. For Lindbeck, the meaning of freedom is "to be free . . . to accept oneself, warts and all" (1985:7). This comes through faith which provides one with a "basic confidence . . . the liberating force" (1985:6). The confidence that the fight between faith and disbelief, or faith versus the world, flesh, and the devil, is already won. For Lindbeck, like Luther, freedom is not libertarian freedom to choose, but the ability to be fully human.

Lindbeck's position is developed as a way out of the aporias of three other types of theology: the classic cognitive type which construes doctrines as assertions of truth, the experiential-expressive type which grounds religion and its doctrines in a prelinguistic experience, and a hybrid of the first two. Indeed much of *The Nature of Doctrine* can be read as defining the nature of doctrine oppositionally by differentiating this view from these other types of theologies.

The cognitivist approach to theology takes doctrines as "informative propositions or truth claims about objective realities" (1984:16). Cognitivists, or propositionalists as he sometimes calls them, insist on the fact that if a doctrine is true it must always be true. This claim makes ecumenical exchange difficult if not impossible to sustain and ecumenical reconciliation difficult if not impossible to attain. It also ignores the fact that doctrines were often called *regula fidei* and did develop in the early church, as well as later. Lindbeck rejects propositionalism not merely for its "fundamentalistic" style, but for its inability to account for Christian history and to sustain ecumenical dialogue.

The experiential-expressivist model takes religious doctrines "as noninformative, nondiscursive symbols of inner feelings, attitudes, or existential orientations" (1984:16). This is the opposite of the cognitivist view. It implies that doctrines simply don't make truth claims. This makes ecumenical discussions practically irrelevant because there's no explaining tastes or attitudes. If the propositionalists are too literal, the experiential expressivists are too figurative.

The third approach is a compromise between these first two. This approach simply attempts to accept both of the other two approaches to the study of doctrine as valid, but in different ways for different purposes. Lindbeck identifies Roman Catholic theologians Bernard Lonergan and Karl Rahner as proponents of this hybrid type (1984:16). But as well as having the advantages of both pure types of theology, they also have the disadvantages as well.

Lonergan in particular serves as Lindbeck's chief foil throughout the book. His works, especially *Method in Theology* and *Insight*, appear repeatedly in Lindbeck's notes both as representing the opposing view and supporting Lindbeck's own positions. Although Lindbeck initially lumps Lonergan in with the hybrid approach, he takes Lonergan's position for a statement of the experiential-expressivist approach at the beginning of his comparison in Chapter 2 of *The Nature of Doctrine*. Thus Lonergan serves as source and foil for the development of the cultural-linguistic position. The importance of Lonergan's influence on *The Nature of Doctrine* is rarely appreciated.

Still Lonergan is not the only opponent. By naming Schleiermacher at the beginning of the experiential-expressivist theologies, Lindbeck is attacking this whole tradition extending from Schleiermacher through Tillich and even through contemporary theologians like David Tracy. Lindbeck's approach is developed in opposition to these other approaches with the purpose of addressing the ecumenical concerns of our time.

Richard John Neuhaus restated Lindbeck's view by suggesting that, "preliberals take a cognitive-propositionalist approach to doctrine, liberals assume an experiential-expressive approach, and post-liberals favor a cultural-linguistic approach" (1985:66). This echoes much of Frei's position. Yet it doesn't tell us enough about Lindbeck because it neglects to consider the foundations, perhaps unrecognized even by Lindbeck himself, of his thought. Lindbeck serves as the foremost theoretician of postliberalism, but his thought cannot fully be understood or appreciated without noting his inheritance from prior modes of thought, a glimpse that finds more of the pre-modern in Lindbeck's postliberalism than of the postmodern.

Two major problems emerge for Lindbeck's work. The first is whether a pure intratextual theology is coherent. "Systematic or dogmatic theology has generally been thought of in the Christian West as especially concerned with faithfulness" to the normative features of the tradition (112). Examining the steps of the path Lindbeck walks in displaying his notion of fidelity as intratextuality shows where the problems lie in intratextuality.

There are five steps on his path. (1) He begins with a formal claim that concepts acquire their meaning not from the entities to which they refer or from some experiences they symbolize, but from how the concept operates in a semiotic system composed of interpretive and communicative signs, symbols and actions (114), what Wittgenstein would call language games embedded in a form of life. (2) He then construes religions as instantiations of such semiotic systems (114-116). (3) Next he construes the canonical writings of religious communities as constituting a distinct semiotic system or world. "For those who are steeped in them, no world is more real than the ones they create. A scriptural world is thus able to absorb the universe" (117). The biblical text is next identified as constituting the world into which all others are absorbed (118). When "extrabiblical material inserted into the biblical universe . . . becomes the basic framework of interpretation" (120), the mainline Christian church rejected the result as heresy, as the early Church did gnosticism. (4) Past interpretive practices are redescribed as intratextual interpretation (117). (5) Finally, he notices the fact that material conditions in late capitalist society are such that it is increasingly difficult for intratextual interpretation to be practiced. This becomes a veiled (or not so veiled) advocacy of reading religions and their scriptures "in terms of their intrinsic sense" rather than attempting to translate them into popular categories (124; cf. 134-135).

Lindbeck's first step makes perfect sense. The second step on Lindbeck's path is not so easily commendable. It is not clear that all religious traditions can always be *independent* semiotic systems. Clearly, "a religion can be viewed as a kind of cultural and/or linguistic framework or medium that shapes the entirety of life and thought" (33). Some persons *can* and do "speak of all life and reality in French, or from an American or Jewish perspective" (114). But do American and Israeli Jews have the *same* semiotic system? Will the entirety of their lives and thought be shaped in the same way, given their different social locations? Do Saint Augustine, Saint Thomas, Luther, and Lindbeck live in the same cultural-linguistic framework? (see Surin 1988:201 for a similar point). While one *could* say they did *if* the three basic rules Lindbeck identified were sufficient to define a cultural system or form of life, those three are not *sufficient*, but only *necessary* for a system to be Christian (see page 95 above). Implicitly, Lindbeck seems to deny any real internal pluralism in the Christian tradition. His view also presumes a normality, a stability, of a religious framework, independent of its actual instantiations in multiple cultural contexts and social locations. But this contradicts the basic insight of a cultural-linguistic model of religion, that the meanings of concepts are determined by their place in the semiotic system which the community uses (114). The problem is that no one can play only the "Christian language game." We are embedded in other forms of life as well, e.g., commerce, education, elective politics, etc., which are independent of religious forms of life. These also determine the meaning of the concepts we use.

Lindbeck skillfully exploits the cultural linguistic model to argue that Buddhist compassion, Christian love, and French Revolutionary *fraternité* are not expressions of a single underlying experience, emotion or attitude. These are "radically (i.e., from the root) distinct ways of experiencing and being oriented toward self, neighbor, cosmos"(40). But what he neglects to note is that the "self, neighbor, cosmos" to which compassion, love, and *fraternité* orient us also differ radically. Not only are the Buddhist cosmoi different from the Christian, but the cosmoi of Jesus, Augustine, Aquinas, Luther, and Lindbeck are radically different. Either the meaning of Christian concepts is determined by a single semiotic system, without regard to the social location in which those concepts are deployed, or it is not clear how they can possibly have the same meanings in those various locations.

Lindbeck opts for a single semiotic system. He proposes a "normal" framework in claiming that the "same content can be expressed in different formulations"(93). His example is the equivalence of "12" in base four to "6" in base ten notation. But to show such equivalence requires that both base systems are commensurable in terms of more general mathematical conventions. He goes on to say that "the only way to show that the doctrines of Nicaea and Chalcedon are distinguishable from the concepts in which they are formulated is to state these doctrines in different terms that nevertheless have equivalent consequences"(93). But a judgment of equivalency of consequences requires a framework in which commensurating consequences of terms drawn from other frameworks is possible. Lindbeck assumes that while no framework can commensurate Buddhist compassion, Christian love, and French revolutionary *fraternité*, one framework can commensurate "hypostasis," "ousia," "prosopon," "persona," "nature," etc. This assumption begs the question. As Richard Rorty put it in another context, "Alternative geometries are irreconcilable because they have axiomatic structures, and contradictory axioms. They are *designed* to be irreconcilable. Cultures are not so designed, and do not have axiomatic structures" (Rorty 1985:9). Lindbeck improperly conflates the *necessary* incommensurability and reconcilability of mathematical systems with the *contingent* incommensurability (and contingent, but real irreconcilability) of cultural "systems." The issue of reconcilability finally is an open question, even if it is one profoundly difficult to resolve in cultural "systems."

The issue is whether the concepts and practices in a religious framework which does not constitute the semiotic system of its cultural location can be understood completely independently of the framework of that location. If those concepts and practices *cannot* be so understood, then non-religious discourses partially constitute those concepts for people in those locations. If those concepts and practices *can* be so understood, then the religious framework alone is sufficient to determine how religious concepts are to be understood. But then the religious framework must be independent of its cultural-linguistic instantiation. This is unlikely, at best, on Lindbeck's own cultural-linguistic grounds.

Lindbeck's third step identifies this culturally independent framework as the "scriptural world." It "absorbs" all the other worlds. It presumes that this one text constitutes a world of its own. It provides, finally, the commensurating paradigm for all Christian concepts. However, this simply won't do. A close examination of the presuppositions which must be true if the "scriptural world" is to be a semiotic system sufficient to determine Christian concepts reveals that those presuppositions are at best dubitable and at worst false.

First, it must be true that texts *alone* are sufficient to establish a "world of meaning." Lindbeck begins his argument as follows:

> Masterpieces such as *Oedipus Rex* and *War and Peace*, for example, evoke their own domains of meaning. They do so by what they themselves say about the events and personages of which they tell. In order to understand them in their own terms, there is no need for extraneous references to, for example, Freud's theories or historical treatments of the Napoleonic wars. Further, such works shape the imagination and perceptions of the attentive reader so that he or she forever views the world to some extent through the lenses they supply (116-117).

Although the metaphor of "lenses" is far too thin to support Lindbeck's points, he is surely correct to say that understanding a text "in its own terms" requires no reference to "extratextual " (e.g., Freudian) analyses of those texts, no matter how useful those "extratextual" analyses may be for disclosing unexpected meanings in the text. But concretely for a reader to understand a text in any terms, those terms must be accessible in the reader's world. In short, getting the point of a strange text, of one that is other than one's own narrative, or learning of a world in which one does not already live, requires intertextual interpretation which Lindbeck, in his opposition to extratextualists and liberal hermeneutics, opposes.

A second, more general, problem also plagues the postliberal approach. A semiotic system cannot be separated from the community which constitutes that system. Frei put the matter nicely in the following:

> The descriptive context, then, for the *sensus literalis* [of Scripture] is the religion of which it is part, understood at once as a determinate code in which beliefs, ritual, and behavior patterns, ethos as well as narrative, come together as a common semiotic system, and also as the community which is that system in use—apart from which the very term ("semiotic system") is in this case no more than a misplaced metaphor. Clifford Geertz calls culture an "acted document," and the term applies also to religion (Frei 1986:70-71).

A religious community may be an acted document. But it is confused to think that document acted is the scripture alone. The scripture is a *part*, in terms Frei adopts, of the "determinate code," not the determinate code itself. It is not sufficient alone to determine the meaning of all the parts of the system or of the semiotic system as a whole. On the cultural-linguistic model, the Bible or the gospel is not and cannot be the only text which determines the semiotic system of a Christian community.

Lindbeck's fourth move, the redescription of past interpretive practices as intratextual practices, doesn't fit the facts. First, classic Christian theologians *materially* did not work within the same text. The writers of the New Testament, the writers of the patristic period, and Protestants in general did not recognize the same canon of scripture. Nor did they interpret it in similar ways: the exercise of the medieval four-fold exegesis differs radically from Luther's work. Lindbeck's step 4 which functions logically to legitimate the claim in step 3 that there is a biblical universe which provides *the* semiotic system for Christian intratextual interpretation, fails. This means that step 5 is misstated. It is not only contemporary society in which the conditions are such that the scriptures can be construed as providing a self-sufficient context for interpretation. Rather, the Christian tradition as a whole has the same "problem." It is intrinsically internally plural in that it has always had a multiplicity of canons and texts in which textual interpretation takes place. It has always been not a single "acted document" but a set of enacted texts. Lindbeck's dichotomy of either reading religions and their scriptures "in terms of their intrinsic sense" or attempting to translate them into popular categories (124) is finally a false dichotomy. Frei's dichotomy of a reading of scripture privatized to the believing community versus readings through extracommunal interpretive lenses is finally a false dichotomy. Both presume that Christian discourse is *essentially* a normal, commensurable, discourse which requires only instantiation. But even if the three identity-giving rules are stable and normal, they are not sufficient to configure all of Christian discourse. The very dichotomy necessary for the postliberal position to make sense is deeply mistaken.

This is not to say that the problem is irreparable. As Richard Rorty persuasively argued (1985), in a post-positivist context the anthropologists' distinctions between the intracultural and the intercultural collapse. The same sort of argument undermines the distinction between the pure intratextual and the intertextual: the worlds in which we live are *internally* plural. Pure intratextuality is a practical impossibility. *Oedipus Rex,* or any other text, is not a single text we "dwell in," but one which we read in extratextual contexts. Hence, a postliberal position which rejects the reductionist interpretations of texts and traditions can be sustained only as a "dirty" intratextuality (see Tilley 1989a; 1989b:1-2). Insofar as their theologies are "dirtier," but no less concerned with the Christian tradition than Lindbeck's, the similar works of Milbank and McClendon are important variations on the postliberal theme.

The second question to be posed to the postliberal project is whether it really engages postmodernism, especially in its strongest geneological form. If modernity can be understood as concerned primarily with the individual, with the subject's powers of instrumental reason, place in the socio-political community, rights under law, ideology of progress and equality, etc., then postmodernism can be seen as not concerned with the *values* of modernity, but with the devastating *effects* of incarnating those values in the warring (Nietzsche) or carceral (Foucault) cultures of modernity.

The claim has been made that post-modernity is the intensification of modernity, the ultimate finishing of the modernism. While postmodernists certainly use some of the analytical strategies and intellectual tools developed in modernity, not all postmodernists can be seen as "completing" or "finishing" the modern project (as Griffin 1989b suggests). Postmodernists recognize that modernity is not finished—its effects continue. We do not live in a "postmodern" world, at least not yet. If modernity was concerned with the rights of the individual, the subject, etc., over against and within the community, postmodernity is concerned more with the oppression and atrocities which occur within and because of modernity. Postmodernism is not concerned with the "rights" of the community especially if the community is seen as a group of individuals (the modernist view of community). Rather, postmodernism sees communities as fields of interrelated power structures and is concerned with the constitution, sustenance, and effects of those structures. In short, postmodern deconstruction, archaeology, and genealogy reveal the malignancies in the structures that present themselves as the benign face of modern, liberal individualism.

Hence, the idea of the community has become quite complex in postmodernity. It is not clear that Lindbeck's cultural-linguistic approach has accounted for this complexity. The problem is not that the "community" doesn't exist, but rather that several interrelated, overlapping, diverse, yet dependent communities exist simultaneously within the same space. Indeed, each of us inhabit or dwell in multiple communities. Postmodernity is in no way concerned with the unifying factors that maintain a community, such as individuals' consent, but rather with those factors that cause its dispersion and division, on the one hand, and that maintain a community's power to develop and sustain itself, on the other. The postmodern world is not characterized by stable foundations, but rather radically unstable and continuous development that is not necessarily progress or even a progression of any kind.

Lindbeck thinks of his work as addressing the concerns of the postmodern era (1988:19). He understands postmodernity to be characterized by a loss of confidence in the categories of reason and progress. He cites a lack of social cohesion and the proliferation of bureaucratic social controls and near-totalitarian management as his evidence of the need for a system of laws or doctrines, rules of discourse governing behavior to serve as a unifying force in the community. Lindbeck accepts that his (and every) theology is without foundations. In this he recognizes themes in and utilizes resources from postmodernist writers. He tries to avoid the overt foundationalism of cognitivist approaches and the covert foundationalism of experiential-expressivism. In this he agrees with part of the picture which power-struggle postmodernists paint.

Lindbeck also avoids wedding his position to any specific epistemology or ontology. Nonetheless, he claims that a cultural-linguistic approach has room for realist truth claims:

> A religion can be interpreted as possibly containing ontologically true affirmations, not only in cognitivist theories but also in cultural-linguistic ones. *There is nothing in the cultural-linguistic approach that requires the rejection (or the acceptance) of . . . epistemological realism and correspondence theory of truth* (1984:68-69; emphasis added).

This statement is developed when he claims that "[T]heology and doctrine . . . assert nothing either true or false about God and his relation to creatures, but only speak about such assertions" (69). Earlier he asserted the definition, "categorially and unsurpassably true religion is capable of being rightly utilized . . . in a way that corresponds to ultimate reality, and of thus being ontologically (and 'propositionally') true" (1984:52). The thread linking these statements is the problem of ontology.

The ontological question will not go away. It haunts the nature of Lindbeck's prose and slips in between his words in the form of the possibility of ontologically true statements. And at this point he takes leave of the postmodern world. The possibility of ontologically true claims presumes what genealogical and deconstructive postmodernism diagnoses as the ontology of presence common to western metaphysics since Plato's cave. Postmodernism claims that foundationlessness lives only in the space opened and defined by an ontology of absence. Whenever an ontology of presence is presumed, premodern and modern concerns about representation and truth slip in. The ontology of absence creates the space which necessitates accepting the play of differences in our writing, our language, but also in our world, our communities.

Lindbeck never meets this challenge head on. His openness to epistemic realism is at home in a premodern or modern assumption of stable presence, not in postmodernity. In effect, Lindbeck sidesteps postmodern concerns. His postliberalism tailors its methodology to be context oriented in response to postmodern foundationlessness. It assumes that doctrines, rules, concepts, etc., only retain their meaning as they are in use and that we cannot study them apart from the place and context of their use. But postliberalism is not an account of doctrine in the world of difference and power structures portrayed by postmodern thought. Nonetheless, his nonfoundationalism allows him to develop the idea of the incommesurability of religious traditions and thus to recognize the postmodern claim to diversity. But all of this is not as simple as it seems.

Lindbeck's concerns are finally not postmodern, but premodern. Wesley Kort put it well:

Lindbeck's project of severing religious doctrines from ties to subjective sources and referents and of locating them in the life of the Christian community is also a project to protect and preserve the objectivist or referential standing or thrust of doctrine.

This unbalanced or incomplete use of postmodernist discourses... is questionable. What goes for the subjectivist side goes for the objectivist, too. To employ postmodern modes of thought is to cut discourses from the security and stability of both poles . . . . Lindbeck is using postmodernist modes of thought selectively, for postmodernism makes more cuts and changes than he admits (Kort 1992:37-38).

This reading places Lindbeck more in the camp of the cognitivist-propositionalists than in the cultural-linguistic space which he wants to inhabit (a point which would have delighted Professor Frei—see Frei 1990). He seeks a stability which postmodernism undermines. He uses postmodernists' techniques, but remains tied to premodernist aims. He tries to reestablish the possibility of a conceptual objectivity, while trying to accommodate postmodernist concerns regarding the unlimitable play of difference. It is not clear that this strategy can be carried out coherently.

Directly related to this problem is the problem of change. Lindbeck accommodates change by claiming that, while the religious community is defined by its doctrines, those doctrines determine the nature of that same religious community. Though this explanation sounds rather circular, Lindbeck points to it as operating on the basic plan of the dialectic, a modernist solution of the problem (Lindbeck 1984:33). Kort points to this when he notes the similarity between Lindbeck and certain structuralist theoreticians, A.J. Greimas for one:

It is not altogether clear if it is the Christian community, as a historically or socially identifiable and particular group, or some structure shaping the community from beneath that gives rise to doctrine. In any case, Christian discourses find their stability and authority [in Lindbeck's system] in something claimed to antedate them (Kort 1992:38).

Kort's point brings up the problem surrounding Lindbeck's conceptions of culture and community.

How are culture and community related? What founds a community? What holds it together? How does it change without disintegrating? As Lindbeck (1988) shows, the problem of the community is linked to the idea of unity. Both of these ideas are finally not rooted in modern concerns, but rather in the premodern era.

Lindbeck (1988) pursues the idea of reestablishing something similar to classical, premodern hermeneutics as the central unifying factor in Christian communities. Lindbeck here emphasizes the polemical nature of his task. He here directly links religious doctrines to the laws of the community in the secular sense. He points to classical biblical hermeneutics as the unifying force within the early Christian church and points to that era as being similarly foundationless as in our own time. He finds that our society needs "texts projecting imaginatively and practically habitable worlds. . . . [in] written form, for they can then have a comprehensiveness, complexity and stability which is unattainable in other media" (1988:21) In a world of diversity and difference he is appealing to a premodern sense of the unifying powers of a text that will occupy the center of the community.

Can a text and the rules it carries unify a disparate group in postmodernity? Can a language conceptualize a nonreducible multiplicity of difference? Or do attempts to unify diversity and conceptualize difference finally run into the limits of language? Hence Wittgenstein's confession, "My whole tendency and I believe the tendency of all men who ever tried to write or talk on Ethics or Religion was to run against the boundaries of language" (Monk 1990:277).

The problem brought to fore by an examination of these boundaries of language is the problem of difference. In relation to language this problem is that "language is a system of differences rather than a collection of independently meaningful units . . . . [It is] constituted by the very distances and differences it seeks to overcome" (Derrida 1981:9). This problem of difference is the problem of diversity. It is a problem that cannot be solved by locating "independently meaningful units," and understanding them as such. The problem of the Jew or the Catholic in America is different from the problem of the Jew in Europe or the Catholic in Africa. These communities are too complex to be understood simply in relation to the books that are at their center. Difference will not submit to any form of unification but rather consistently subverts any idea that reduces what can only remain a noncentered heart of a fundamental multiplicity. Thought in the postmodern age requires acceptance of the problem of difference and the freedom from conceptual reduction necessary for the thinking of this thought.

> The freeing of difference requires thought without contradiction, without dialectics, without negation, thought that accepts divergence; affirmative thought whose instrument is disjunction; thought of the multiple—of the nomadic and dispersed multiplicity that is not limited or confined by the constraints of similarity; thought that does not conform to a pedagogical model (the fakery of prepared answers), but that attacks insoluble problems—that is, a thought that addresses a multiplicity of exceptional points, which are displaced as we distinguish their conditions and which insist and subsist in the play of repetitions (Foucault 1977:185).

The cultural-linguistic approach which takes the world of the biblical text as unifying and stable does not account for, at least in Lindbeck's development of the idea, the problem of institutions as control agents, the problem of the law as defining both the limits of freedom and the domain of man's self, or the even more complex power structures that define the problem of families. Even a Roman Catholic thinker who is not an advocate of such genealogical analysis recognizes this inadequacy: Lindbeck's neglect of institutional authority would make a postliberal Catholic theology "quite akin to the theological positivism expected by Pius XII in his encyclical *Humani Generis*" (Thiel 1991:162). In short, postliberalism, at least in its "clean" versions, seems to be a bastion of premodern thought in a postmodern world.

Yet another postliberal thinker has suggested that there is a possibility which might not allow the postliberal merely to "sidestep" the postmodern critique, but to analyze and oppose postmodernism in the name of a retrieval of legitimate and graceful premodern concerns. John Milbank sees three items as constituting genealogical and deconstructive postmodernism: an absolute historicism, an ontology of difference, and an ethical nihilism" (1990:278). He then goes on to argue that

> differential ontology is but one more *mythos*, and that the postmodern realization that discourses of truth are so many incommensurable langauge games does not ineluctably impose upon us the conclusion that the ultimate, overarching game is the play of force, fate and chance (1990:279).

Milbank's trenchant analysis of postmodernism is difficult to summarize (but see Burrell 1992). It begins with recognizing that postmodernism is radically and absolutely historicist. Postmodern historical genealogies uncover the relationship of constellations of power, knowledge, and "freedom" in any and every disciplinary structure or institution. But these genealogies lead to a theoretically insoluble problematic: the relation of genealogy and justice.

The problem is surreptitiously resolved by the hidden construction of a postmodern narrative or *mythos* incorporating premodern motifs: Nietzsche's *übermensch* owes much to Homeric heroes. Milbank's brilliant summary of the problem which emerges from postmodernism must be quoted at length:

> The claim, then, is that genealogical accounts are objective, but then at the same time they stand in an intimate relationship to the question of justice. As Foucault points out, the earlier Nietzsche related "scientific history" to the exposure of unjust social structures. The later Nietzsche, on the other hand, came to regard every regime of power as necessarily unjust, yet now believed still more strongly in the liberating role of history, which exposes this fact of injustice. By

revealing the injustices, the arbitrariness, of every power-constella-
tion, history leads us gradually to the realization that this state of
affairs proper to "life" is not to be condemned, but rather celebrated.
Hence, genealogy is not an intepretation, but a new "joyfully" nihilistic form of positivism which explains every cultural meaning-com-
plex as a particular strategy or ruse of power. No universals are
ascribed to human society save one: that it is always a field of warfare.
And yet this universal history of military manoeuvres is also to be
regarded as in some sense liberating, as assisting the emergence of an
übermensch, or a post-humanist human creature (1990:281-82).

The question is whether this story of universal warfare as liberating is
convincing as a *mythos*, as a universal story.

If it is not claimed to be a universal story, then it cannot consistently be
claimed to undermine another possibility, that a community of shared faith
might recognize the violence and nihilism of a world without God and
create a countercommunity with a countermemory and a counterstory in
which to dwell nonviolently in the knowledge, love, and service of God. It
might accept all that postmoderns reveal, but claim that the world of
modernity so revealed is not "normal," but aberrant, perhaps sin infected,
as Lindbeck suggests. A postliberal might accept Kort's analysis as basically
correct, that postliberalism borrows much, but not all, from postmodern
writing. What postliberal Christianity refuses to accept is only the postmoderns' surreptitious claim that the war of each against all or the vicious play
of differential power is a "normal" state of affairs which always and
everywhere obtains (even if it is hidden by apparently stable structures). If
it is not a universal story, it necessarily leaves room for another radical
possibility: a remnant community, sociologically if not theologically sectarian (see Frei 1990:281). Non-universal postmodernism thus can be side-
stepped. However, if postmodernism claims to tell a universal story, is it
credible?

Is the postmodern story one where justice and liberation unite? Finally,
as Milbank argues, that is incredible. For if "every cultural meaning-com-
plex [is] a particular strategy or ruse of power," then why presume *any*
cultural formation can ever be supported as just or truly liberating? Ethical
nihilism is not a contingent effect of genealogical postmodernism, but a
necessary one. There can be no moral good in the world (and, indeed, it is
hard to see how there can be moral evil). But is this credible?

The story of postmodernism has been told without surreptitious ruse
and in all its terrifying clarity. Bertolt Brecht's libretto for the opera, *The Rise
and Fall of the City of Mahagonny,* is the story. As Augustine wrote *The City
of God,* Brecht has written its inverse, *Cities Without God.* Mahagonny, City
of Nets, city of entrapments, city which valorizes absolute individual
freedom, city with no *don'ts,* city which destroys itself.

The opera begins. The city where anything is available is established by the sheer willpower of thieves on the run from the law at a desolate spot where their truck happens to break down. Here is the joyful acceptance of fate so valorized by Nietzsche. The town flourishes as a city of pleasure under the complete and arbitrary control of the founders. The first act concludes with the town's impending destruction by a violent hurricane while Alaskan gold-miner and snared tourist Jimmy Mahoney (Gallagher in Auden's translation) historically defies both civic convention and the natural storm in singing joyfully of absolute freedom, "just do it." This becomes the new regnant civic ideology.

The second act has the storm "miraculously" bypass the city. The act then displays the results of living in absolute freedom. The chorus tells the story:

> One means to eat all you are able;
> Two, to change your loves about;
> Three means the ring and gaming table;
> Four, to drink until you pass out.
> Moreover, better get it clear
> That Don'ts are not permitted here.
> Moreover, better get it clear
> That Don'ts are not permitted here!
> (Brecht 1976:68)

One man eats himself to death; Jimmy and Jenny the whore sing of true love after a quick tryst in a brothel; another miner is killed in a fixed fight where all but Jimmy know to bet on the winner, one of the founders of the city, Trinity Moses; Jimmy and the boys get drunk when Jimmy buys rounds for the bar. But the second act ends with Jimmy arrested for the only capital crime in Mahagonny: being broke. Jimmy bought drinks he couldn't pay for!

The third act begins with the following superscribed over the stage: "Every city has its own notion of what is just, and Mahagonny's was no sillier than that of any other place." The Mahagonny "establishment" sits in judgment. They take a bribe in their first case to acquit a murderer. But Jimmy is broke and his "friends" won't pay his debts or offer bribes in his case. He is sentenced to death for not paying his bar bill. Jimmy appeals to God, but the didactic playlet, "God Comes to Mahagonny," displays the citizens' refusal of God. The final scene has rioters bearing Jimmy's coffin. They march in various groups, bearing placards with competing slogans, and conclude with the happy chorus, "No one can do nothing for a dead man: Can't help him or you or me or no one" (Brecht 1976:107).

Brecht's libretto is often taken as a Marxist's critique of late capitalist society where the only crime is being broke. But in Mahagonny, *money is power*. The only crime is being *powerless*. "As you make your bed, so you lie on it, The bed can be old or brand-new: So if someone must kick, that is my part, And another get kicked, that part's for you" (105; oft repeated with

variations). Money power can buy justice, love, food, and anything else
Mahagonny has to offer. The city of absolute freedom, the city where Trinity
Moses and his cohort are the ruling establishment, is the city without God.
It is constructed in and by power relations. It may seem fine for those who
have money power, who can kick; but as the crooks found out, it was their
part to get kicked, too. Power slides away as it is spent.

Finally, Mahagonny is hell (104). Here the logic of postmodernism is
uncovered: Brecht's point is that every city based on power is hell; every
city is based on power; we are all citizens, as Augustine noted; we thus all
live in hell. Is this state to be grasped and celebrated? Isn't the celebration
of freedom in such a city the vilest of all illusions?

Mahagonny displays the silliness of justice in every city of power. Milbank's point can be sharpened: the postmodern mythos renders the world
as hell. It creates a world of warfare, where each is kicker and kicked. It
creates a world of incarceration, where jailers and inmates are bound
together in destruction. Its freedom is illusion for it is controlled by the
powerful; its good or its justice is equally illusory for it is dispensed by the
powerful. There is only power: some kick, some are kicked.

The point is that the freedom of ludic celebration cannot exist if all cities
are Mahagonny. The freedom and the celebrations are controlled by new
establishments who institute new constellations of power. Ludic celebration seems possible only for the (temporarily) powerful. But this celebration
is not free, but bought. And to be powerless—or broke—is a death sentence.
Worse yet, real power can be more deeply concealed in a city where
everyone buys into an ideology of absolute freedom than where the power
is transparent. When everyone sees freedom, who can even ask which ones
supply it for purchase?

The establishment figures of Mahagonny—Everycity—are magicians.
They deceive the marks who shop there by distracting them from seeing
their ownership, their control, their power. The suckers see only a bought
freedom. Are the deceptions of hell to be celebrated, desired, recreated
universally and eternally once one knows one lives in hell? The tourist-citi-
zens and establishment in Mahagonny do. Must we? This is what postmodernism comes to.

Or is there another option? Wherever else options might be found,
Milbank argues that Christianity surely provides one:

> Because Christianity is the precise opposite of nihilism, the nihilist
> genealogists are forced to narrate Christianity as the operation of the
> ultimate ruse of power, the final "training" of humanity which pro-
> duces a modern military (Nietzsche) or carceral (Foucault) society,
> and yet also prepares the transgression of this society by the *über-
> mensch* or the "aesthetic individual". However, I have shown that the
> interpretation of Christianity as *ressentiment*, and of its historical role
> as primarily the promotion of asceticism, are both, at least, highly

questionable. This has an important consequence: if nihilism cannot "position" Christianity in its genealogy, in a way that amounts to more than interpretation, then it emphatically cannot—as we already suspected—justify historically its reading of every event as an event of warfare. The possibility of a different counter-history (the counter-history given by Augustine) which reads war as an absolute intrusion, an ontological anomaly, remains still intact (1990:293-94).

Both Brecht and Milbank can follow Augustine to identify and display the politics of the city without God: the politics of sin and death. Sin is especially the creation of illusions, more especially illusions of absolute freedom in the city of control, most especially the Nietzschean declaration that there is nothing but illusions. The death is the death of self-destruction: neither God nor nature can destroy Mahagonny. Only the city can—to be recreated again wherever the truck carrying the fleeing citizens (who became kicked instead of kickers) breaks down.

Genealogical postmodernism, then, valorizes Mahagonny. Is the better response to this situation "just do it," just grasp the film of illusion and live in it, just celebrate the city that begins in breakdown and ends in self-destruction, just live in a community with no enduring rules? Or is the better response to find another way to live which eschews the power of violence and relies on another Power for its order? That, finally, is the question a postliberal can pose in opposition to genealogical postmodernism.

Postliberal theology, then, can sidestep postmodernism. Critiques like Kort's are partly correct: postliberalism uses archeological tools of genealogical postmodernism, but not to excavate a universal story, but to show that communities of a Power which makes for Righteousness can live even in the interstices of hell. In this sense postliberalism can use postmodern tools without being committed to what postmodernists valorize in their use of those tools. If this is "premodern," a postliberal should say, then "hurray" for the preservation of an oasis in the desert.

Whether such communities can be structured so simply as "intratextual" communities and thus render their members free of the world is another question, one which seems unlikely, at best. The criticisms we made of postliberalism (pp. 100-109 above) suggest such pure intratextualism is impossible. But perhaps in communities of solidarity and resistance (Welch) counterstories of peace and cooperation can be lived midst the violence. Indeed, that is just where positions to be discussed in Part 4 are centered.

PART 4

THEOLOGIES OF COMMUNAL PRAXIS

The patterns in contemporary theologies are as fluid as wild rivers running in the spring. Each analyst or historian of the theological flood composes a snapshot of the contemporary scene in order to capture a pattern in the chaos and to draw connections and reveal oppositions between the "types" of theologies he or she "discovers." But no pattern is final or definitive. As one who has structured a book with four patterns, I can imagine other interesting ways (e.g., David Griffin's) of setting off the differences and similarities among postmodern theologies. The situation is indeed fluid.

The present picture differs from more typical ones in various ways. For instance, it separates liberation theology from European political theology; to many, these seem to fit together. It joins process theism with Habermasian critical theory, which don't seem to fit together well. It pries the American anabaptist-based theology of McClendon apart from the postliberal work of Lindbeck and the communalism of Griffin—two of his apparent allies in theology. It juxtaposes postliberalism to the genealogical and deconstructive streams of postmodernity rather than to postliberals' perceived revisionist opponents. Why join and sunder this way, rather than that? There are two reasons.

First, Kort's oppositional method of discourse analysis has influenced the present analysis strongly. His work helps to bring out the central and distinctive features of different theologies in very helpful ways. The method shows connections across denominational and traditional lines that other approaches fail to highlight. Even if Kort's strong claim that theological discourses define themselves oppositionally cannot be fully sustained, a weaker claim that unacknowledged facets of these discourses can be revealed when placed in an oppositional light is practically indubitable—at least by the present author who has engaged in the exercise of doing just that. Moreover, Kort's refusal to reduce the discourses of contemporary theology to harmony or to choose one theory over another is not merely strategically important, but the proper upshot of his analysis. He warns his readers about this early on in his text:

> Readers who know my previous work may expect that, if I do not resolve the question with a theological position, I will turn to narrative as providing coherence in the face of theological dissonance. But that is also a move I do not make, although a "narrative theology," one construed differently from those now largely available, can provide an antidote to the present situation created by propositional theologies. But I am just as eager to point out that a narrative, because it is also discourse, participates in the play of differences and in the situation of conflict. No, I end with the situation of differences and conflicts, one I characterize, however, in a positive mode (Kort 1992:7-8).

The position which Kort reaches is a postmodern one, characterized in the following:

> What becomes clear, after release from the addiction [to certainty and coherence in the culture] of identity, is that things are authoritative, real, and valuable for people because they believe them to be so. What nonfoundationalism and postmodernism adumbrate is a culture characterized not by appeals to certainty, fact, the indisputable, and the actual unconditioned by belief but, rather, a culture characterized by shared and differing beliefs (139).

Yet what we share and differ over finally is not best understood as "beliefs," but as "practices," including the practice of believing.

Kort simply asserts that "every person, group, and society has scriptures, that is, texts that grant and articulate their world's contours, contents, possibilities, and norms" (140). He also claims that such texts are never wholly available to a reader. But this seems mistaken. It seems more accurate to say that every particular culture dwells in a myth that creates a world. Such a myth thus provides a way of directing religious energy, places the present time in specific relationships with human origins and destinies, specifies proper (moral, legal, etc.) and improper (immoral, illegal, etc.) relationships between various members of the culture, and provides individuals with a place in cosmos and society—although not always a comfortable or desirable place (Tilley 1985:40-46). However, a claim that these myths are fully ensconced in texts or scriptures which are known to or knowable to the members of the culture is unsustainable. All too often the stories which drive a culture are hidden even from the view of the participants—a point the social scientific study of religion has often reiterated and which we made in our own way with regard to the mythos of postmodernism in the previous chapter. Cultures are structured by myths; but often a myth is implicit, hidden in a culture's presuppositions and practices. The myth may be invisible and yet real—and made visible only when it is abstracted from the cultural practices which it envelops. Such is the case with the myth of the Enlightenment: the official "myth" said one thing; the hidden and operative myth had and has quite a different shape, as proponents of a second enlightenment and their nihilistic opponents would both tell us. In sum, although I cannot follow Kort to his final position, his practice has enlightened the present analysis, and engaging in it has shown that there is no simple theoretical or narrative resolution to the problems created for religious thought by modernity and revealed or extended in and by postmodernists.

Second, even if no theoretical or narrative resolution is available, that does not mean that no resolution at all is available. The postmodernists of completion are united in their valorization of an overarching theory, whether a theory of communicative action, a process-relational theistic ontology, or a hermeneutics of the manifestation and proclamation of classics in contemporary contexts. If theory is not their foundation, it is their bread and butter. The dissolute postmodernists portrayed in Part 2 are also highly theoretical. For them traditional theory solves no problems, so all theoretical constructs are to be deconstructed and transcended or jettisoned. Whether the turn is to radical incarnationalism, to ultimate religious nihilism or to an attempted retrieval of sanctity, these are all rejections of theory—even though the rejections come from wildly different directions. Even if theory from Hegel to Foucault controls their discourses, it does not resolve the modern and postmodern problems. The postliberals leave us in a remarkable position in which we are forced (if we take the discourses of the previous four chapters seriously) to choose almost arbitrarily between absorbing the modern world into a traditional, premodern text (which promises a real possibility of self-deception of the worst sort) and destroying any allegiance to any value save that of raw power (which construes the world in which we live as truly hell).

The positions considered in the present part are united by a shared central and distinctive conviction or theme: that the clue to resolving the question is neither theory nor narrative, but the turn to shared practice or praxis (terms which, in the present context, will be used as synonyms even though advocates of praxis often oppose such a move because practices are thought to be merely repetitive or oppressive; but see MacIntyre 1981; McClendon 1986; and Tilley 1994). It is not that these theological discourses fail to valorize either theory or narrative. Nor do they fail to recognize the dialectics of theory and practice as mutually influencing and changing each other in various patterns (see Lamb 1982). Liberation theologians, for instance, are deeply indebted—too deeply indebted some would say—to theory. And theologies of communal practice like McClendon are often associated with narrative theology and postliberalism. But the difference is that for the discourses in these three chapters, shared praxis is, if not foundational to theory, finally given priority over theory. In this, they are to be grouped over against the other positions surveyed in the previous three chapters, wherein theory is, if not foundational for practice, finally prior to, and seemingly more important than, practice.

Chapter 8

Gustavo Gutiérrez and Praxis in Christian Communities

with C. Bradley Morris

The Incarnation . . . an irruption that smells of the stable.
—Gustavo Gutiérrez

In a remarkable and underappreciated article analyzing the methods of Peruvian liberation theologian Gustavo Gutiérrez and Uruguayan liberation theologian Juan Luis Segundo, Joseph Kroger differentiates two tasks which Latin American liberation theologians seek to accomplish. Kroger writes:

> In performing its prophetic-critical task, liberation theology functions as a critical theory which *precedes and promotes* the praxis of faith, but the praxis it promotes is the liberating self-reflection on the part of the Christian community, or what Gutiérrez and Segundo, following Paulo Freire, characterize as "conscientization." On the other hand, in carrying out its practical-strategic task, liberation theology functions as a critical theory which *follows and reflects* the praxis of the Christian community, and here the praxis includes strategic activities and pastoral involvement in the political process (Kroger 1985:17; emphasis added).

What Kroger points out here is that liberation theologies include two dialectical moments. To neglect either moment and to construe any of the liberation theologies as either simply reflection on practice or merely theory for praxis is inadequate.

The first moment is a "prophetic *annunciation* of the good news of God's kingdom and a critical *denunciation* of every dehumanizing social condition" (Kroger 1985:17). But this prophetic-critical task is simply insufficient to establish what the present practice of the present community should be, that is, what the church should do. Rather, it clears the ground by bringing forward a scriptural vision and raising the awareness of aspects of our life where this vision is not only not realized, but undermined or overthrown. The good news is the affirmation of the God of life, the God who makes life worth living, to whom we are called to respond by making life worth living. "The kingdom [of God] is a gift but also a demand" (Gutiérrez 1991:118). But the content of that demand *in the present circumstances* cannot be determined by the scriptural vision alone or the diagnosis of evils alone. Prophetic criticism is not enough.

The second task, the practical-strategic task, is the crucial one. The prophet details the vision. The critic displays the present situation. At this point the "Church should rise to the demands of the moment with whatever lights it has at that moment and with a will to be faithful to the Gospels" (Gutiérrez 1973:34; Kroger 18). We take this to be a version of Augustine's very deep and difficult admonition to "love, and do what you will." Theologians are not to prescribe what the Christian community should *do*, but first to act as a member of the church by whatever lights they have and with a will to be faithful to the good news of the reign of God. The theologians cannot *say* what the church is to do, but can *show* what should be done by doing it with the community. Then the theologians can describe, analyze, and criticize (when necessary) what the Christian community has done and has believed as a result of what it does. Gutiérrez puts it this way:

> By preaching the Gospel message, by its sacraments, and by the charity of its members, the Church proclaims and shelters the gift of the Kingdom of God in the heart of human history. The Christian community professes a "faith which works through charity." It is—at least ought to be—real charity, action and commitment to the service of men. Theology is reflection, a critical attitude. Theology *follows*; it is the second step. What Hegel used to say about philosophy can likewise be applied to theology: it rises only at sundown. The pastoral activity of the Church does not flow as a conclusion from theological premises. Theology does not produce pastoral activity; rather it reflects upon it. Theology must be able to find in pastoral activity the presence of the Spirit inspiring the action of the Christian community (Gutiérrez 1973:11-12).

Gutiérrez goes on to reflect on the claims of Yves Congar and Edward Schillebeeckx to show the necessity of Christians' social and political involvement. But what makes Gutiérrez's point truly radical is masked by the abstract language he uses about "theology." The concrete theologian must act in and with the other members of the church and then reflect on that shared praxis. Without participation, the theologian is in no position to undertake reflection.

Kroger finds that Gutiérrez tends to emphasize the prophetic-critical task of theology and Segundo the practical-strategic task of theology. But, as the quotations from Gutiérrez above and the analysis below show, his work also includes a very strong version of the practical-strategic moment. A similar point could be made using texts from Segundo's writings or from the texts of other liberation theologians, but here we will concentrate on Gutiérrez, not as a "representative" of liberation theology (as if one person's work could "represent" a whole varied movement), but as a postmodern theologian of communal praxis.

Gustavo Gutiérrez was born in 1928, in Lima, Peru, to a poor mestizo family. As a child he was ill with osteomyelitis and bedridden for six years. After completing some medical studies, he entered the seminary. He was sent to Louvain for work in philosophy and psychology and, in 1959, he received a Ph.D. in theology from the University of Lyons, France; he was ordained the same year (Brown 1980:22; Ferm 1988:155). As a pastor in Lima and instructor at the university, he had to rethink completely the theology he had been taught. He moved to a small apartment in the slums of Lima. He learned experientially, as had the worker priests of France over a decade before, that poverty was destructive of persons and their relationships and that poverty was not a mere accident that happened to some people, but a structural social condition (Brown 1980:23). At the Medellín Conference of Latin American bishops in 1968, where Gutiérrez was an advisor, the theology of liberation was born. However, "conservatives excluded Gutiérrez from the 1979 conference of Latin American bishops" held at Puebla, Mexico (Ramsay 1986:55). Nonetheless, he was present outside the conference and talked with friends on the inside (another experience, perhaps, of doing theology effectively from the margins).

Liberation theology reconceives the tasks of theology and highlights the relevance of the social location of the theologian. Theology grows out of the theologian's experience, out of the theologian's own authenticity, and out of the theologian's social location. Classic theologies grew out of theologians' experience in the monastery, the university, the seminary, the episcopal palace, the court, etc. Liberation theologians find another place where theology can and should be done: the barrio, the slum, the ghetto, the prison. Whereas premodern theologies tended to be unmindful of social location and whereas modern theologies (Lonergan) tended to obscure the importance of social location while valorizing theologians' authenticity, liberation theologians see the theologians' roots in the practices of their communities.

Liberation theology does not simply reject the theologies which grow in other times and places. Presumably, they too, reflect on the practices of the church in those situations. Nonetheless, each theological enterprise must be recognized as being as "situated" as liberation theology is. Every theology is a local theology of inculturated practice (compare Schreiter). Each must be "tested" for its relevance to other social locations. None can possess a complete system of theological truth unless it identifies itself as God's own truth—a diagnostic sign of theological hubris. Each can seek to be faithfully relative to the Truth that is God and God's alone. For liberation theologians, the social location for doing theology is the shared experience of Christian life on the margins of society, that is, with the poor and oppressed.

But this social location means that the theologian must show what it means for a church to be in solidarity with the poor. In practice, it means being one with them to overcome the conditions—personal and social, practical and theoretical—which contribute to their oppression. Hence, Gutiérrez writes that "we cannot separate our discourse about God from the historical process of liberation" (Gutiérrez 1988:xviii). Theology is the second step; and that constructive and critical theoretical step is always shaped and necessarily conditioned by the first practical step we take.

Gutiérrez defines liberation theology as "a critical reflection on Christian praxis in the light of the word of God" (Gutiérrez 1988:xxix). "The aim of the theology of liberation is to be a language about God, and to be this in the communion of the church. It is an effort to make the word of life present in a world of oppression, injustice, and death" (Gutiérrez 1990:18). Gutiérrez explicitly chose *liberation* as his qualifying term over *development* because he says that development has become "synonymous with economic growth." *Liberation* could include "social, political, and cultural aspects" as well as the economic ones (Gutiérrez 1973:24).

The key for Gutiérrez's theology is not a theoretical methodology, but reflection on the practice of Christian discipleship incarnated in particular situations. Unlike modern and other postmodern theologies, liberation theology is not based in the academy. "The course to be followed if one is to be a Christian is the basis for the direction in which one must move in order to do theology. It can therefore be said that our methodology is our spirituality" (Gutiérrez 1990:5). Although present in his earlier works, the practical basis of Gutiérrez's theology in spirituality became clearer with the publication of *We Drink from Our Own Wells* (1984).

The focus of this spirituality is found in the biblical text: the narratives of the Exodus, the Magnificat of Mary, Jesus' proclamation of the kingdom of God in deed and word, the Beatitudes, and the Cross and Resurrection. But it is not merely that we read those narratives. "The scriptures are not a passive store of answers to our questions. We indeed read the Bible, but we can also say that the Bible 'reads us' " (Gutiérrez 1984:34). The biblical text does not merely provide prophetic and critical insights into the present situation, but can transform the very questions we ask.

Gutiérrez points out that "according to the biblical sources the following of Christ is a communal experience" (Gutiérrez 1990:6) and one that must be carried out in practice: "Love and do what you (together) will." In commenting on *We Drink from Our Own Wells*, Gutiérrez made it clear that the practice of discipleship is communal: "My concern was to bring out the point that the following of Jesus always supposes membership in the assembly, the *ecclesia*. The following is, of course, a personal, free decision on my part, but I cannot live it out except in a community" (1990:49). If "our method is our spirituality," then the method is basically one of discipleship in community. Discipleship is, of course, not understood as slavish imitation of the past, but as creative response to the present situation in fidelity to the past and in hope for the future. That creative response is not passive but active. It is Christian praxis.

Praxis denotes the ongoing interaction of reflection and action. Praxis occurs when "we act, reflect on the action, and then act in a new way on the basis of our reflection" (Brown 1980:34). Liberation theologians are wary of the term "practice" because they think that term is used in the sense of "practice makes perfect," i.e., learning how to do something like singing a song until one can do it the same way again and again. However, in contemporary Anglo-American philosophy influenced by Wittgenstein, understanding a practice is understanding how to go on, how to engage in the practice in new circumstances. The contrast between this sort of practice and praxis is a distinction without a difference—no real difference at all.

Gutiérrez writes "all the political theologies, the theologies of hope, of revolution, and of liberation, are not worth one act of genuine solidarity with exploited social classes" (1988:174). The fact is that theories *do* grow out of practice. The problem is that some theories, some theologies, fail to grow out of an authentic practice of charity, an authentic spirituality, in solidarity with the poor. Academic theologies live on in the academy, but all too often lose touch with the communities whose theology they were.

Classic European theology has been not only the dominant theology, but the theology of the dominant. Here Robert McAfee Brown's analysis captures the liberationists' claims quickly and sharply:

> Dominant theology responds "from above," from the position of the privileged, the cultured, the affluent, the bourgeois; liberation theology responds "from below," from the "underside of history," from the position of the oppressed, the marginated, the exploited . . . . Dominant theology has links "with western culture, the white race, the male sex and the bourgeois class": liberation theology is linked with "the condemned of the earth," the poor, the marginalized races, despised cultures and sex, exploited classes (Brown 1980:47).

Even the gains of modernity have been gains only for some and have come, all too often, by others "paying the price" for the gains, but not reaping the benefits of those gains.

In light of this, the challenge which liberation theologians address is quite different from those of modern European or North American theologians. In secularized or pluralistic societies, the challenge may be understood as "unbelief" or "loss of faith." The "cultured despisers," as Schleiermacher named them in 1799, challenge the credibility of faith. The problem is different in Latin America, as Gutiérrez notes:

> But in Latin America *the challenge does not come first and foremost from nonbelievers but from nonpersons*—that is, those whom the prevailing social order does not acknowledge as persons: the poor, the exploited, those systematically and lawfully stripped of their human status, those who hardly know what a human being is. Nonpersons represent a challenge, not primarily to our religious world but to our economic, social, political, and cultural world; their existence is a call to revolutionary transformation of the very foundations of our dehumanizing society.
>
> In this context, then, the question is not: How are we to talk of God in a world come of age?, but: How are we to proclaim God as a Father in a nonhuman world? What is implied when we tell nonpersons that they are sons and daughters of God? (1990:7; emphasis added).

The world in which Gutiérrez lives is as dehumanizing as any world portrayed by the Nietzscheans. Like the postliberals, Gutiérrez seeks a way to be Christian in a dehumanizing society. But unlike some postliberals, the question is not concerned with finding a way of discipleship which can resist the lures of a comfortable materialistic life, but with finding a way of discipleship in a world which denies any status to the poor. The answer begins, of course, with praxis.

Christians have always struggled "with the tension between reflection and action, work and study, prayer and picketing" (Brown 1980:34). The tension is hardly new. But Gutiérrez finds that the relevant action is "the praxis of the poor in history." Influenced by a prophetic-critical moment which identifies the God portrayed in the biblical text as a God who liberates humanity from oppression in every sphere, Gutiérrez identifies the despised and rejected of the earth as those with whom and for whom a liberating God is working. And in light of the eschatological parable of the sheep and the goats (Matt. 25:31-46), the Christian should be engaged wherever the power of sinful oppression can be seen. It is the practice of learning how to act in such situations, learning how to go on as a disciple of Christ, that is central.

Arthur McGovern has noted that what "Gutiérrez and other liberation theologians reflect upon, in their growing emphasis on learning from the poor, is the 'action' of the poor in confronting their lives" (McGovern

1989:34). But the poor from whom Gutiérrez and others identify with are not just any poor people, but primarily Christians. Unlike the "poor" of the NATO countries, almost all the "poor" members of Latin American society are at least nominally Christian—as are the "rich." Although criticized by NATO theologians for an excess of concern with political and social issues, the liberation theologian can respond clearly: that is *our* problem. Latin Americans are at least nominally Christian; but they are so impoverished that they are nonpersons. " 'Oppressed' and 'Christian' are two aspects of one and the same people" (Gutiérrez 1990:8). When Gutiérrez writes of the poor, he is writing about one huge segment of the Christian community.

In this context, the aim "of the theology of liberation is to be a language about God, and to be this in the communion of the church. It is an effort to make the world of life present in a world of oppression, injustice and death" (Gutiérrez 1990:18). Hence, when Gutiérrez finds solidarity with the poor to be a social location for doing theology today, he is pointing up the need for solidarity with local communities of Christians, for the oppressed poor just are Christian—a point too often unnoticed by those who base their criticism on an unnuanced and decontextualized understanding of the texts of liberation theology (e.g., Milbank). Liberation theology grows out of the community of Christians treated as nonpersons by the society in which they live.

If poverty is more a result of oppressive social structures than a lack of initiative by the poor, then the social structure is the first problem and as such must be changed. To bring about change calls for "subversive" action. This is not necessarily violent revolution. As Brown notes, history can be subverted from below,"which means that the poor take charge of their own lives, or it can be changed 'from above' (*super-vertir*) by 'super-versive action,' which means that the rich ensure that their position of privilege is not challenged" (Brown 1980:31). Subversion is not necessarily an over-throwing of social structures, but a counteraction of them. In contrast, armed revolution is often superversive, not subversive, an action in which one elite fights to supplant another.

One way to counteract (but not violently overthrow) the structures of oppression is to form basic Christian communities, *communidades de base*. These are grass-roots groups of "sometimes fifteen to fifty people who share in Bible study, discussion of religion, teaching each other skills in farming or mechanics or even literacy, and political action, perhaps of a quite local nature" (Ramsay 1986:54). *Communidades* are typically led by catechists rather than priests and may effectively become communes. Generally, most commentators find over 100,000 such communities in Latin America; 80,000 in Brazil alone (Lernoux 1982:40). Liberation theology, then is "an under-standing of the faith and a re-reading of the Word as it is lived" among the poor "Christian community" (Galilea, et al. 1974:57).

Not just the Bible, but history must be read from the underside, from the perspective of those who have been marginalized in the historical process.

Nor can we talk about a privatized kingdom of God in some sense outside of public history. Indeed, it is just on this point of a unified history of salvation/liberation that Gutiérrez in particular, and liberation theologians in general, depart from the classic modern construals of religion.

Gutiérrez's reading of history is similar to the postliberals' reading. For Gutiérrez, secular history is not something separate from God's dealings with the world, but part of it. While not insisting that the text of the scriptures absorbs the world, he does insist that we cannot talk about the kingdom of God as outside of history, in a "sacred history" isolated from human, profane history:

> Historically and concretely we know humanity only as actually called to meet God. The basic statement here is that from the viewpoint of faith "the history of salvation is the very heart of human history." Consequently, "the historical destiny of humanity must be placed definitively in the salvific horizon" (Gutiérrez 1990:124).

At another point he writes, "There is only one history—a 'Christo-final-ized' history" (Gutiérrez 1988:86). This history is not a sacred history, nor a private history, nor a spiritual history, but the one real history. It is constituted by

> ... the defense of the rights of the poor, punishment of the oppressors, a life free from the fear of being enslaved by others, the liberation of the oppressed. Peace, justice, love, and freedom are not private realities; they are not only internal attitudes. They are social realities, implying a historical liberation (Brown 1980:55).

Liberation theology sees history as a process of total and integral salvation. "Salvation in Christ gives human history ... its ultimate meaning and elevates it beyond itself" (Gutiérrez, 1990:117). For Gutiérrez, there are not two or ten histories, but one:

> [T]here is not a history of nature and another history of grace, a history of fellowship and another of sonship and daughterhood. Rather, the connection between grace and nature, between God's call and the free response of human beings, is located within a single Christo-finalized history (Gutiérrez 1990:126).

Liberation theologians see liberation as comprehensive. Nonetheless, there are important distinctions to be made within this view. For Gutiérrez there are three dimensions of liberation.

First, there is the "liberation from social situations of oppression and marginalization" that oppress and destroy people, forcing many to live in sub-human conditions (Gutiérrez 1988:xxxviii). "The structures may be political, economic, or cultural; they may grow out of warped attitudes based on race, class, nation, or sex; they may also be embodied in church structures" (Brown 1990:104). The second dimension is that of "a personal transformation by which we live with profound inner freedom in the face of every kind of servitude" (Gutiérrez 1988:xxxviii). Third is "liberation from sin, which attacks the deepest root of all servitude; for sin is the breaking of friendship with God and with other human beings" (Gutiérrez 1988:xxxviii). In short, Gutiérrez's theology offers a multi-faceted and integral theology of salvation. Christ is savior-liberator. Christ's saving action is actualized in those areas where we need liberation: social, personal, spiritual.

One common criticism of liberation theologians is that they pay too much attention to social evils and not enough to personal sin. But too often this criticism is phrased not as a disagreement about the "balance" of liberation theology, but as a critique which implies that liberation theology practically ignores personal sin. The former point is always debatable, as "balance" is hard to find in theology, but the latter is simply unfounded, unless the critic is gripped in an ideology which is so thoroughly individualistic as to see that the individual human being's willing is the necessary and sufficient cause of sin without regard to the conditions in which the individual finds herself or himself. The issue *is* one of balance, and is, finally, a judgment call.

However, the Roman Catholic bishops of the United States, hardly liberation theologians, have recognized that one way to reduce personal evils is to ameliorate social evils. Consider the following:

> The severe human costs of high unemployment levels become vividly clear when we examine the impact of joblessness on human lives and human dignity . . . . Unemployment takes a terrible toll on the health and stability of both individuals and families. It gives rise to family quarrels, greater consumption of alcohol, child abuse, spouse abuse, divorce and higher rates of infant mortality. People who are unemployed often believe that society blames them for being unemployed. Very few people survive long periods of unemployment without some psychological damage even if they have sufficient funds to meet their needs. At the extreme, the strains of job loss may drive individuals to suicide (United States Catholic Conference 1986:141).

Certainly child abuse, spouse abuse, and suicides can be personal sins. Increased infant mortality, family quarrels, and divorce may not often or ever be sinful, but are human tragedies. Citing extensive literature from social scientists, the bishops do not directly claim that structural evils cause personal sin. But they clearly imply that the structural evil of increased unemployment is a condition in which personal sin and tragic evils do increase.

In this pastoral letter, the bishops recognize the connections between structural evil and personal sin—not a "causal" connection, but a statistical and conditional one. Ameliorate the social conditions, and you ameliorate the personal evils and sins. The liberation theologians are not alone in noting that ameliorating social conditions reduces incidences of sin and evil; if they are out of balance, so must be the American Catholic bishops.

As much as any other postmodern or postliberal position, Gutiérrez's version of liberation theology is concerned to address the destructive consequences of modernity. However, the consequences are quite different in the societies of Latin America which, for the most part, have not been profoundly affected by the theoretical issues of the Enlightenment, but by the social stratification engendered by the industrial revolution. Given the different context, the theology developed will be different. Whether Latin American versions of liberation theology are finally irreconcilable with contemporary Vatican and mainstream theology (as Min 1989 argues), the context in which the theology has developed is crucial.

As liberation theology has developed, it has shifted its emphases. Many of the traditional criticisms leveled against it have been defanged. As even an unsympathetic critic like David Neff noted in 1988, Gutiérrez has made it clear that liberation theologians have come to recognize the evils of racism, sexism, and cultural idolatries, as well as political and economic evils. Even those economic evils might possibly have non-socialist solutions; and clearly the Marxian tools which liberation theologians have used for social analysis are disposable. Yet Neff finds that "liberationism" has "a basic flaw—it defines theology as *praxis,* or application of truth, downplaying the orthodoxy that undergirds any solid grasp of the truth" (Neff 1988:15). The profound confusion of Neff's view should be obvious by now: Neff wants to keep all theology in the classic modern and premodern motif wherein theory *controls* practice. But in the end, theory cannot control practice—or we would have no need for Aristotle's virtue of phronesis, Aquinas's virtue of prudentia, or what we can call "practical wisdom" (Tilley 1989c; 1995). For no theory can finally say how the theory is to be applied in practice.

Moreover, as the present analysis (indebted to Kroger's insights) shows, liberation theology is a postmodern theology of communal praxis which sees that knowing the truth is possible only for those who first make the vision of the kingdom come true, at least in part, despite the structures of evil which work to make that incarnation impossible. We may err in our actions, but errors can be corrected for the future, even if they cannot be "undone." However, if we take no action to ameliorate, subvert or counteract structures of evil, we can do no good and cannot help to make the hope for the reign of God to come true.

Chapter 9

Sharon Welch and an Ethic of Risk in Communities of Resistance and Solidarity

Solidarity does not require self-sacrifice but an enlargement of the self to include community with others.

—Sharon Welch

Much feminist thought in North America in the final third of the twentieth century has been marked by concerns with and for community. Radical feminist writers like Mary Daly stress not only structural sexism, but also the creation of women's spaces to resist oppression. Societies dominated by male-centered ideologies have developed discriminatory gender roles and allowed degradation of women to be routine "business as usual." Nonetheless, women in solidarity with each other have been able to create pockets of resistance guided by an alternate vision. Feminist writers, like Latin American liberation theologians, have thus offered diagnoses of the contemporary situation and prescriptions for radical or ameliorating changes.

Some contemporary feminist writers, even those less radical than Mary Daly, have noted a contradiction in much popular and academic feminism. When feminists attempt to ground theories of women's rights as the foundation for human liberation on the basis of liberal theories of equality and freedom, an aporia emerges. As Rebecca Chopp notes:

Feminists have used liberal claims about equal rights to place women in professions, to work for affirmative action, and to assert the equality of women with men. Yet . . . there has been relatively little change in the patriarchal ordering of the private and the public. The success of liberal egalitarianism has been limited to minimal opportunities for a few women to enter professions; women who do enter traditionally male professions find themselves operating, time and time again, like men. Most women . . . must take low-paying jobs of institutional mothering such as nursing, teaching, and secretarial work that merely continue in the public realm what women do in the private realm (Chopp 1989:108).

To be accepted in the historically male professions, women must become like men. Even if there were not a "glass ceiling" in those professions, simply to work successfully requires that an individual behave in a "professional" manner. But male-centered traditions have defined professional behavior patterns, dress codes, authority structures, etc., whether in trial law, in surgery, in wholesale sales, in business marketing and real estate, in stock brokerage, or other professions. Each of these take the male as central and normative. To be accepted as a professional, an individual, whether male or female, must conform to masculine norms.

Moreover, the vast majority of working women remain in the traditional "women's work." Here they receive inferior wages and prestige. Here female models dominate and individuals—whether male or female—often have to be or become "feminine" to take these roles (nursing provides a prime example). Chopp's point is that this discrepancy in power and money between humans' (men's) work and women's work is encoded in the ideology of liberalism. Enlightenment liberalism and the industrialization of the economy have combined historically to construct a society which sharply distinguishes public and private spaces, the world of the working man and the domestic woman. Working women are employed more in public extensions of the domestic sphere than in the public sphere itself. Feminist advocates who utilize liberal or humanistic claims to further women's claims to fair and equal treatment fail to see that liberal individual ideology, including liberal construals of human rights, is part of the problem, not the solution (cf. Chopp 1985:108-109). In short, a critical feminist theology cannot remain mired in modern liberalism, but needs to enter the space of postliberal and postmodern writing.

It is unfortunate that feminist philosophies and theologies are often labeled as works of "women's liberation." For once they are so categorized, they can too easily be dismissed from "serious" consideration by "mainstream" writers. Such disdain occurs in the academy as well as in society in general. The contemporary academy, despite protests to the contrary, remains dominated by a male-centered pattern. "Women's studies" programs in general and courses on "women and religion" in particular are marginalized in an insidious way. Such programs and courses were and are dreadfully needed because women's voices and experiences have been notable by their absence from many "mainstream courses" in the humanities and social sciences. But once "women's studies" like "African-American studies," achieves an institutional status, women's experiences can again be marginalized in practice by being labelled the work of just another "interest group" competing for money and power in the academy. The voices they raise can be forgotten or obscured in mainstream courses. This is because "I" as a mainstream teacher know that "someone else" is attending to women's particular experiences and "I" don't need to do more than give it a token of representation in my own program or classroom. I can continue business as usual, because the voices of the others are heard in other places even if they are silent or weak in my classroom or program. My "tokenism" fulfills my "duty" to their particular needs as an "interest group." The result is that the pattern so established encourages us to treat "women's theology" as if it were a particular concern relevant primarily or exclusively to an interest group and to treat "theology" as at least a concern for the whole Christian community or as at most a universal concern.

Some who devote their teaching and research to "women's studies in theology" then find it difficult to be taken seriously by the "mainstream" because their concerns are "narrow" and they are part of a particular "interest group." Others find academic administrators cooperating with strident feminists in expecting that feminists will do "women's courses" and opposing those who choose to do "mainstream" courses, but to do them in a different voice. This sort of situation, found in many academic institutions, admits of no obvious solution because the academy (and often the society) defines "women's studies" as a particular interest group. We're damned if we do go our separate ways and we're damned if we don't!

One possible way to finding a solution is to see that the mainstream just is a shifting set of particular perspectives and to notice that all perspectives are particular, but need not be treated as the "property" of an interest group. The practice that would appropriately ensue would be what Habermas would call the discursive redemption of claims where each voice was heard and discourse occurred until a working agreement could be achieved. That such is rare in the academy indicates how systematically distorted the lifeworld of academe has become.

Among Christian theologians who identify themselves as feminists, Sharon Welch has developed a theology and an ethic which are both rooted in narratives, especially women's narratives. She constructs her position also in oppositional dialogue with postliberalism, Latin American liberation theology, Habermas's critical theory, and postmodern genealogical writers (see Welch 1985:32-54; 1990:123-36,148-51). Welch does not here "stand in" for "feminist theologies" in general. Her particular perspective is feminist and does offer a postmodern path in theology which also emphasizes communal praxis. What makes her work remarkable is the depth of her acceptance of postmodernity and the recognition that the only possible theological and religious responses to the post-age risk capitulating to madness or illusion.

Welch has worked with Clergy and Laity Concerned and other peace groups. Her academic career brought her to a Ph.D. from Vanderbilt and teaching at Harvard Divinity School and the University of Missouri, Columbia. More revealing, however, is her brief portrayal of her own journey in writing *A Feminist Ethic of Risk*:

I began this exercise from a particular vantage point, that of a member
of the Euro-American middle class committed to lessening the threat
of nuclear war. In working on this political problem with African-
American women and men, I found my theological and political
analyses fundamentally challenged. I was confronted by African-
American women and men with a critique of the nuclear arms race
that was inseparable from a critique of my racism, the racism of the
Euro-American middle class. I found myself involved in communicative ethics, a political involvement and dialogue that evoked a foundational critique of Western philosophical and theological
understandings of responsible action (1990:156).

Welch's ethic is neither an ethic of rights (characteristic of liberalism) nor
an ethic of care (characteristic of one major strand of contemporary feminism) but an ethic of solidarity and resistance—quite literally and seriously
an ethic of *risk*.

Like many postmodern theorists and their theological and atheological
fellow travelers, Welch's basic theological position seems paradoxical. She
writes of her work that it

. . . has two contradictory strands: on the one hand, a relativist
limitation of truth claims and a qualified nihilism, an acceptance of
the fact that might does shape reality, if not make right. On the other
hand, nihilism and relativism are held in tension with a strong normative claim, an attempt to identify values and structures that can
transform society and end oppression. Both strands are necessary. The
tension between the two constitutes genuinely liberative theology
and critical theory (1985:84).

In this way of construing the matter, Welch places her work in a position
not totally dissimilar from either Latin American liberation theology or
North American postliberal theology, save that she more clearly embraces
a radical relativism than the others and more clearly recognizes the power
of might to shape the world in which we live.

The rationale for her acceptance of relativism is basically pragmatic.
"The ideal of universal or absolute truth is intrinsically correlated with
oppression" (1985:72). The correlation occurs because seeking to have an
absolute truth is a seeking for security. But in an inevitably insecure world,
bounded by powers beyond individual or communal control (both natural
forces and social structures which bring people to "place" each other
according to class, race, and gender even if these are irrelevant), security is
never absolute. Postliberal theologies are vulnerable to a form of seeking
security by valorizing one narrative structure or grammar and ignoring the
fact that no grammar is absolute and that each of us are formed in multiple
communities of discourse (1990:104-106). Rather, what postmodern gene-

alogists reveal is that alleged truths are stabilized and rendered secure by power and wealth. And this means repression. Might *does* make reality, if not truth; wishing to have absolute truth means wishing to have almighty power which can absolutely secure reality if it will. Hence, the quest to possess ultimate absolutes, to be in control of them, is inherently problematic as it legitimates almighty repression.

Although she learns much from Habermas, Welch finally cannot accept the portrayal of the discursive validation of claims that he gives. Following Anthony Giddens (whom she quotes in the following), she finds that there is good reason to see not consensus, but universal solidarity—which may be realized despite a lack of overall consensus—as the proper goal of a communicative theory.

> Giddens poses a thought-provoking alternative to Habermas: " 'Our first sentence,' you once wrote, 'expresses unequivocally the intention of universal and unconstrained consensus.' Why not say that our first gesture of recognition of another person promises a universal solidarity of human beings?"
>
> The intention of universal solidarity is potentially more inclusive and more transformative than is the goal of consensus. Many liberation ethicists argue that the search for consensus is a continuation of the dream of domination (Welch 1990:132-33).

Citing Habermas's "dismissal of oral cultures," Welch suggests that the "ideal speech situation" is closed not only to people of the past and future, as Peukert notes, but even to those in the present who cannot "measure up" to Habermas's standards (1990:134). In opposition to Habermas, Welch finds that a communicative ethics must be based not in continuing surreptitiously the dream of domination by seeking consensus, but, like Peukert and Arens, in an unlimited solidarity which recognizes the other and hears their voices even if consensus is not reached.

Welch identifies a pattern in the Western tradition which she calls "the erotics of domination." She finds that

> . . . oppressive power gains much of its force through the claim of submission to a greater moral purpose. The claim of moral purpose blinds both oppressor and those who acquiesce to oppression. The valorization of absolute power is constitutive of the dreams of the oppressors and the capitulation to force on the part of others (Welch 1990:114).

Welch finds that theologians Paul Tillich, Karl Barth, and H. Richard Niebuhr explicitly oppose domination by tyrants, whether human or divine tyrants, yet they all legitimate coercive power which can absolutely achieve results. However, "the only type of power that is guaranteed to be successful is destructive power" (Welch 1990:120). One can guarantee that one can stop one's enemies if one kills them or forces the to stop being or doing what makes them enemies; one can never guarantee that an enemy will cooperate with one—or even that an enemy will enter into discourse with one.

Welch links this erotics of domination with belief in an omnipotent God. An omnipotent God can ensure "the right" outcome of things. Theodicist Charles Journet makes this even clearer than the (mostly Protestant) theologians Welch cites. In finishing his book on evil, Journet writes his comforting final words that "if ever evil, at any time in history, should threaten to surpass the good, God would annihilate the world and all its workings" (Journet 1963:289). Journet's belief in God's goodness and omnipotence leads him to claim that it is possible that the destruction of the world God created could be a good thing for an all-good God to do! That the love of God could be destructive of all creation indicates that the human desire to dominate and control is mirrored in a belief in a God who could dominate and destroy all—while yet being all-good and all-loving.

In lieu of the quest for absolutes which leads to the unwanted goal of domination, Welch finds that liberation theologies provide a model for a different path. They do not uncover universal truths, in Welch's view, but do something even more revolutionary: They surface dangerous memories.

> The dangerous memory expressed in liberation theology is not only a memory of conflict and exclusion, . . . [but] also a memory of hope, a memory of freedom and resistance . . . . In order for there to be resistance and the affirmation that is implied in the preservation of the memory of suffering, there must be an experience that includes some degree of liberation from the devaluation of human life by the dominant apparatuses of power/knowledge. Even to resist implies a modicum of liberation and success. Domination is not absolute as long as there is protest against it (Welch 1985:39).

Such memories are preserved among communities of solidarity and resistance, i.e., *communidades de base*, African American churches, and women's communities.

These communities are constituted and characterized by the particular and local practices of solidarity. "Solidarity takes the place of traditional notions of redemption: it is evoked or enabled by the grace of God; it is the evidence and the result of God's incarnation; it is the fulfillment of creation" (Welch 1985:46). These communities develop theologies which not only describe the experience of the members, but also offer ways of thinking profoundly different from the dominant views. These patterns of intellectual practices free people "to name their own experience and shape their world" (Welch 1985:57). The solidarity in these marginal communities gives their members vision and voice. Instead of being passive victims of oppression, they can become agents of justice and dream of and act for an unlimited solidarity.

> The claim that solidarity and justice are impossible arises when those ideals are posed conceptually or abstractly—as achieved already in the life of Jesus, as givens—and not rooted in a particular form of ecclesia. The ideals of a liberating faith are not duties or imperatives; they emerge naturally from identification with the oppressed, from the experience of community with the oppressed. The power of relatedness in ecclesia does not demand love and solidarity, but enables and evokes it (Welch 1985:66-67).

In such contexts, power is not a "zero-sum game" in which any gain I make is your loss and vice versa. Rather, power here is seen as fecund and creative. It is empowerment, but not empowerment to "win over" the other, but to "win with" the other (compare Welch 1990:6) in solidarity.

The classic academic ethical question of the relationship of the normative to the descriptive simply does not arise in this approach. People do what is fitting in the circumstances. If it turns out they err, then they correct themselves by listening to each other. As in Latin American liberation theology, praxis is the first step. But in Welch's view the praxis of communal solidarity is one that can evoke a power that is other than the problematic power over the other, the power of oppression.

Welch learns from Michel Foucault that it is always easy to evade the problem of oppression. One can explain it away as a result of a theoretical anomaly or of historical causes. But oppressions are not accidental or incidental and to explain them away leaves them unexplained. But the most insidious move is to allow one's vision to move from the particular to an allegedly universal form of oppression, e.g., the universality of sin. Even if sin is a "universal," its practical effects in actual circumstances are what is crucial.

The common temptation, especially among academics, is to think that attending to universal imperatives will solve practical problems. This temptation turns out to be part of the problem, for it is a strategy of distraction. "Universal discourse is the discourse of the privileged" (Welch 1985:80). The universal claim that all men [sic] are created equal has not given rise to the inclusion of women, African Americans, and other marginalized groups into the privileged center, save that the marginalized use the universal claim as a prophetic and strategic weapon, as did the American civil rights movement a generation ago. To think that universal claims have some intrinsic universal power beyond their use in particular circumstances is to evade the problems of oppression.

Yet utopian hope and universal discourses are not *necessarily* oppressive. Welch seeks to rescue them in the following:

They are liberating when they express a concern for the well-being of all people, when they lead us to care about justice for other groups of people, when they move us beyond a concern for our small social world. These ideas are not, however, liberating in their attempt to articulate that which is universal. Their liberating function lies in the concern they express for other people. This concern is, ironically, distorted by the very concepts which express it. To work for human rights, but to base our definition of those rights solely on the experience of one race, gender, or class, is itself oppressive.

The ambiguity intrinsic to a universal basis for resistance to injustice can be mitigated if the concern is expressed in terms of universal accountability rather than in terms of what is universally true about human being (Welch 1985:81).

What is right and useful about universalism is not its truth value, but its recognition that our practices have effects beyond the narrow confines of our everyday lives and that our solidarity must extend indefinitely. Welch, like Peukert and Arens, finds that seeking justice in particular entails a commitment to justice that is unlimited. This universal justice is not given a foundation in some theory of human nature, but implicated by the very practices in which we engage.

Yet perhaps this is all nothing but a nice story, a comforting fiction which blinds us to the truth about humanity: that humanity is constituted by the will to power, that might does make right, and that the momentary and local "actualizations of peace, justice, and freedom could be mere aberrations in the experience of a people incapable of survival" without oppression. "To speak of Christian ideals of love for the neighbor being in any sense true, or of the benefits of the rule of reason in an age gone mad in its acceptance and justification of oppression and exploitation is an unspeakable outrage" (Welch 1985:88).

As argued in Chapter 7 above with regard to postliberalism, Welch finds that the world of Mahagonny may be the real world. Perhaps our valorization of love is a paper screen hiding the ugly truth. Practicing love may be no more than slaking lust. Perhaps we need illusions to preserve our sanity. For Welch, a theology which does not seriously consider the possibility that nihilism paradoxically is the truth about the human condition fails to face the real issue in our postmodern world.

The resolution of the issue is not, however, theoretical. It is practical. Shall we live in solidarity with those who resist oppression and bet their lives that the fleeting glimpses of peace are the "real thing" horribly distorted in a world where might makes right? Or shall we live as individuals who seek satisfaction and blind ourselves to any oppression in which we engage force knowing that the only peace is escaped?

The "middle class" ethic that "fits" with nihilism (as well as with the theologies of radical transcendence which remove any divinity from the actual, historical world) is an ethic of cultured despair. This ethic has two features:

> (1) the despair is cultured in the sense of its erudite awareness of the extent and complexity of many forms of injustice; and (2) the knowledge of the extent of injustice is accompanied by despair, in the sense of being unable to act in defiance of that injustice (1990:104).

The ethic may take the form of ludic celebration, of resignation, of self-destruction, or of cooptation and cooperation with "business as usual" no matter how destructive that business is. Symptoms of this ethic in practice can be seen in conspicuous consumption, in withdrawal from the commonweal, in excessive use of alcohol, drugs, etc. In local politics, people may recognize the need for new schools or waste treatment facilities, but reject them. "Yes, we need them, but NIMBY (not in my back yard); build them 'somewhere else.' " In the face of massive social and ecological problems, the ethic and politics of cultured despair teaches that the first response is "leave me alone; it's not my problem; it's not my job to fix it."

Welch's constructive answer is to explore an ethic of resistance and risk: "The ethic of risk is characterized by three elements, each of which is essential to maintain resistance in the face of overwhelming odds: a redefinition of responsible action, grounding in community, and strategic risk-taking" (Welch 1990:20).

Responsible action is not defined by the goals or motives of action nor is it measured by direct results. Rather, responsible action is "the creation of a matrix in which further actions are possible, the creation of the conditions for the possibility of desired changes" (Welch 1990:20). Welch finds that these gains may often be small, e.g., the founding of a clinic or school. However, these provide a model for larger social actions, e.g., the implementation of a system of public health which works to make real those conditions in which people can thrive and which provides basic medical care for all the members of a society. "Partial victories" are often the key here. Responsible action is that action which "gets the ball rolling" and keeps it rolling toward a goal which, realistically, may never be reached, but which, realistically, can be approached. "The measure of an action's worth is not, however, the willingness of someone to risk their life but the contribution such an action will make to the imagination and courage of the resisting community" (Welch 1990:22).

But responsible actions are impossible for individuals to take alone. Reflecting on the work of womanist author Paule Marshall, Welch makes this point clearly by arguing that

> Marshall helps whites see that we do have the power to act alone and decisively. Yet such decisive action is intrinsically immoral. We do have the power to act alone to repress, to exploit, to blow up the world.

We do not, however, have the power to make the world peaceful and just. That is a qualitatively different task and requires a qualitatively different exercise of power. Justice cannot be created for the poor by the rich, for it requires the transfer of power from the oppressors to the oppressed, the elimination of charity, and the enactment of justice (1990:51).

Responsible action requires grounding in a community of critical support. One acts responsibly not for oneself or for an interest group, but in action taken in and as a member of a community. The illusion that we can act responsibly alone is generated by the illusion that we really are "individuals" who are not constituted as persons by the networks of relationships that form the communities in which we live. Rather, responsible action is taken on behalf of the community. Welch is not denying the reality of personal agency, but claiming that a responsible agent is a person-in-community.

Strategic risk-taking is neither pragmatic nor self-destructive. As Welch put it:

While the consequences of actions are taken into account so that one does not risk death over every offense, the approach is not narrowly pragmatic, acting only when one is sure of the consequences of that action. Risks are taken—both risks of immediate harm and risks that what is done will provide the foundation for victory later on (1990:78).

Utilizing womanist narratives of resistance and risk, Welch provides no theoretical guidelines for risk-taking. She notes that a "risk-benefit" analysis won't work because just as one cannot calculate the risks of radical actions, so one cannot calculate the benefits. Nor is martyrdom to be sought. The guidelines that are available are brought out in reflections on Toni Cade Bambara's novel, *The Salt Eaters:*

. . . Bambara encapsulates the process that leads to the healing of community. She describes three aspects of persistent joyful communal resistance to structural evil: an abiding love for other people, an acceptance of the need for taking risks in political action, and an active commitment to the "ancient covenants" with life (1990:95).

Overall the key is that the risk is finally a shared risk based in love, acceptance, and fidelity. Resistance to the encroachment of structural evils into the community is an act that is risky, but necessary if the community is to be able to live on.

The ethic of risk requires a politics of both difference and solidarity. Welch endorses postmodern rejections of "grand narrative" because those rejections overturn the pretense of universality without domination. Moreover, the reasons Foucault gives for dialogue are more compelling than Habermas's, in Welch's eyes:

> Foucault argues that we can see a system of logic as a particular system and not as truth itself only when we are partially constituted by different systems of producing truth. We can transcend the blinders of our own social location, not through becoming objective, but by recognizing the differences by which we ourselves are constituted and, I would add to Foucault, by actively seeking to be partially constituted by work with different groups. Thus the condition of overcoming ideology is difference, a mutually challenging and mutually transformative pluralism (1990:151).

And in this sort of politics the real risk emerges: by seeking to reconstitute ourselves by incorporating—literally—the powerful practices which constitute others differently from us, we take the chance of losing our selves. But just as an absolute truth or other safe enclave can be maintained only by the logic and practice of oppression, perhaps an absolute self can be maintained only by the logic of exclusion, by the ethic of cultured despair that results in the isolation of oneself from all others and the rejection of difference. Such isolation is finally possible only by exercising not the power of oppression, but of exclusion—a direct rejection of solidarity. And if I reject solidarity with those different from me, the implied end of this practice is solipsism or suicide. Welch notes that the politics of solidarity and difference is difficult to sustain; but the only alternatives are absolute exclusion or arbitrary boundaries. In an ethic that legitimates NIMBY, where does one build the security fence which encloses one's own back yard?

To maintain the difficult alternative, an ethic of risk and a politics of solidarity, Christians can turn to a theology of resistance and hope incarnated in communities of solidarity. But as the quotation heading the chapter suggests, these are not communities of "self-sacrifice." Risks and dangers abound. Yet self-sacrifice is not the correct characterization of those who live in such communities which bear dangerous memories. Welch writes:

> The concept of self-sacrifice is faulty in two fundamental ways. First, the term "sacrifice" is "reviewer-language": it reflects how an outside observer sees someone's actions, and it rarely is used by those actually bearing the costs of resistance. To those resisting, the primary feelings are those of integrity and community, not sacrifice. Second, what is lost in resistance is precisely not the self. One may be deprived of the accoutrements of a successful self—wealth, prestige, and job security—but another self, one constituted by relationships with others, is found and maintained in acts of resistance. *When we begin from a self created by love for nature and for other people, choosing not to resist injustice*

would be the ultimate loss of self (Welch 1990:165; second emphasis added).

What one is left with is, in Welch's view, divine.

Welch's theology concludes by finding that "god" is totally immanent. "While [Carter] Heyward claims that 'god' is the source of our relational power, I argue that the divine *is* that relational power . . . ." Welch finds that "positing" a One beyond that immanent power as its ground is "neither necessary nor liberating" (1990:173). She celebrates a "presence that is both healing and fragile, constitutive of life and unambiguously present in the human condition . . . [but] absent in the atrocities of history and in human-kind's despoliation of the earth" (1990:177). She worships "the web of life or the dance of life" (1990:120). The positing of a transcendent God opens up the problems of theodicy and is in danger of valorizing oppression.

Although she distinguishes her view from Feuerbach's (1990:177), Welch's position is thoroughly naturalistic. This opens an aporia at the heart of her theology. Universal solidarity becomes not merely a utopian goal, but an impossibility. As Peukert notes with regard to Habermas, so we can note with regard to Welch: that without God there is no reason to think that universal solidarity is a possible state of affairs. All solidarity will remain local because it cannot include anything other than nominal or imaginary solidarity with the dead and the future. Welch opts for a "universal account-ability" as a basis for resistance to injustice, rather than some universal truth about human beings. But without the possibility of a real universal solidar-ity, what can that mean? By denying the reality of a living God in solidarity with all that there is and who keeps solidarity alive even in the face of the reality of death, Welch undermines the possibility of an unlimited solidarity and accountability.

Welch is quite aware of the problems of accepting the reality of a transcendent God. However, the problem of evil does not require a "theodicy" for its solution. Indeed, theodicies are part of the problem, not part of the solution (Tilley 1991). The attempts to write theodicies contribute to the neglect of real evils and reinforce the erotics of domination (see Noddings 1989:227-228). One way to avoid some, if not all, of the evils typically associated with belief in an omnipotent God is to refuse to attempt to write any theodicy that shows why that God allows evils in God's world. Technically, all that is needed to show that it is not incoherent (1) to believe or hope in the reality of a God who can keep solidarity with all creatures and (2) to recognize the real evils in the actual world is a minimal defense of the compossibility of these (Tilley 1984,1991). The problem of divine omnipotence may not be with the affirmation of divine power, but with the sort of dominating power we use as a model for divine power. If our model for power is the power to sustain relationships rather than the model of the bulldozer able unilaterally to move mountains, the concept of omnipotence can be disconnected from the erotics of domination.

Moreover, Welch neglects the possibility that the world in which we live is a sacramental universe. In celebrating a presence "both healing and fragile, constitutive of life and unambiguously present in the human condition . . . [but] absent in the atrocities of history and in humankind's despoliation of the earth" (1990:177), why is one not recognizing the local presence of a transcending power which is omnipotent not as a bulldozer is, but omnipotent in the ability to heal all that can be healed? A sacramental universe is not one where ritual somehow "magically" cures, but one in which, at certain times and places, the presence of a power to heal and unite all is real. In short, the choice is between a Feuerbachian view valorized by Welch and a Rahnerian view: both are fully naturalistic, but the latter recognizes the natural as also sacramental.

In that universal solidarity is possible in a sacramental universe and impossible in a nonsacramental universe, I would claim that a sacramental theism is both reasonable intellectually and liberating practically. It is also fully consistent with the thrust of Welch's ethic of risk incarnated in communities of solidarity and resistance. For it is in these sorts of communities where communion is sacramental. In sum, what Welch advocates is a risky vision of communal praxis which Christians should endorse; but what Welch denies—the reality of a God who creates and sustains conditions for universal solidarity—weakens, rather than strengthens, her work.

Chapter 10

The Baptist Theology of J. W. McClendon, Jr., and Practical Faith in a Pluralistic Context

How Christlike are disciples' lives to be?
—J. W. McClendon, Jr.

The polity of the United States allows many free (voluntary) churches in a free (no establishment of religion) society. Nonetheless, much Christian thought has been developed in the context of a different polity. An aspect of the social location of most Christian theologians outside of the United States is that they work in the context of religious establishment, whether formal or informal, legal or traditional. Thus, contemporary theological views rooted in German, French, Spanish, Italian, British, Scottish, Latin American, or even Swiss theology, are rooted in a position where a church is "established."

Much modern and postmodern thought is conditioned by the presumption of establishment. The Enlightenment's desire to escape from tutelage by priests would make little sense in the context of nonestablishment and religious pluralism. Gutiérrez's rejecting the theologies of the dominant, his recognizing the primacy of praxis, and his requiring theologians to act with the oppressed Christians, rather than with the oppressing Christians, makes most sense where there is an establishment Church.

Issues about the limits of tolerance for various religious views and practices arise whether or not a church is established in a society. But in contemporary Western societies of whatever polity, participating in any religion is truly optional for individuals. One is not required or expected to participate. One must opt for them—and most postmodern writers, of course, opt out of them. For modernity, freedom of religion is a problem needing to be politically resolved. In a postmodern context, freedom of religion is taken for granted both in the personal sense (one must opt for religion) and in the political sense (a community is free to practice its faith, within the limits of public decency and order).

142

What makes the work of James Wm. McClendon, Jr., of distinctive interest is that he has sought to write a theology which presumes a free-church polity rather than an established one. In *Ethics*, the first volume of his projected three volume *Systematic Theology*, McClendon provides a free-church theology "in light of the baptist [sic] vision" especially accessible to those beyond the free-church traditions. The roots of this accessibility are biographical and theological. After completing a Th.M. at Princeton (1952) and a Th.D. in theology and philosophy of religion at Southwestern Baptist Theological Seminary (1953), McClendon taught at Golden Gate Baptist Seminary in California (1954-66) and undertook further graduate study in philosophy in Berkeley (1958-62) and Oxford (1962-63). From 1966-69 he taught in a Roman Catholic college, the University of San Francisco, and from 1971-89 was Professor of Theology at the (Episcopal) Church Divinity School of the Pacific in Berkeley. He has also held visiting appointments at Stanford, Temple, St. Mary's (Moraga, Calif.), Penn, Goucher, Notre Dame, and at Fuller Theological Seminary. For the past thirty years McClendon has explored his (free church) baptist vision while teaching in mainstream Protestant, Catholic, and secular institutions.

McClendon offers what he has called a "practical" theory of religion. He portrays this theory in the following:

> [A] religion is a set of powerful *practices* that embody the life-forming convictions of its practitioners. There *is* no "essence" of religion; religions are neither . . . all more or less true nor . . . all more or less evil. It follows that generalizations about religion are generally mistaken, since religions differ in kind, and only concrete, sympathetic historical and empirical study can tell us about any particular religion. We may call this the *practical theory* of religion . . . in the sense that its concern is the life-shaping (as I will say, the convictional) *practices* religions embody. So religions are not to be identified with their abstract teachings, far less with their "errors" (1994:42).

In McClendon's usage, "practice" is a technical term, akin to Alasdair MacIntyre's understanding of "practice." McClendon writes:

> [S]ocial practices, like games, strive for some *end* beyond themselves (health for the practice of medicine, livable space for architecture), require intentional participation on the part of *practitioners*, employ determinate *means*, and proceed according to *rules*. [So] a "practice". . . is a complex series of human actions involving definite practitioners who by these means and in accordance with these rules together seek the intended end (McClendon 1994:28).

McClendon differs from MacIntyre in allowing that the *teloi* of practices are not necessarily internal to those practices and in claiming that practices, even if one engages in them properly, do not necessarily require morally good means, develop virtuous practitioners, or lead to good ends. In short, Christian theology is reflection on Christian practices.

But those practices are not necessarily exclusive or merely repetitive of the past. In his earlier work McClendon devoted himself to finding the connections between his anabaptist vision and other perspectives. In philosophy of religion, he and "secular atheist" J. M. Smith, wrote *Understanding Religious Convictions*, still the only book in philosophy of religion fully co-authored by a Christian and an atheist. Using the speech act analysis of J. L. Austin (who lectured in Berkeley during McClendon's time there), they jointly worked out an account which preserved the cognitive, expressive, and affective aspects of religious belief. Although written long before Richard Rorty sponsored anti-foundationalism and philosophy as conversation in *Philosophy and the Mirror of Nature* (1979), and before Habermas's ideal speech situation of unconstrained discourse was well known in this country, *Understanding Religious Convictions* anticipated these influential positions and used basic strategies they would later use to account for reasonable disagreement in and adjudication of differences about convictions, those deep and persistent beliefs which shape individuals and communities into the kinds of people they are (McClendon and Smith 1975:7).

The work behind and in *Understanding Religious Convictions* led naturally in two theological directions. One was a rich sacramental theology (McClendon 1966;1967). Speech act theory fits with sacramental realism and the recognition that communities engage in sacramental practices (also see 1974:98-99; 1986:32,106,214-218; 1994:373-416). The concern with convictions led naturally to describing their place in the shared and individual lives of those who are formed by Christian convictions.

If Christianity has a most central and distinctive doctrine, it is the atonement. But no doctrinal formula or slogan ("substitutionary atonement," "ransom theory," "exemplarism") can plumb its depths. It requires narratives to say what it could mean ("He died in our place. . . ." "He paid a ransom to the devil to redeem us from pawn. . . ." "He showed us the way and opened the gates of heaven. . . .") and how it could be put into practice. *Biography as Theology* took up this challenge by exploring how atonement could be a conviction central in variously shaping four individuals' lives: Dag Hammarskjöld, Martin Luther King, Jr., Clarence Jordan, and Charles Ives.

But religious convictions cannot be separated from moral ones (1974:28-38). Both are woven into the fabric of our lives and pulling one kind out for examination destroys the pattern to be seen there. He argued that Christian ethics cannot be reduced to a single principle, but must represent the complexity of the Christian ethos (1978). But to discover, understand, and transform the thought and practice of Christians—Christian ways of life or praxes—is just to do Christian theology. Thus *Ethics* begins a major systematic theology.

To *begin* a systematics by painting a complex portrait of Christian practice and to write an ethics without casuistry is courageous. McClendon is also provocative as he includes two eighteenth-century American Puritans, a German Lutheran and a convert to Roman Catholicism as exemplars for a free-church ethic. In doing so he startlingly redraws the lines of the Christian traditions.

The basic vision of *Ethics* is that "a threefold cord is not quickly broken" (Ecclesiastes 4:12). Christian ethics is not a chain of argument, strong as its weakest link, but a woven rope of life. Its three strands are distinguishable, but inseparable in practice. At some points a single strand may carry the whole moral load; at others friction between or within strands may erupt into destructive flames, but each is necessary to constitute the breadth and length of Christian praxis.

The first strand is the organic and the natural, where the pulls of the body predominate. A theoretical chapter portrays moral reactions (delight and disgust), moral emotions (shame, blame, and guilt), moral needs (basic bodily needs), and a moral virtue (presence) appropriate to a Christian somatic ethic. Each of these can be distorted, e.g., any who fail to react with horror to some of the scenes in the film *Night and Fog* or who feel tremendous guilt over trivial matters have something important wrong with their moral equipment. In a remarkable biographical chapter McClendon connects the erotic love of Sarah and Jonathan Edwards through their narratives of their own conversions to Jonathan's most profound philosophical theology. His account restores the determining narratives and pastoral practices unacknowledged in recent Edwards scholarship to the center of the picture. An application chapter discusses sex, love, and marriage. It contains no casuistry or rules, but rather shows how Christians all too often exalt Augustinian ambivalence about sex, romantic accounts of love (from Tristan and Iseult to *Love Story*), and Freudian analyses over the Christian story of the love of God. Aided by Edwards, McClendon sketches another story of love as feeling, virtue, and gift, a three-stranded love based in the narrative of creation, redemption, and reconciliation. We are bodily beings and our embodied practices are crucial for our lives.

The second strand is social ethics. In the theoretical chapter McClendon joins the biblical notion of the principalities and powers to produce an account of social structures remarkable for its ability to explain the power of practices to shape people and communities. The biographical chapter portrays Dietrich Bonhoeffer as an emblem of the failure of German Christianity to be a community able to resist the powerful and attractive practices which molded German Protestantism into an established *Reichskirche*. The chapter's theological success is its persuasive use of a view sympathetic to the ancient personification of the *power* of practices as daemonic. It reveals a richly biblical way to understand the *force* of "social sin." The application chapter uses the practices which form the community whose literary legacy is the gospel of Matthew to show the internal and external social ethics of early Christianity. This leads McClendon to reject monochromatic models of the relation of church and society. The church cannot adapt to or resist the world wholesale, for the world is not a unity independent of the church, but is "an indefinite congeries of powerful practices, spread over time and space, so that any number of these practices may impinge upon believers in a variety of ways, while our witness to them will necessarily take a corresponding variety of forms" (1986:231). Moreover, Christians have always had to try to shape alien practices to fit the Christian story, so a Christian social ethic of sectarian withdrawal is historically and theologically wrong. Christians together must finally practice a politics of forgiveness, a theme reminiscent of *Biography as Theology*. We are social beings and the practice of forgiveness must play a central role if we are to be able to live together.

The third strand is the anastatic, where the incredible gift of resurrected life is key. An exclusively second strand ethic too easily degenerates into a Christian sectarianism or "comports too well with the comfortable wasteland of that numerous tribe, the half-Christians, busy about their little cares and wants, unquestioningly accepting the hand fate has dealt them, conformed to the mores of their own society or the fashions of the present age" (1986:243). The theoretical chapter shows that a Christian ethic which consigns the resurrection to moral irrelevance runs the danger of investing created religious or secular practices and powers with ultimacy—a violation of the first commandment. Conversely, a pure "anastatic" ethic without the ballast of body and community is easy prey to the winds of gnosticism. The biographical chapter tells of Dorothy Day—a woman in no danger of losing touch with somatic or communal life, and the shaper of a community with eschatological peace at its center ("Heaven can begin here" [1986:296]). The application chapter discusses the centrality of peacemaking for Christians. The differences between pacifists and just warriors are displayed, but the contrast between the story of Jesus and the narratives of crusades and justifiable war to preserve or overthrow social structures is only briefly sketched ("If war stories can capture or subvert the Jesus story, it can happen the other way around as well" [1986:314-15]). In contrast to those who feel responsible for the fate of the earth or who would lose everything if that fate were destruction, not only do Christians invest (proximately) in this world, but they are also invested by their God with an eschatological hope which can enable them to make peace even though the violent bear them away. We are beings with soul, if not souls, and in a sacramental universe we can be carried outside ourselves.

Like Sharon Welch, McClendon finds that theology is a task which requires struggle, even resistance, especially against the comforting illusion that our "unchallenged beliefs are self-evident truths" (1986:17). Without accepting her endorsement of relativism, he recognizes the particularity and the communal nature of each theological view:

> [This volume] takes seriously the existence of a plurality of convinced communities, not only the Christian one (or the "baptist" one) that is this book's community of reference. It does not assume that the others are all false and this one alone true. Nor on the other hand does it assume that all are moving toward a common truth along different roads (1994:22-23).

McClendon's method is also pluralistic and based in narratives, although the narratives central for his work are not fictional (like Wyschogrod's), but biographical. In a manner similar to other theologians of communal praxis, the community which begets theology is not the dominant of the world; yet McClendon recognizes (unlike the postliberals), that Christian lives are structured not only by the church and its narratives, but also by the world. "The struggle begins with the humble fact that the church is not the world. This means that Christians face an interior struggle, inasmuch as the line between church and world passes through each Christian heart" (1986:17). The practice of theology, then, holds up the mirror to the community (analogous to Gutiérrez's second step) so as to reveal the shape of the communal practices in which the theologian shares and to ask the question of whether the community does practice what it preaches (1986:35).

The anastatic strand in McClendon's ethics distinguishes his notion of practices from the repetitive, repressive, "practice makes perfect" view excoriated by liberation theologians. One of the "rules" which guides Christian practices can be formulated in Wittgensteinian terms as "the ability to go on" by creatively (and in sometimes unexpected ways) following a rule in new situations; or in Augustinian terms "love and do what you will"; or in the paradoxical rule "break the rules when necessary." There is no rule available to tell when the anastatic strand should inform our practices. Rules come to an end and we must go on beyond them; thus Christian practice must be a creative praxis.

McClendon rejects the decisionism characteristic of modern ethics (debating with Methodist P. Wogaman and Catholic T. O'Connell) in favor of an ethic of character (virtue) in community (Christian practices). He defends the primacy of narrative in Christian ethics against those who would base ethics on principles or values, adapting both the speech act theory of *Understanding Religious Convictions* and Hans Frei's account of the biblical narrative. Here the connection of truth with truthfulness, also characteristic of Stanley Hauerwas's work, is crucial.

Volume II of McClendon's systematics, *Doctrine*, asks what the Church must teach to be the community of discipleship. Teaching is a form of practice; theology reflects on what the community actually teaches—and

sometimes exercises the prophetic and critical task of recalling the community to the vision which informs it. As with *Ethics*, McClendon finds that
doctrine falls comfortably into three strands.

The first strand is "the rule of God." Christians are properly ruled by an
eschatological vision that sees that "what history is about is the formation
of a new race of human beings, a race made of all races, a people made of
all peoples" (1994:98). This is not a vision of universal agreement, but of
universal solidarity. In anticipation of that final realization of solidarity,
each Christian community is to be open to others and each Christian is to
act in anticipation that the universal solidarity is eschatologically realized.
Despite that vision, Christians fail to realize—to make real—that salvific
reality. Socially and personally, that is sin. But the God who created this
world is not a God of domination. While McClendon affirms that the church
must practice a faith that recognizes God is reliable, it also must refuse to
construe that reliability as tyranny or domination, for God is the creator of
co-creators:

> God the Creator is not remote from these developments [of struggle,
> suffering and evil], and is supremely the passionate (rather than
> impassible) God. The freedom of human co-creators is in part freedom
> to struggle . . . and to suffer, to be a Jacob at the ford of Jabbok,
> wrestling *with* God the Creator (1994:168).

The rule of God is one in which struggling with the Ruler is not only
possible, but may be necessary; in McClendon's view, the God who acts is
the creator of creativity.

The second strand is "the identity of Christ." Christ is first identified by
his atoning work. The story of the gospels is the story of blundering
disciples coming to new life together in his death and resurrection. The risk
of forming a community of trust even unto death is the risk of incarnating
atonement. To identify Christ as redeemer is to be a disciple; one is finally
in no position to make the identification unless one participates in the story.

> Discipleship meant (and means) commitment to the social radicalism
> of a non-conformist Christ; it required (and requires) not inner tor-
> ments . . . or guilty consciences but entire reorientation to a life with
> Jesus that will necessarily collide again and again with the powers,
> with the world's "no," that is, with a cross (1994:279).

Discipleship is risk in and of community and often failure—but not
ultimate failure, for the God who Jesus identifies with is a saving God with
whom and for whom all risks can be redeemed.

The third strand is the fellowship of the spirit. That fellowship is celebrated not as a closed community, but as a community open to solidarity
with all. Like Wyschogrod, McClendon sees the practice of the reformed

and baptist community of Chambon during the holocaust as one partial exemplification of Christian community. The community gathers and disperses, and as it travels must take its bearings from the dangerous memory and transforming hope where the divine shows through the ordinary.

McClendon's theology is politically post-Constantinian and intellectually postmodern in ways too complex to display here. McClendon's beginning his systematics with an ethic of character-in-community has deep resonance with the practical-strategic and prophetic-critical patterns of Gutiérrez. His continuation with doctrine suggests that only in the shared practices of a community is it possible for the Good News to be practically proclaimed. In reflecting on a story by William Saroyan, "On the Train," in which a group of draftees is being sent to the war front, McClendon notes that these strangers talk, sing bawdy songs and eventually turn to singing "Leaning On the Everlasting Arms."

> The story presents the fears of such as these, fear of the future, of war, of alienation, of death. Against war, there is for soldiers the hope of lucky survival; against alienation, sometimes there are friends. Against death, there is nothing. Nothing but the Good News. Most striking for us is the song's text: it announces itself as a song about "...a fellowship . . . a joy divine."
>
> Now by our present account, these two are the very ends of the Spirit's mission—they are the creative goal of the great suffering divine holy Creator God. In the song, "joy divine" is what we have called ecstasy; "fellowship" is our *koinonia*, our congress one with another in Jesus. Together these constitute the intimacy that wipes away every tear, and gathers every lost sheep home.
>
> > Leaning, leaning, safe and secure from all alarms;
> > Leaning, leaning, leaning on the everlasting arms.
>
> As Saroyan says, "By this time everybody was singing" (1994:452).

Even on troop trains, the reign of God can be proleptically realized by engaging in the practices that fit properly in that reign. And they sang quite a different song from that sung in Mahagonny: "No one can do nothing for a dead man!" In the reign of God, Someone can.

Epilogue to Part 4

Requiem Aeternam, Lux Perpetua

In profoundly different ways, Gutiérrez (a Peruvian Catholic priest), Welch (a radical feminist from the United States from mainstream Protestantism) and McClendon (another North American academic, but from the anabaptist heritage of the radical reformation) all turn to communities formed by those whom the powers of this world reject in order to see and show an incarnation of salvation. Gutiérrez finds the praxis of the community of the oppressed to incarnate the irruption of liberation in every sphere. Welch finds communities of solidarity and resistance make possible abandoning an ethic of domination and control practiced by the powers of this world—at best James's "prudence" (p. 78 above)—and accepting an ethic of risk for new and better life for the future—James's saintly charity. McClendon finds that the character of discipleship can develop in those communities which enjoy the love of God, write and read of the grace of Christ, and gather in the Spirit's fellowship (1994:488) despite the fact that the powers of the world know that "no one can do nothing for a dead man" (see p. 78 above). As John Shea once put it, they all see that the only alternative in a world come of age is that "We gather together and tell stories of God to calm our terror and hold our hope on high" (Shea 1978:39).

Each uses wildly different language to tell those stories and promote the gatherings. Gutiérrez borrows terms from Marxism as well as the Scripture. Welch takes words from the postmodern genealogists as well as the modern theological tradition. McClendon uses expressions from American philosophy as well as the anabaptist and other Christian traditions. Gutiérrez's and Welch's stories are less traditional than McClendon's. McClendon and Gutiérrez are far more scripturally oriented than Welch. Welch and McClendon are far more conscious of religious diversity than Gutiérrez is. It is not that they all tell the same tale. To claim that they do would be a false irenicism, a silencing of distinctive voices, a denial of diversity. They tell

different tales, have different hopes, advocate different patterns of practice—but also overlap interestingly in their diversity.

Each also recognizes that the lures and the terrors of the world are "living
options" for each and all. The communities of solidarity, resistance, and
fellowship are not composed by people unattracted by the charm of the
cultures which valorize dominance, exclusivity, and comfort. The community of struggle is where eternal rest is found and where perpetual light can
be found—if rest and light are available anywhere in a postmodern world.

PART 5

POSTMODERN THEOLOGIES
AND
RELIGIOUS DIVERSITY

Chapter 11

The Challenge of Religious Diversity

In a pluralistic society like that of the United States, religious diversity is taken for granted. As part of the American polity, the soil of religious freedom yields a luxuriant growth of religious bodies. Many Americans are proud of this diversity because it marks the United States as a tolerant society. People can believe and practice the religion they think right, without coercion by government authorities or fear of violent attacks from armies on crusade. Although America has a heritage of discriminating against non-Protestants, from colonial laws against Catholics and their priests, through the various anti-immigrant and anti-Semitic biases characteristic of nineteenth- and early twentieth-century America, to opposition to "cults" in recent years, the national myth is one of "civility" in religious disagreement. Even if the problem of religious diversity is "solved" in political theory, it has hardly been resolved in civic practice, in philosophy of religion, and in Christian theology. Religious diversity remains a problem for both political practice and religious thought.

I have grouped the postmodern theologies we have considered into categories where comparisons seem feasible. I have also compared the theologies on specific points where comparison seemed useful. However, honest and fair attempts to compare the theories in any overarching way across categories seem difficult to execute, if not impossible. Even when comparing theologies that are in dialogue with each other like Tracy's and Lindbeck's (Stell 1993; Lints 1993), the conclusions authors reach seem to be a function of their initial predilections for oppositions (Stell) or harmonization (Lints), as much as of their analyses of the texts considered. If we think all the theories are commensurable, we have pretty much given the prize to the Habermasians (or other constructive postmodernists), since their view is that an "ideal speech situation" in which all could be considered would show which is best—thus validating one of the theories on trial. If we think they are radically incomparable, we have practically named the postliberals the winners, for they find the grammar of each tradition to be different enough to make them incomparable. If we think the problem is not really a theoretical one, but one constructed by oppositions which need to be explored and deconstructed, we have found the genealogists the winners of the game, for they would point out that it simply is a matter of power relations. If we think that the problem is to be first solved in practice and allow theory to follow as it will, then the theorists of communal praxis are the victors. In short, it seems that any *direct* attempt to compare and evaluate such different theologies cannot avoid the problem of prejudicial judgment.

But this does not necessarily apply to indirect comparisons. What I propose to do in this chapter is to examine how representatives of each of the patterns developed above deal with the challenge of religious diversity. This will not yield a "knock down" claim that one or the other pattern or exemplar is "better" than the rest. However, if we can find that some of them deal more adequately with a problem that plagues contemporary philosophical theology, then we have a sign that suggests some patterns may well be superior to others, at least with regard to coping with one significant problem for theory and challenge to practice. But even to engage in such indirect evaluation we need to place the issues of religious diversity in their own proper contexts.

THE PROBLEM OF RELIGIOUS DIVERSITY

Religious diversity is one of three major interrelated problems which have been the subject matter of much modern philosophy of religion and, hence, of philosophical theology. The first is the reasonableness of religious belief. "How can any reasonable person believe in God?" is the homely question which lies behind the sophisticated debate in this first area. The attempt to answer this sort of question has led philosophers of religion to seek a secure and rational foundation for religious belief—or to argue that such a foundation is neither necessary nor sufficient for a reasonable person to believe religiously or be religiously active. Debates over the proofs of the existence of God, over the rationality of accepting the deliveries of religious experience, over whether it is prudent to believe in God even if there is no proof are topical foci of the problem of reasonableness. Indeed, excellent contemporary college textbooks (e.g., Geivett and Sweetman, Audi and Wainwright) center on this problem. Yet the academic debate in this area has focused almost entirely on the rationality of belief in God. I have argued that this approach finally cannot resolve the real issue in this area, the wisdom of commitment in and to a tradition of religious practice and belief (Tilley 1989c; 1995).

The second area of debate in modern philosophy of religion is the problem of evil. The question, "How can anyone believe in an omnipotent, omniscient, omnibenevolent God in the face of all the real evil in the actual world?" moves this issue. However, the problem of evil is not one, but many. The *logical* problem of evil has been solved. Various successful defenses of the logical compatibility of propositions like "There is a God as traditionally conceived" and "There is real evil in the world" are available (e.g., Plantinga 1974:7-64). A person's beliefs are not logically inconsistent if she believes both of those propositions. The *evidential* problem of evil is more difficult. It is not clear how real evils should or should not "count against" the reasonableness of belief in God. Contemporary philosophers simply disagree on the logic of the argument concerning the evidential problem. Plantinga argues that on any objective account of probability, the reality of evil does not render belief in God improbable; Hick has claimed that evil does count against belief in God and must be explained (see Tilley 1984). The evidential problem seems more to have to do with the (subjective, personal) plausibility of belief in God than with the (objective) probability that God exists; if that is the case, the problem is not philosophical and, properly understood, cannot be resolved philosophically. I have argued (Tilley 1991) that the whole project of theodicy, the modern attempts to offer an explanation of the "evidence" of evil against God, finally creates more evils than it resolves, especially because theodicies' abstractions efface evil as a *social* problem.

The third problem is that of religious diversity. "Since so many religions say so many different things, how can they all, or any one of them, be rationally credible?" This philosophical problem is often conflated with a Christian theological problem of religious diversity, "Can people be saved if they do not believe in the name of Jesus?" Much confusion in theology and philosophy of religion has resulted from not keeping the first, epistemological question separate from the second, soteriological question.

The epistemological question of religious diversity has been helpfully addressed by American philosopher William Alston. Generally speaking, Alston finds that religious beliefs are produced by people participating in religious practices. These practices have no more and no less "rational support" than does the practice of sense perception, save that each of the religious practices is "local" and the practice of perception is practically "universal." That the local religious practices produce contrary or contradictory beliefs is finally neither very surprising nor does it count against the reasonableness of forming such beliefs. If this sounds unlikely, consider the fact that psychological and social theorists today provide theories which yield contradictory or contrary beliefs; this does not count against the rationality of their practices, but only highlights that their "sciences" are young and not exact. That there is disagreement is neither surprising nor does it show psychology or sociology irrational. So religious believers and theorists engaging in varied practices develop contradictory or contrary beliefs; perhaps religious practices—and especially interreligious dialogue—is "young" given what it seeks to understand and "inexact" by the nature of that which concerns religious life. Disagreement need not be

construed as showing religious practices irrational (Alston 1991) or religious beliefs, on the whole, unfounded. Alston's great contribution is that
he has placed the epistemological question in the right location and thus
pointed the direction for its resolution (see Tilley 1995:77-89).

Soteriological concerns have been prominent in both philosophical and
theological discussions (see Hick 1989; Knitter 1985; Hick and Knitter 1987;
d'Costa 1990; DiNoia 1992). Indeed, the basic pattern for theories which
seek to account for religious diversity offered by religion scholars has its
roots in Christian soteriological issues. *Exclusivism* is a theory which
emerges in the premodern era and claims that only those who believe in
"our way" can be saved (and have true beliefs, too). *Extra ecclesiam nulla
salus*, taken in its narrowest sense, expresses one form of exclusivism.
Inclusivism is a modern improvement on exclusivism which extends the
power of our way or savior to others, although they are not aware that they
have been saved; Karl Rahner's account of the "anonymous Christian" is
taken to be one typical example of an "inclusivist" paradigm. *Intra ecclesiam
vera salus*, with "church" extended to include all or practically all of creation
expresses one form of inclusivism. *Pluralism,* as a theory about the diversity
of religion (it is also used as a synonym for the fact of religious diversity,
although I will avoid that usage here) is a typical liberal, modern view
characteristic of what Lindbeck has labeled "experiential expressivism." It
claims that there are many paths to the same One who shows him/her/it-
self in myriad ways, so that each should walk her or his own path as
devotedly as possible in order to be saved. Pluralism is *not* "indifferentism";
pluralism claims we can't know for sure which, if any, path is the best way
to the center (although we are nonetheless right to count on our own path
at its best as a way we can and should follow) while indifferentism is a
"lazy" belief which implies it makes no difference which path one walks or
whether we walk it well. Pluralism comes in two varieties: one claims that
religious traditions finally all do say the same thing; we'll call this *reductive
pluralism,* since it reduces the variety of religious views to one basic or
hidden truth. The other version we can dub *phenomenal pluralism,* for it
claims that religions finally refer to the same noumenal and transcendent
reality, but appear different and conceive of that noumenal reality as it is
related to us in profoundly different ways. Huston Smith tends toward the
former sort of pluralism, John Hick to the latter.

Finally, a new and important view has emerged recently which is best
called *particularism* (e.g., DiNoia 1992). Associated especially with postliberalism, it takes differences most seriously. Like exclusivism, it finds each
of the religious traditions substantially different. However, a particularist
typically does *not* ask the soteriological question as an overarching one.
Any complete answer to the question "who can be saved?" will be a
universal answer which inevitably undermines the particular patterns of
some religious traditions. Moreover, such an answer is presumptuous in
the extreme, making a claim to know how God finally disposes of every-

thing there is. Hence, particularism rejects reductive pluralism and is suspicious of phenomenal pluralism, exclusivism, and inclusivism, much preferring to espouse more modest particular theological claims.

Having set the issue of religious diversity in its contexts as an epistemological problem and a soteriological problem, briefly shown its dimensions, and characterized the typical solutions, we can turn to seeing how various postmodern theological positions would address the problem.

CONSTRUCTIVE POSTMODERNISM

Francis Schüssler Fiorenza, a theologian influenced by Habermas, clearly states the problem religious diversity creates for Christian theology:

> The task for theology is both to take pluralism seriously and to explore the particularity and significance of the Christian vision without reducing religious language to an isolated language-game that neglects other religious visions and the global situation of humanity (Schüssler Fiorenza and Galvin 1991:I,68).

Yet in the text from which that quotation is taken and in his other most important work (1984), he hardly addresses the problem of religious diversity. In these texts, as in those of other theologians influenced by Habermas (e.g., Arens 1992:162-74), diversity is part of the context for doing theology, and Christians are to be in solidarity with those of other classes, traditions, cultures, and religions. Yet how religious diversity materially affects the task of theology and how Christians are to undertake the task of solidarity with those who are religiously other remain territories underexplored.

Although David Ray Griffin is in practice richly open to dialogue with others, his own position is, as noted in Chapter 2, in danger of advocating a reductionism of the most serious kind. His foundational process metaphysics and his romantic communalism finally seek the conversion of others to his vision. For Griffin, religious diversity is, at a metaphysical level, a problem to be overcome.

In contrast, David Tracy has been exploring the issues of religious pluralism directly and extensively. Indeed, it is difficult to separate this issue from Tracy's theology more generally because almost the whole of his career has, in some sense, been devoted to the theological implications of religious diversity.

Dialogue with the Other: The Inter-Religious Dialogue (1990) is Tracy's first book-length attempt to deal with global diversity and non-Christian religions. This short work is a refined, nuanced program for dealing with extra-Christian diversity. Tracy draws on insights from Sigmund Freud, William James, and Mircea Eliade, among others, to construct a theologically grounded method for or approach to interreligious dialogue.

The basic framework for Tracy's argument is provided by a division of religious discourse into "prophetic" and "mystical" categories. The prophet hears a word, not his own, but from an Other, "which demands expression through the prophet" (1990:18). This word can tend to go out in two directions: a generalizing and ethical direction and, by radical contrast, "in favor of the intensification, indeed transgression of the prophetic form into a radically apocalyptic form" (1994:113). The mystic denies that any word can be spoken that tells truly of what is ultimate. Yet it is Tracy's hope that dialogue with the Buddhists can be mutually illuminating of these different "rhetorics" and even produce a reconciliation between these trends within his own Christian tradition: the "pervasive religious dialectic of manifestation and proclamation is best construed theologically as mystical-prophetic" (Tracy 1990:7).

One of Tracy's major concerns is to develop criteria for dialogue. He writes:

> There is no more difficult or more pressing question on the present theological horizon than that of interreligious dialogue. Part of that question must be the question of possible criteria for the dialogue itself. Such criteria, if available, must not claim to replace the dialogue but, at best, heuristically to inform it (Tracy 1990:27).

Tracy "revisits William James" to provide a new set of criteria for dialogue (Tracy 1990:28). Based on James's philosophy and psychology of religion, Tracy articulates a concept of experience as something which "is not limited to sense experience (as in British empiricism) but includes feelings, mood, and what Whitehead (here influenced by James) named non-sensuous perception" (Tracy 1990:37). For Tracy, James is a useful starting point because he not only focuses on the experiences which stimulate religious response, but also considers the social ramifications of those experiences, via his concerns with mysticism and saintliness, respectively (Tracy 1990:37-38).

Tracy notes the peculiar "fit" of Buddhism with the postmodern consciousness, finding its closest analogue in Deleuze and Derrida (Tracy 1990:70), though he also considers the more familiar analogy with Eckhart (Tracy 1990:87-91). What matters here is less the support he has to offer for such comparisons or interaction, or even the program for Buddhist-Christian dialogue, than the conclusion of his chapter on this subject:

> Clearly . . . the Buddhist and the Christian [are not] saying the same thing. But the radically relational *structure* of Ultimate Reality would be commonly affirmed . . . . Clearly the Buddhist and the Christian are not the same way. But neither are we two, in any easy way, merely other to one another. Perhaps, as the Buddhists suggest, we are neither the same nor other, but not-two (Tracy 1990:93,94).

From the perspective of the development of the problem of pluralism, Tracy seems to be sitting on the fence. He seems both to want to avow phenomenal pluralism and particularism. Yet he also rejects John Hick's key move in his phenomenal pluralism:

> The "answer" is unlikely to be, as some suggest, by shifting from a "christocentric" to a "theocentric" position. This Christian response seems more a postponement of the issue rather than an adequate response to it. For insofar as Christians know the God (as pure, unbounded Love) that all Christian models of theocentrism demand, they know *that* God in and through the decisive revelation of God in Jesus Christ (Tracy 1990:96-97; also see 1994:111).

Here, the particularistic insistence on honest appraisal of difference is quite forcefully stated. If Tracy is a pluralist, then his is a "revisionist" pluralism which recognizes the basis of religious experience in some loosely defined Ultimate Reality. Nonetheless, he insists on the distinctiveness of any expression of that Reality by its particular linguistic formation and situation. For Tracy, Christian theology must be "christomorphic" (1994:111). The pluralism of Tracy is not one which swallows up diversity and difference into an overarching or foundational absolute identity of experience.

Tracy's comparison between Christian and Buddhist concepts of "salvation" also distinguishes him from both the phenomenal pluralist and radical particularist stances:

> [T]he challenge from the different Buddhist ways to this Christian way of even posing the question [of salvation as total liberation] much less proposing a response seem to me as necessary for Christians to hear as they are unnerving. At the same time, I hope that at least part of our joint discussion may illuminate how modern Buddhist ways account in their own fashion for the social and political liberation we all need (Tracy 1987a:138).

Tracy seeks a pluralism which allows him to maintain the real diversity of religious traditions as well as his dialogue-correlation model of theology. Moreover, by retaining in an attenuated form the pluralist insistence on the experience of Ultimate Reality, Tracy continues to support a "public" theology, so that the enterprise of discussion and debate has some grounding in a shared experience (however tenuous or minimal that sharing might be) and is not an exercise in difference *tout court*, as it might appear to be, for example, in a radically particularist approach.

Moreover, the practice of dialogue is not centrally an academic or theoretical practice. Dialogue participants are not engaged in a purely descriptive exercise for the benefit of outsiders. Discussion and dialogue as Tracy would envision it entails both a commitment to recognize the authentic diversity and difference of the participants' traditions and a commitment normatively to ground the findings of the discussion in an experience which all do or can share (hence "common human experience"). The hope is that the debate not be endless and consensus be possible—a consensus which, as noted above, Tracy sees as the goal of public discourse in a pluralist society (Tracy 1989a:202). Yet that consensus might well always remain partial—for the other always remains irreducibly other (Tracy 1994:112).

David Tracy, then, with his revisionist model for postmodern theology—his emphasis on the correlation between the plural and ambiguous received tradition and the apparently shared experience of contemporary humanity—has produced a subtle "middle way" for understanding the diversity of today's religious world which is neither radically particularist nor phenomenally pluralist, but which recognizes and celebrates diversity. His focus on dialogue means that the central problem of religious diversity is a practical one of understanding "the other," rather than an epistemological or soteriological problem. In this, Tracy departs from, and in his most recent work (1994) clearly moves beyond the typical modern worries—hence, his work charts a way beyond the pitfalls of the modern problematic and commends a christomorphic theology that values the others.

THE DISSOLUTION OF DIVERSITY INTO PRACTICALLY NOTHING

Although it seems odd to do so, perhaps the most paradoxical position taken on religious diversity of the various views considered in this text would be Thomas Altizer's. He is obviously well-versed in interreligious dialogue, as his early studies of Buddhism attest. Yet his position is that of a reductive pluralist who finds that Nothing is that which is "behind" the variety.

Altizer sought to "uncover" a basic commonality in religious experience. In the tradition of his mentors, he spoke of all religions' interest in positing a *coincidentia*, a union of sacred and profane realities. Mystical attention, of course, fared prominently in his assessment. The upshot of his investigations led him to believe that all religions seek a redemption of "opposites." However, he commends Christianity's distinctiveness for being emphatically teleological. His account of other religions sees them as calling for a *backward*-moving eternal return. Christianity, on the other hand, radically envisions its goal as the eternal recurrence of time, always pressing *forward* though to an ending of an end. Christianity, especially in its Catholic version (1994) has anticipated the fully eternal return.

Altizer's own unique version of a radically atheistic Christianity places him in the ranks of past gnostics who reflected on their visions as though *gnosis* came to them alone. Besides passing over the corporate nature of most religious traditions, Altizer reduces their distinctive aims or ultimate goals to one. He thus solves the problem of religious diversity by identifying one aspect of religiosity as the primal or basic component of religion and reducing all the diversity to the *coincidentia oppositorum*.

Although Wyschogrod recognizes the real diversity of saints (e.g. 1990a:13,39) and the differences between saints and mystics, the problem of religious diversity is not central for her work. Yet one paragraph is highly illuminating:

> It is worth noting in the context of the problem of saintly life that the distinction drawn by Deleuze and Guattari—a distinction between God as an ultimate principle of being and truth as well as the energy of the productive forces—can be reframed in traditional theological language. The God of love has been distinguished from the God of wrath, the God of Abraham from the God of the philosophers, the God beyond God from the creator and governor of the universe, the *arhat* or the *pratyeka* buddha who seeks individual release from suffering from the bodhisattva who works for the release of all. *These disjunctions were intended to mark off differences between normative theological constructs and the burning center of things.* To be sure, each pairing requires careful historical elaboration and arises in a unique socio-historical context (1990a:197; emphasis added).

While this paragraph occurs in an expository section in an uncanny text, and so its claims cannot be simply treated as Wyschogrod's, the italicized comment suggests that she, like Altizer, may accept a reductive pluralism as a way to respond to the challenge of the diversity of religions.

Mark C. Taylor also does not directly address the diversity of religion. He shows in his writing elsewhere that he is aware of other cultures and religions and how their views of humanity differ. In "The Broken Image" of humanity, he addresses Asian cultures and religions and says that among the reasons for question traditional foundations in the eighteenth and nineteenth centuries was "an increasingly global awareness of the alien cultures of South and East Asia" (Raschke et al. 1977:226). Taylor goes on to discuss how the breakdown of conventional images in the West was paralleled in Asia.

Yet because of the main themes in his a/theology, Taylor finally seems also to be a pluralist. Altizer says about *Erring* that "Taylor seeks a genuine Christian theology, a theology centered in Incarnation and Crucifixion . . . [and that he] is also in quest of a purely Biblical or Scriptural theology, a theology that will know Scripture or Writing and Scripture alone" (Wyschogrod 1986:525). Taylor is addressing Christian concepts as the traditional foundations of the Western world. *Erring* is dedicated to discovering a new "Christology," and in it Taylor uses the images of the cross and the crucifixion throughout, but his a/theology is not necessarily Christian. The Christian imagery is used to illustrate self-sacrifice for the sake of the self.

Taylor is more like what George A. Lindbeck refers to as an "experiential expressivist." "For experiential-expressive symbolists . . . religiously significant meanings can vary . . . [and doctrines are] subject to changes of meaning or even to a total loss of meaningfulness" (Lindbeck 1984:17). As we have seen, meaning is, for Taylor, always dependent on interpretation. Since experiential-expressivists are typically pluralists, Taylor would seem to be so also.

Taylor's relativistic approach does appear to classify him as a pluralist. However, what is different about Taylor is his notion of religion. For him, there are not only different versions of knowledge and truth, but there are *not* any absolute truths. It is not just that humans can not "know" it, but that it "is" not. "[W]e can attain unity within plurality, Being within becoming, identity within difference" (Wyschogrod 1986:524). The divine, for Taylor, lies in the milieu, in the space of nothingness. Religious reflection hovers in the acceptance of erring within the divine tear. Hence, Taylor's position can be seen as a variant on phenomenal pluralism: not one who posits a One at the center, but who finds no center at all.

In short, the problem of religious diversity is not important for postmodern theorists of dissolution. Each of them have similarities to modern phenomenal and reductive pluralists, but with one key difference: they deny that there is any unity at the heart of plurality. This suggests that their work is "ultramodern" or "mostmodern" rather than postmodern, as Griffin has argued, in that they accept a main constituent of liberal modernism in their implicit approaches to the challenges of religious diversity.

POSTLIBERAL PARTICULARISM

George Lindbeck makes an appeal to diversity that frees him from characterization as either an exclusivist, inclusivist or pluralist theologian. Lindbeck is a particularist. Comparing religions is an academic task and the real question to be asked is their own categorical adequacy to meet the challenges of their own particular community. Lindbeck remains rooted firmly within a Christian, and specifically Lutheran, tradition. He has no special need to develop an account of the radical differences between traditions that his intratextualist theory shows. Lindbeck early on writes that if a religious community does not have the linguistic means to conceptualize the experience of another community, then this experience will remain as nonsense, outside the bounds of understanding that defines that first community (1984:48). He later tempers, or perhaps overlooks, this idea with the claim that the function of ecumenical discussion in his methodology is to help those outside our own religious community to learn to better understand the grammar of their own religious language framework. He uses the not altogether convincing example of the student of foreign languages who understands the grammar of those languages better than the natives of the foreign community (1984:61). Lindbeck's particularity distinguishes him from the other approaches (exclusivist, inclusivist, pluralist, etc.), but it is not a particularity that is so radical as to allow Christianity to be isolated from the rest of the religious world.

J. A. DiNoia, O.P., working in the particularist tradition of postliberalism develops the question of religious pluralism in this way, "Can Christian theology of religions affirm the universality of salvation in a way that is consistent with Christian determination to engage in interreligious dialogue?" (1992:x). DiNoia rejects Rahnerian inclusivism as well as pluralism. His view is that a Christian can strongly affirm

> the doctrine of the divine universal salvific will without prejudice to central Christian doctrines and without prejudice to the distinctive claims put forward by other communities. The Christian community will not regard itself "as the exclusive community of those who have a claim to salvation, but as the historically tangible vanguard" of a coming destiny it hopes to share with the whole human family (DiNoia 1992:108; quoting Karl Rahner).

DiNoia suggests that instead of a foundational inclusivism or pluralism which blurs the differences among particular traditions, a *prospective inclusivism* might be a way Christians could affirm the hope for all people without denying their distinctiveness (166; compare Lindbeck 1984:59).

Postliberals tend to respond to the epistemological issue of religious diversity by simply acknowledging the diversity of religious traditions. On the whole, they would tend to accept the position Alston has proffered in his practical account of religious diversity. The various traditions are irreducibly different; they are not static; and given that each articulates different origins for, paths in and goals of life, they are not directly commensurable. Nonetheless, insofar as one learns another tradition as one learns another language, one's understanding of one's own tradition may (and perhaps must, at least slightly) shift in light of one's new ability.

THEOLOGIES OF COMMUNAL PRACTICE

Given the social context for Gutiérrez's theology, it is not surprising that the issues of religious diversity are rarely found in his work. The epistemological issue is not significant and the soteriological focus is on empowering the nonperson to become a person, rather than on how God can save the nonbeliever. Nonetheless, Gutiérrez's reflections on history suggest that his view is finally inclusivist. "The history of salvation is the very heart of only one history—a 'Christo-finalized' history" (Gutiérrez 1988:86). "Salvation in Christ gives human history . . . its ultimate meaning and elevates it beyond itself" (Gutiérrez, 1990:117). Although Milbank finds that Gutiérrez has a conceptual debt to Rahner's form of inclusivism (Milbank 1990:229, citing Gutiérrez 1973:66-72), Gutiérrez actually cites Rahner more as an authoritative forerunner than as a theoretician of religious diversity. Although Gutiérrez cites Rahner, it is not to acknowledge a theoretical debt. Rather than construing Gutiérrez as a classic inclusivist, his position emphasizing the finality of Christ fits more closely with DiNoia's prospective inclusivism.

Like Gutiérrez, Welch is not directly concerned with the issues of religious diversity. Yet her ethic of risk and the anthropology embedded in it suggests that her position will be comparable to those of Tracy, DiNoia, and Gutiérrez. Welch writes, "Our bodies are formed from the bodies of two other people; our personalities are created by the regard given us by others" (1990:162). Welch's anthropology is profoundly social and requires difference if we are to become distinct selves. Welch also writes:

> Accountability, not guilt, is the response to critique when our selves are constituted by love for others.
>
> This love for others is holy and is rightly referred to as grace, a power that lifts us to a large self and a deeper joy as it leads us to accept blame and begin the long process of reparation and recreation (1990:174).

Her ethic also requires solidarity in difference and points the way to this solidarity with the unalterably other: to take the world as graced and joyous. Welch's naturalism leads her to a theology less distinctively "christomorphic" than postliberals' or liberationists' discourses. Nonetheless, the particularity of resistance and the hope for solidarity with the irreducibly other also mark her view as both particularist and prospectively, not foundationally, inclusivist.

McClendon proposes to deal with problems of religious diversity in the yet unwritten third volume of his systematic theology. Yet his own writing practices in the past have made clear that he, too, is a particularist of sorts who has recognized that we have all in various ways internalized some degree of diversity (see 1986:1; 1994:21-22). In the context of a book dealing with the justification of religious belief in a pluralistic world, fully co-authored with a "secular atheist" (1975:vii), McClendon writes:

> [I]f I believe in a God (am convinced of God) in a pluralistic world, a world in which I know there are men [sic] of good will who do not so believe, then my faith, if justified at all, must be a faith which takes account of that very pluralism which in part denies my faith. It must be faith justifiable . . . *in a world which includes unfaith* . . . . The pluralism

be faith justifiable . . . *in a world which includes unfaith* . . . . The pluralism we envisage, then, does not obviate justification nor require narrowness of outlook, but it does require that the pluralism itself shall be internalized, so that it becomes a factor which my convictions take into account (McClendon and Smith 1975:183).

Moreover each person is not formed simply in one community, but in many. Internal pluralism is unavoidable.

For McClendon, the other has entered "our" world. Like many of the dissolute postmodernists, McClendon recognizes the radical uncertainty in which we live. There is no membrane which we can use to keep the "other" out of our lives; our theological yards are unfenced and unfenceable. He also recognizes that we truly need the other as other if we are to be ourselves (1994:447-49).

Yet his work, like Tracy's and Gutiérrez's is clearly "christomorphic." Hence, McClendon also seems to take up the pattern of particularity and prospective inclusivism which they share with postliberalism. The practice of unity is a practice of unity-in-diversity which is not achieved by self-serving knaves who seduce others into unity nor "externally imposed by a dictator God" (1994:449). Rather it emerges—or will emerge—through the power of the Spirit of love, the Spirit Christ sent.

CONCLUSIONS: PATTERNS OF ACCOUNTING FOR RELIGIOUS DIVERSITY

When research for this book began in earnest many months ago, its main author did not expect that examining how postmodern theologies responded to the challenge of religious diversity would enable us to single out one position as superior to others. Rather, I expected a variety of accounts which would simply provide us with one interesting, but not final, standard by which to measure the discourses we discussed. However, as the research and analysis proceeded, it has become clear that the authors considered have fallen into two basic patterns. One group minimizes or erases the differences among religious traditions by a reductive or phenomenal pluralism. The other group is rooted in irreducibly diverse and particular positions which, unlike the premodern exclusivist positions they seem to emulate, aspire to inclusivism or universalism, but refuse to deny the otherness of the "other."

The first group would include Habermas (but not necessarily his theological followers), Griffin, Altizer, Taylor, and Wyschogrod (if not supplemented as we have argued in Chapter 6). The second lumps together the postliberals, Tracy, Gutiérrez, Welch and McClendon.

This indirect comparison finally leaves us with an unexpected conclusion: although the members of the first group are surely postmodern *writers,* they fail to take religious otherness seriously and are not writers of post-modern *religious* thought. Consider David Tracy's comments:

> Postmodernity begins by trying to think the unthought of modernity. Beyond the early modern turn to the purely autonomous, self-grounding subject, beyond even the more recent turn to language (the first great contemporary challenge to modern subjectism) lies the quintessential turn of post-modernity itself—the turn to the other. It is that turn, above all, that defines the intellectual as well as the ethical meaning of postmodernity. The other and the different come forward now as central intellectual categories across all the major disciplines, including theology. The others and the different—both those from other cultures and those others not accounted for by the grand narrative of the dominant culture—return with full force to unmask the social evolutionary narrative of modernity as ultimately an alibi-story, not a plausible reading of our human history together. Part of that return of otherness . . . is the return of biblical Judaism and Christianity to undo the complacencies of modernity, including modern theology (1994:108).

The first group recognizes the otherness of God and the otherness of other humans, but fails to recognize the otherness of, the radical diversity in, religious difference. Their writing erases that diversity.

Postmodern Christian theology must also recognize the remarkable otherness of God. Divine "otherness" is not the "wholly otherness" of a God so transcendent of the world that God is finally absent from the world. That is the God of modernity. Rather, postmodern theologies construe the otherness of God as unavowably, remarkably present-as-radically-other to us in the worlds in which we live. The language may be one of sacrament or of manifestation or of prophecy or risk of solidarity. While the world in which we live may no longer be "enchanted"—modernity has seen to that—our world can be one where amazing grace and divine joy can be healingly present and where the one who is present as radically Other to us is present paradoxically in solidarity with us.

Or what's an Incarnation for?

Works Cited

Aichele, George, Jr.
  1991   "Literary Fantasy and Post-Modern Theology." *Journal of the American Academy of Religion* 59/2:323-337.

Allen, Charles W.
  1990   "Between Revisionists and Postliberals: A Review Article." *Encounter* 51:389-401.

Alston, William P.
  1991   *Perceiving God: The Epistemology of Religious Experience.* Ithaca, N.Y.: Cornell University Press.

Altizer, Thomas J.J.
  1961   *Oriental Mysticism and Biblical Eschatology.* Philadelphia: Westminster.
  1963   *Mircea Eliade and the Dialectic of the Sacred.* Philadelphia: Westminster.
  1966   *The Gospel of Christian Atheism.* Philadelphia: Westminster.
  1970   *The Descent into Hell: A Study of the Radical Reversal of the Christian Consciousness.* Philadelphia: Westminster.
  1972   "An Inquiry into the Meaning of Negation in the Dialectical Logics of East and West." In *Religious Language and Knowledge,* edited by R.H. Ayers. Athens, Ga.: University of Georgia Press.
  1980   *Total Presence: The Language of Jesus and the Language of Today.* New York: Seabury.
  1985   *History as Apocalypse.* New York: State University of New York Press.
  1990a   *Genesis and Apocalypse: A Theological Voyage to Authentic Christianity.* Louisville: Westminster/John Knox.
  1990b   "Is the Negation of Christianity the Way to its Renewal?" *Religious Humanism* 24.
  1990c   "The Beginning and the End of Revelation." *Theology at the End of the Century,* edited by Robert P. Scharlemann. Charlottesville: University Press of Virginia.
  1993   *Genesis of God: A Theological Genealogy.* Louisville: Westminster/John Knox.
  1994   "The Contemporary Challenge of Radical Catholicism." *The Journal of Religion* 74/2:182-198.

Arens, Edmund
    1992   *Christopraxis: Grundzüge Theologischer Handlungstheorie.*
            Quaestiones Disputatae 139. Freiburg: Herder.
Audi, Robert and William J. Wainwright, editors
    1986   *Rationality, Religious Belief, and Moral Commitment: New Essays
            in the Philosophy of Religion.* Ithaca, N.Y.: Cornell University
            Press.
Bambara, Toni Cade
    1981   *The Salt Eaters.* New York: Vintage.
Brecht, Bertolt
    1976   *The Rise and Fall of the City of Mahagonny.* Translated by W. H.
            Auden and Chester Kallman. Boston: David R. Godine.
Brown, Robert M.
    1980   *Gustavo Gutiérrez: Makers of Contemporary Theology.* Atlanta, Ga.:
            John Knox Press.
    1990   *Gustavo Gutiérrez: An Introduction to Liberation Theology.* Mary-
            knoll, N.Y.: Orbis Books.
Burrell, David, C.S.C
    1992   "An Introduction to Theology and Social Theory." *Modern
            Theology* 8/4:319-329.
Chopp, Rebecca
    1985   *The Praxis of Suffering: An Interpretation of Liberation and Political
            Theologies.* Maryknoll, N.Y.: Orbis Books.
    1989   *The Power to Speak: Feminism, Language, God.* New York:
            Crossroad.
Cobb, John B., Jr., and David Ray Griffin
    1976   *Process Theology: An Introductory Exposition.* Philadelphia:
            Westminster.
Comstock, Gary
    1987   "Two Types of Narrative Theology." *Journal of the American
            Academy of Religion* 55/4:687-717.
Contemporary Authors
    1990   *Contemporary Authors.* Volume 125. Detroit: Gale Research
            Company.
Cunningham, Lawrence S.
    1983   *The Catholic Heritage.* New York: Crossroad.
d'Costa, Gavin, editor
    1990   *Christian Uniqueness Reconsidered: The Myth of a Pluralistic
            Theology of Religions.* Maryknoll, N.Y.: Orbis Books.
Derrida, Jacques
    1981   *Dissemination.* Translated by Barbara Johnson. Chicago:
            University of Chicago Press.
DiNoia, Joseph A., O. P.
    1992   *The Diversity of Religions: A Christian Perspective.* Washington,
            D.C.: Catholic University of America Press.

Farley, Edward
1990   *Good and Evil*. Philadelphia: Fortress.
Fenton, John Y., et al.
1988   *Religions of Asia*. Second Edition. New York: St. Martin's Press.
Ferm, Deane W.
1988   *Profiles in Liberation: Thirty-six Portraits of Third World Theologians*. Mystic, Conn.: Twenty-Third Publications.
Foucault, Michel
1977   *Discipline and Punish: The Birth of the Prison*. Translated by Alan Sheridan. New York: Pantheon.
Frei, Hans
1974   *The Eclipse of Biblical Narrative*. New Haven, Conn.: Yale University Press.
1986   "The 'Literal Reading' of Biblical Narrative in the Christian Tradition: Does It Stretch or Will It Break?" *The Bible and the Narrative Tradition*, edited by Frank McConnell. New York: Oxford University Press.
1990   "'Narrative' in Christian and Modern Reading," in *Theology and Dialogue*, edited by Bruce Marshall. Notre Dame, Ind.: University of Notre Dame Press.
Galilea, Segundo, et al.
1974   *The Mystical and Critical Dimensions of Christian Faith*. New York: Herder and Herder.
Gareffa, Michael, S.J.
1991   "Saints and Postmodernism: Revisioning Moral Philosophy." *Theological Studies* 52.
Geivett, R. Douglas and Brendan Sweetman, editors
1992   *Contemporary Perspectives on Religious Epistemology*. New York: Oxford.
Geertz, Clifford
1973   *The Interpretation of Cultures*. New York: Harper and Row.
Griffin, David Ray
1973   *A Process Christology*. Philadelphia: Westminister.
1977   *Mind in Nature: Essays on the Interface of Science and Philosophy*. Washington, D.C.: University Press of America.
1985   *Physics and the Ultimate Significance of Time: Bohm, Prigogine and Process Philosophy*. Albany: State University of New York Press.
1988   *Spirituality and Society: Postmodern Visions*. Albany, N.Y.: State University of New York Press.
1989a   "Charles Hartshorne's Postmodern Philosophy." *Hartshorne, Process Philosophy, and Theology*, edited by Robert Kane and Stephen H. Phillips. Albany, N.Y.: State University of New York Press.
1989b   *God & Religion in the Postmodern World: Essays in Postmodern Theology*. Albany, N.Y.: State University of New York Press.

1990a   *Archetypal Process: Self and Divine in Whitehead, Jung, and Hillman.* Evanston, Ill.: Northwestern University Press.

1990b   *Sacred Interconnections: Postmodern Spirituality, Political Economy, and Art.* Albany, N.Y.: State University of New York Press.

1992   "Green Spirituality: A Postmodern Convergence of Science and Religion." *Journal of Theology* 96:5-20.

1993   *Postmodern Politics for a Planet in Crisis: Policy, Process, and Presidential Vision.* New York: State University of New York Press.

Griffin, David Ray and Huston Smith

1989   *Primordial Truth and Postmodern Theology.* New York: State University of New York Press.

Griffin, David Ray, William A. Beardslee and Joe Holland

1989   *Varieties of Postmodern Theology.* Albany, N.Y.: State University of New York Press.

Gutiérrez, Gustavo.

1973   *A Theology of Liberation: History, Politics, and Salvation.* Translated by Sister Caridad Inda and John Eagleson. Maryknoll, N.Y.: Orbis Books.

1984   *We Drink from Our Own Wells: The Spiritual Journey of a People.* Translated by Matthew J. O'Connell. Maryknoll, N.Y.: Orbis Books.

1988   *A Theology of Liberation: History, Politics, and Salvation.* Second Edition. Maryknoll, N.Y.: Orbis Books.

1990   *The Truth Shall Make You Free: Confrontations.* Translated by Matthew J. O'Connell. Maryknoll, N.Y.: Orbis Books.

1991   *The God of Life.* Translated by Matthew J. O'Connell. Maryknoll, N.Y.: Orbis Books.

Habermas, Jurgen

1984   *The Theory of Communicative Action.* Volume I: *Reason and the Rationalization of Society.* Translated by Thomas McCarthy. Boston: Beacon Press.

1987   *The Theory of Communicative Action.* Volume II: *Lifeworld and System: A Critique of Functionalist Reason.* Translated by Thomas McCarthy. Boston: Beacon Press

1992   "Transcendence from Within, Transcendence in This World." *Habermas, Modernity and Public Theology,* edited by Don S. Browning and Francis Schüssler Fiorenza. New York: Crossroad.

1994   " 'Moral Humility, Fewer Illusions'—A Talk between Adam Michnik and Jürgen Habermas." *New York Review of Books* 41/6 (March 24): 24-29.

Harvey, Van A.

1989   "On the Intellectual Marginality of American Theology."

Religion and Twentieth-Century American Intellectual Life, edited by Michael J. Lacey, 172-192. Cambridge: Woodrow Wilson International Center for Scholars and Cambridge University Press.

Hawks, James
    1990   "Juan Luis Segundo's Critique of David Tracy." *Heythrop Journal* 31:277-294.

Hick, John
    1978   *Evil and the God of Love.* Second Edition. New York: Harper and Row.
    1989   *An Interpretation of Religion.* New Haven, Conn.: Yale University Press.

Hick, John and Paul Knitter, editors
    1987   *The Myth of Christian Uniqueness.* Maryknoll, N.Y.: Orbis Books.

High, Dallas
    1967   *Language, Persons and Belief.* New York: Oxford University Press.

James, William
    1961   *The Varieties of Religious Experience.* New York: Collier.

Journet, Charles
    1963   *The Meaning of Evil.* Translated by Michael Barry. New York: P. J. Kenedy and Sons.

Knitter, Paul
    1985   *No Other Name?* Maryknoll, N.Y.: Orbis Books.

Kort, Wesley
    1992   *Bound to Differ: The Dynamics of Theological Discourses.* University Park: The Pennsylvania State University Press.

Krell, David F.
    1977   *Martin Heidegger: Basic Writings from* Being and Time *(1927) to* The Task of Thinking *(1964).* New York: Harper and Row.

Kroger, Joseph
    1985   "Prophetic-Critical and Practical-Strategic Tasks of Theology: Habermas and Liberation Theology." *Theological Studies* 46/1:3-20.

Kurtz, Lester
    1986   *The Politics of Heresy: The Modernist Crisis in Roman Catholicism.* Berkeley: University of California Press.

Lakeland, Paul
    1990   *Theology and Critical Theory: The Discourse of the Church.* Nashville, Tenn.: Abingdon.

Lamb, Matthew
    1982   *Solidarity with Victims.* Maryknoll, N.Y.: Orbis Books.

Lernoux, Penny
    1982   *Cry of the People.* New York: Penguin.

Lindbeck, George.
    1984   *The Nature of Doctrine.* Philadelphia: Westminster.

1985 "Modernity and Luther's Understanding of the Freedom of the Christian." *Martin Luther and the Modern Mind,* edited by Manfred Hoffmann. Toronto: The Edwin Mellen Press.

1988 "Scripture, Consensus, and Community," *This World* 23 (Fall): 5-24.

Lindbeck, George, editor

1965 *Dialogue on the Way.* Minneapolis: Augsburg.

Lints, Richard

1993 "The Postpositivist Choice: Tracy or Lindbeck?" *Journal of the American Academy of Religion* 61/4:655-677

MacIntyre, Alasdair

1981 *After Virtue.* Notre Dame, Ind.: University of Notre Dame Press.

McClendon, James Wm., Jr.

1966 "Baptism as a Performative Sign." *Theology Today* 23/3 (October):403-16.

1967 "Why Baptists Do Not Baptize Infants," *Concilium* 24.

1974 *Biography as Theology.* Nashville, Tenn.: Abingdon.

1978 "Three Strands of Christian Ethics." *Journal of Religious Ethics* 6/1 (Spring):54-80.

1986 *Ethics: Systematic Theology.* Volume I. Nashville, Tenn.: Abingdon.

1994 *Doctrine: Systematic Theology.* Volume II. Nashville, Tenn.: Abingdon.

McClendon, James Wm., Jr., and James M. Smith

1975 *Understanding Religious Convictions.* Notre Dame, Ind.: University of Notre Dame Press (revised edition: *Convictions: Defusing Religious Relativism.* Philadelphia: Trinity Press International, 1994).

McGovern, Arthur F.

1989 *Liberation Theology and Its Critics: Toward an Assessment.* Maryknoll, N.Y.: Orbis Books.

Milbank, John

1990 *Theology and Social Theory.* Oxford: Basil Blackwell.

Min, Anselm Kyongsuk

1989 *Dialectic of Salvation: Issues in Theology of Liberation.* Albany: State University of New York Press.

Monk, Ray

1990 *Ludwig Wittgenstein: The Duty of Genius.* New York: The Free Press.

Murphy, Nancey and James Wm. McClendon, Jr.

1989 "Distinguishing Modern and Postmodern Theologies." *Modern Theology* 5/3:199-212.

Neff, David.

1988 "Gustavo's Surprise." *Christianity Today* 32/13:15.

Neuhaus, Richard John
1985   "Is There Theological Life after Liberalism: The Lindbeck
        Proposal." *Dialog: A Journal of Theology* 24:66-72.
Noddings, Nel
1989   *Women and Evil.* Los Angeles: University of California Press.
Ochs, Peter
1990   "A Rabbinic Pragmatism." *Theology and Dialogue,* edited by
        Bruce D. Marshall. Notre Dame, Ind.: University of Notre
        Dame Press.
O'Leary, Joseph
1985   *Questioning Back: The Overcoming of Metaphysics in Christian
        Tradition.* Minneapolis: Winston.
Percy, Walker
1961   *The Moviegoer.* New York: Popular Library.
Peukert, Helmut
1984   *Science, Action and Fundamental Theology: Toward a Theology of
        Communicative Action.* Translated by James Bohman. Cambridge,
        Mass.: MIT Press.
1992   "Enlightenment and Theology as Unfinished Projects."
        Habermas, Modernity, and Public Theology, edited by Don S.
        Browning and Francis Schüssler Fiorenza. New York: Cross-
        road.
Plantinga, Alvin
1974   *God, Freedom and Evil.* New York: Harper and Row.
Ramsay, William M.
1986   "Gustavo Gutierrez and Liberation Theology." *Four Modern
        Prophets: Walter Rauschenbusch; Martin Luther King, Jr.; Gustavo
        Gutierrez; Rosemary Radford Ruether,* edited by W. Ramsay.
        Atlanta: John Knox Press.
Raschke, Carl A., et al.
1977   *Religion and the Human Image.* Englewood Cliffs, N.J.: Prentice
        Hall.
Ricoeur, Paul
1988   *Time and Narrative.* Volume III. Translated by Kathleen Blamey
        and David Pellauer. Chicago: University of Chicago.
Rorty, Richard
1979   *Philosophy and the Mirror of Nature.* Princeton, N.J.: Princeton
        University Press.
1985   *Contingency, Irony, Solidarity.* Cambridge: Cambridge University
        Press.
Schleiermacher, Friedrich Daniel Ernst
1928   *The Christian Faith.* Translated by H. R. MacIntosh and J. S.
        Stewart. Edinburgh: T. and T. Clark.
Schreiter, Robert
1985   *Constructing Local Theologies.* Maryknoll, N.Y.: Orbis Books.

Schüssler Fiorenza, Francis
1984   *Foundational Theology: Jesus and the Church.* New York: Crossroad.
1992   "The Church as a Community of Interpretation: Political Theology between Discourse Ethics and Hermeneutical Reconstruction." *Habermas, Modernity, and Public Theology,* edited by Don S. Browning and Francis Schüssler Fiorenza. New York: Crossroad.

Schüssler Fiorenza, Francis and John Galvin, editors
1991   *Systematic Theology: Roman Catholic Perspectives.* Two Volumes. Minneapolis: Fortress.

Shea, John
1978   *Stories of God: An Unauthorized Biography.* Chicago: Thomas More.

Shields, Philip R.
1993   *Logic and Sin in the Writings of Ludwig Wittgenstein.* Chicago: University of Chicago Press.

Silverman, Hugh J., editor
1990   *Postmodernism—Philosophy and the Arts.* New York: Routledge.

Stell, Stephen L.
1993   "Hermeneutics in Theology and the Theology of Hermeneutics: Beyond Lindbeck and Tracy." *Journal of the American Academy of Religion* 61/4:678-703

Stout, Jeffery
1981   *Flight From Authority.* Notre Dame, Ind.: University of Notre Dame Press.

Surin, Kenneth
1988   " 'Many Religions and the One True Faith': An Examination of Lindbeck's Chapter Three." *Modern Theology* 4/2:187-209.
1990   "A Certain 'Politics of Speech': 'Religious Pluralism' in the Age of the McDonald's Hamburger." *Modern Theology* 7/1:67-100.

Taylor, Mark C.
1980   *Journeys to Selfhood: Hegel & Kierkegaard.* Los Angeles: University of California Press.
1984a   *Erring: A Postmodern A/theology.* Chicago: The University of Chicago Press.
1984b   "Altizer's Originality." *Journal of the American Academy of Religion* 52/1:569-584.
1986   *Deconstruction in Context.* Chicago: The University of Chicago Press.
1988   "The Anachronism of A/theology." *Religion and Intellectual Life* 5:22-36.
1992   *Disfiguring: Art, Architecture, Religion.* Chicago: University of Chicago Press.

Thiel, John
 1991 *Imagination and Authority: Theological Authorship in the Modern Tradition.* Minneapolis: Fortress.

Thomas, Owen C.
 1992 "The Challenge of Postmodernism." *Anglican Theological Review.* 72/2:209-219.

Tilley, Terrence W.
 1984 "The Use and Abuse of Theodicy." *Horizons* 11/2:304-319.
 1985 *Story Theology.* Wilmington, Del.: Michael Glazier, Inc.
 1989a "Incommensurability, Intratextuality and Fideism." *Modern Theology* 5/2:87-111.
 1989b "Dying Children and Sacred Space." Winooski, Ver.: Saint Michael's College.
 1989c "The Prudence of Religious Commitment." *Horizons* 16/1:45-64.
 1991 *The Evils of Theodicy.* Washington, D.C.: Georgetown University Press.
 1994 "In Favor of a 'Practical Theory of Religion': Montaigne and Pascal." *Theology Without Foundations: Religious Practice and the Future of Theological Truth,* edited by Stanley Hauerwas, Nancey Murphy and Mark Nation. Nashville: Abingdon.
 1995 *The Wisdom of Religious Commitment.* Washington, D.C.: Georgetown University Press.

Tillich, Paul.
 1951 *Systematic Theology.* Volume I. Chicago: University of Chicago Press.

Tracy, David
 1975 *Blessed Rage for Order: The New Pluralism in Theology.* New York: Crossroad.
 1981 *The Analogical Imagination: Christian Theology and the Culture of Pluralism.* New York: Crossroad.
 1983 "The Foundations of Practical Theology." In *Practical Theology,* edited by Don Browning. San Francisco: Harper and Row.
 1985 "Tillich and Contemporary Theology." *The Thought of Paul Tillich,* edited by James Lather Adams, et al. San Francisco: Harper and Row.
 1987a "The Christian Understanding of Salvation-Liberation." *Buddhist-Christian Studies* 7:129-138.
 1987b "Exodus: Theological Reflection." *Exodus: A Lasting Paradigm,* edited by Bas van Iersel and Anton Welter. Concilium 189. Edinburgh: T & T Clark.
 1987c *Plurality and Ambiguity: Hermeneutics, Religion, Hope.* San Francisco: Harper and Row.
 1989a "Afterword: Theology, Public Discourse, and the American Tradition." *Religion and Twentieth-Century American Intellectual Life,* edited by Michael J. Lacey. Cambridge: Woodrow Wilson

International Center for Scholars and Cambridge University
Press.

1989b   "The Uneasy Alliance Reconceived: Catholic Theological
Method, Modernity, and Postmodernity. *Theological Studies* 50/
4:548-570.

1990   *Dialogue with the Other: The Inter-Religious Dialogue.* Louvain
Pastoral and Theological Monographs 1. Louvain: Peelers;
Grand Rapids, MI: Eerdmans.

1994   "Theology and the Many Faces of Postmodernity." *Theology
Today* 51/1:104-114

United States Catholic Conference

1986   *Economic Justice for All.* Washington, D.C.: United States
Catholic Conference.

Waismann, Friedrich

1979   *Wittgenstein and the Vienna Circle: Conversations,* edited by
Brian McGuinness; translated by Brian McGuinness and
Joachim Schulte. New York: Barnes and Noble.

Welch, Sharon

1985   *Communities of Resistance and Solidarity: A Feminist Theology of
Liberation.* Maryknoll, N.Y.: Orbis Books.

1990   *A Feminist Ethic of Risk.* Minneapolis: Fortress.

Wittgenstein, Ludwig

1958   *Philosophical Investigations.* Translated by G. E. M. Anscombe.
Third Edition. New York: MacMillan.

1966   *Lectures and Conversations on Aesthetics, Psychology and Religious
Belief,* edited by C. Barrett. Oxford: Blackwell.

Wyschogrod, Edith

1974   *Emmanuel Levinas: The Problem of Ethical Metaphysics.* The
Hague: Martinus Nijhof.

1983a   "The Cunning of Language: Derrida, Kristeva, Eco on Interpretation." *Religious Studies Review* 9 January.

1983b   "Man-Made Mass Death: Challenging Paradigms of Selfhood."
Union Seminary Quarterly Review 38.

1985   *Spirit in Ashes: Hegel, Heidegger, and Man-Made Mass Death.* New
Haven, Conn.: Yale University.

1986   "On Deconstructing Theology: A Symposium on *Erring: A
Postmodern A/theology.*" *Journal of the American Academy
of Religion* 54/3:523-557.

1990a   *Saints and Postmodernism: Revisioning Moral Philosophy.* Chicago:
University of Chicago Press.

1990b   "Man-Made Mass Death: Shifting Concepts of Community."
Journal of the American Academy of Religion 58/2.

Acknowledgments

The Department of Religion of the Florida State University, my former academic home, has been very supportive in making this book possible. We are indebted to Leo Sandon, the chair, and the faculty of the department for their willingness to help this project to see the light of day.

Louise Hind helped make some of the final corrections to the manuscript and Stuart Kendall brought terribly needed order to the citations and the list of works cited. G. Anthony George participated in the seminar, and although his own research developed a pattern different from the ones presented here, his participation in our ongoing conversations was invaluable.

The staff of the Strozier Library at Florida State was very helpful with bibliographical work and inter-library loans. The office staff at the University of Dayton's Department of Religious Studies, my current academic home, has also been very helpful in its collaborating in the final proofreading, citation checking and other necessary tasks in bringing this book to completion.

A few paragraphs in chapter seven are based on "Incommensurability, Intratextuality, and Fideism," *Modern Theology* 5/2 (1987) and a few paragraphs in chapter ten are based on "Why American Catholic Theologians Should Read 'baptist' Theology," *Horizons*, 14/1 (1987). Thanks to L. Gregory Jones and Stephen Fowl, editors of *Modern Theology*, and Walter Conn, editor of *Horizons*, for permission to rework this material.

Index